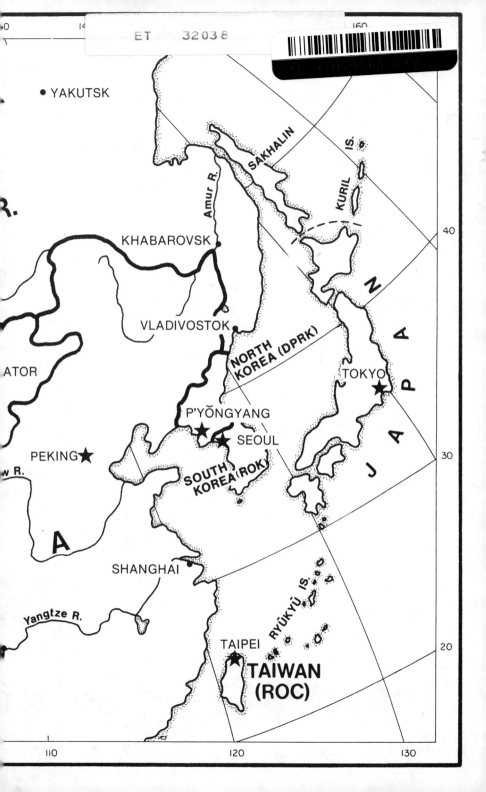

• YAKUTSK

R.

Amur R.

SAKHALIN

KURIL IS.

KHABAROVSK

40

VLADIVOSTOK

NORTH KOREA (DPRK)

J A P A N

TOKYO

ATOR

P'YŎNGYANG

SEOUL

PEKING ★

w R.

SOUTH KOREA (ROK)

30

A

SHANGHAI

RYŪKYŪ IS.

Yangtze R.

TAIPEI

TAIWAN (ROC)

20

110

120

130

P'YŎNGYANG
BETWEEN
PEKING AND MOSCOW

TO MY PARENTS

P'YŎNGYANG
BETWEEN
PEKING AND MOSCOW:
NORTH KOREA'S
INVOLVEMENT IN THE
SINO-SOVIET
DISPUTE, 1958–1975

Chin O. Chung

The University of Alabama Press
University, Alabama

Library of Congress Cataloging in Publication Data

Chung, Chin O   1938–
    P'yŏngyang between Peking and Moscow.

    Bibliography: p.
    Includes index.
    1.   Korea (Democratic People's Republic)—Foreign
relations—China.   2.   China—Foreign relations—Korea
(Democratic People's Republic)   3.   Korea (Democratic
People's Republic)—Foreign relations—Russia.   4.   Rus-
sia—Foreign relations—Korea (Democratic People's Re-
public)   I.   Title.
DS935.5.C6   327.519′3′051   76–44261
ISBN 0–8173–4728–3

CONTENTS

v

TABLES

ACKNOWLEDGMENTS

I would like to acknowledge my indebtedness to Professor Willard N. Hogan of the University of Nebraska and Professor Soon Sung Cho of the University of Missouri for their unfailing encouragement and guidance during an early stage in the writing of this manuscript. I also extend grateful thanks to my colleagues in the Political Science Department of The University of Alabama for their invaluable assistance graciously rendered to me.

My debt to the many scholars whose works I have consulted is acknowledged in the footnotes and bibliography. In particular, I wish to express my gratitude to Professor Byung Chul Koh of the University of Illinois at Chicago Circle, Professor Chong-Sik Lee of the University of Pennsylvania, and Professor Robert A. Scalapino of the University of California at Berkeley, whose pioneering works on North Korea have been drawn upon freely herein.

Responsibility for the interpretations made and for any shortcomings of this book is solely mine.

The Research Grants Committee of The University of Alabama provided faculty summer grants for typing and for the later stages of research.

To my wife, Young Cha, and my children, Jane Ewha, John Jongmun, and Eugene Jongpil, for their patience, encouragement, and inspiration, I owe more than words can express.

P'YŎNGYANG
BETWEEN
PEKING AND MOSCOW

ABBREVIATIONS

CCP   Chinese Communist Party
CDSP Current Digest of the Soviet Press
CEMA Council of Economic Mutual Assistance
CPSU Communist Party of the Soviet Union
CPV   Chinese People's Volunteers
DPRK Democratic People's Republic of Korea (North Korea)
KCNA Korean Central News Agency
KWP   Korean Workers' Party (North Korean Communist Party)
NCNA New China News Agency
NKWP North Korean Workers' Party
NPP   New People's Party
PLA   People's Liberation Army (China)
PRC   People's Republic of China
ROK   Republic of Korea (South Korea)

INTRODUCTION

At first, the Sino-Soviet dispute posed a serious dilemma for Communist regimes and parties in Asia. On the one hand, they were confronted with the need to "choose" between the People's Republic of China (PRC) and the Soviet Union; on the other, they could not afford, for political and other reasons, to alienate either of the two powers. It can be seen, however, that in the course of time the dispute afforded Communist regimes and parties in Asia an opportunity to enhance their independence by means of adroit maneuvering between Moscow and Peking, each of which had to court them in competition for their support.

The purpose of this book is to analyze how one such Communist regime, that of North Korea, dealt with the situation. This work is not intended, however, to be an exhaustive study of North Korea's relationship with Peking and Moscow. Nor does it include detailed discussion of the Sino-Soviet conflict as such, though some aspects of the dispute are summarized when they are necessary for an understanding of the content of this study. Primarily, this book is concerned with the examination of North Korea's attitude in the dispute and of why and how the North Korean regime has reacted to the specific issues and events in Sino-Soviet relations from 1958 through 1975.

The eight major divisions of this study are arranged chronologically, corresponding to changes in P'yŏngyang's attitudes toward Moscow and Peking, respectively. The first chapter sketches a brief historical background covering the period from the end of World War II to 1957. Here the chapter examines how the Democratic People's Republic of Korea (DPRK) and the Korean Workers' Party (KWP) were established, to what extent they were controlled by the Soviet Union, and how much the PRC increased its influence over North Korea during and after the Korean Conflict.

Chapter two is devoted to North Korea's relations with the Soviet Union and the PRC from 1958 through 1959, the period just prior to the outbreak of open controversy between Moscow

1

and Peking. During this time Soviet and Chinese influence on North Korean decisions had reached a state of equilibrium. Particular attention is given to a discussion of North Korea's growing emulation of Chinese economic policies and its attitude toward Khrushchev's "peaceful coexistence" policy.

Chapter three takes up with the beginning of open polemics between the Soviet Union and the PRC and continues through 1961, a period during which North Korea remained neutral. An attempt is made to explore both the North Korean neutrality on the growing Sino-Soviet conflict and the Soviet-Chinese competition for P'yŏngyang's support.

The fourth chapter is primarily concerned with the year 1962, when North Korea inclined toward Peking on the various issues that characterized the dispute in Sino-Soviet relations. Although the P'yŏngyang regime still tried to maintain a neutral posture publicly in the Sino-Soviet conflict, it was put to new and strenuous tests by such issues as the Sino-Indian border dispute and the Cuban missile crisis in the fall of 1962.

In the fifth chapter, an attempt is made to cover the period from 1963 until Khrushchev's ouster in October 1964, during which North Korea became Peking's most outspoken Asian ally in the dispute. The chapter also examines the main motivations of the P'yŏngyang-Peking alliance as well as the deterioration of relations between North Korea and the Soviet Union.

The sixth chapter deals with North Korea's attitude toward the Soviet Union and the PRC from Khrushchev's fall to early 1969. During this period, North Korean-Soviet relations improved considerably, while P'yŏngyang-Peking relations underwent some stress during the Chinese Cultural Revolution. The question of North Korea's "independence" from both Moscow and Peking is also discussed. The change in P'yŏngyang's behavior reflects both North Korea's national interests and a polycentric trend in the Communist world.

Chapter seven examines restored friendly relations between P'yŏngyang and Peking following Mao's Cultural Revolution. It also analyzes the impact on North Korea of President Richard Nixon's Peking and Moscow visits.

The final chapter deals with North Korea's friendly relations with both the Soviet Union and the PRC during the 1973–1975 period. This chapter also discusses the important issues and developments that have a significant bearing on North Korea's relations with the two neighboring Communist powers. The approach employed in this study is a combination of the historical descriptive and the analytical interpretive. The source materials which have been used in the preparation of this book fall roughly into the following categories: official statements and speeches of the leaders of North Korea, the PRC, and the Soviet Union; newspapers, articles, and books published by the three Communist regimes; and secondary sources published in the United States, South Korea, and Japan. In the romanization of Korean names and terms, the McCune-Reischauer system was used unless an official transliteration was available or an individual has done his own romanization. Chinese words were largely rendered according to the standard Wade-Giles transliteration system.

CHAPTER 1
HISTORICAL BACKGROUND
TO 1957

The official Communist Party in Korea was founded in Seoul as a secret organization on April 17, 1925, and was admitted to the Comintern in 1926.[1] Almost immediately, a multitude of factions developed within the Communist movement resulting in internal strife which, during the years 1925–1928, led to the dissolution of the party and its expulsion from the Comintern in December 1928. When subjected to Japanese police surveillance, most of the Korean Communists were forced to base themselves abroad in China, the Soviet Union, or even in Japan itself. Thus, the Communist movement in Korea became fragmented and eventually went underground. Although various efforts were made to revive the defunct party, it was not reorganized until 1945. The pre-1945 Communist movement in Korea thus appears to have been characterized by the clandestine activities of tiny Communist factions.[2]

By agreement with the United States, the Soviet Union accepted the surrender of Japanese forces in Korea pursuant to the terms of surrender which called for a temporary demarcation of Korea at the 38th parallel.[3] As a result of this agreement, the northern half of Korea was placed under Soviet occupation after the Japanese surrender on August 15, 1945. By the beginning of September 1945, the Russians had established their authority over the whole of North Korea and were cautiously working toward the organization of a strong pro-Soviet Communist party as a reliable political force.[4]

However, the Russians' task was far from easy due to the confused state of the North Korean political scene in 1945. Numerous local Communist and nationalist elements were competing with each other for power. The influx of Communists and nationalists from Manchuria and other parts of China and the Soviet Union further complicated the confusing situation in

North Korea. After the liberation from Japanese control, five major distinctive factions appeared: (1) the indigenous nationalist (non-Communist) group; (2) the domestic Communist group; (3) the returnees from China, later identified as the Yenan faction; (4) the returnees from the Soviet Union; and (5) Kim Il-sŏng's personal followers called the Kapsan group.[5]

FIVE FACTIONS

The indigenous nationalist group, led by Cho Man-sik, a well known Christian teacher, held great potential for becoming a major political force. Cho's popularity among the North Koreans was such that the Soviet authorities found it expedient to appoint him as chairman of the Five Provinces Administrative Bureau, which governed the entire Soviet zone of occupation. In November 1945, Cho formed the *Chosŏn Minju-dang* (the Korean Democratic Party, or KDP) which was composed of comparatively well-to-do workers and peasants, Christians, intellectuals, and businessmen. But Cho Man-sik inevitably clashed with the Russian authorities. In January 1946, he was arrested by the Soviet authority because he had opposed the decision of the Foreign Ministers' Conference (the United States, the Soviet Union, Great Britain, and the Republic of China) in Moscow (December 1945) to place Korea under the trusteeship of the four powers for five years. Since Cho's arrest signalled the Soviet intention to prevent or eliminate nationalist activities in North Korea, the leaders of the group began to flee to the South. Although the KDP's central headquarters was moved to Seoul by April 1946, the Communists permitted a skeleton of the party to remain in the North to help maintain the façade of a "new democracy."[6]

As already noted, the domestic Communist group had been striving to build up a viable political force since the 1920s but had been unsuccessful, due largely to both its internal strife and Japanese suppression. In September 1945, Pak Hŏn-yŏng, a veteran Communist since the 1920s, established the Korean Communist Party in Seoul. Pak became the chairman of the party and proceeded to revitalize the regional and local branches of the Communist organization throughout Korea. Pak's followers came largely from the small labor class in the South. When the party was banned in the South by the American military government, Pak fled to the North in mid-October, 1946.[7]

In the North, the principal leaders of the domestic Communist group were Hyŏn Chun-hyŏk, O Ki-sŏp, Yi Chu-ha and Chŏng Tal-hyŏn. Shortly after the liberation of Korea, Hyŏn formed the South P'yŏngan District Committee of the Korean Communist Party. He was very prominent among radical intellectuals and militant nationalists as well as among Communists. The Soviet occupation authorities, however, did not approve of either Hyŏn or his programs. His assassination on September 28, 1945, on the way back from a conference with the Soviet and other Communist leaders, came at a suspiciously convenient time for both the Soviet command in P'yŏngyang and Kim Il-sŏng.[8]

The Yenan group was the strongest of the four in terms of membership and prestige. Based in the Chinese wartime capital of Yenan and composed of people oriented toward the Chinese Communist Party, the Yenan group had engaged in resistance struggles against the Japanese troops. Kim Tu-bong, a noted literary scholar who had been exiled to China since 1919, was the leader of this faction. The Yenan group entered North Korean politics with its old designation of *Chosŏn Tongnip Tongmaeng* (the Korean Independence League). In March 1946, however, it changed its name to *Sinmin-dang* (the New People's Party, or NPP). Its membership included mainly workers, peasants, intellectuals, and small businessmen. At the end of July 1946 the NPP was merged into the North Korean Workers' Party.[9]

The Soviet faction consisted of Soviet-Koreans who were descendants of Korean immigrants in the Soviet Union and mostly held dual citizenship. A large number of these Russianized Koreans were brought into North Korea by the Soviet occupation forces.[10] They had not been active in the Korean independence movement and were not popular in North Korea.[11] Within the North Korean apparatus about 200 critical positions were held by the Soviet-Koreans as a result of the efforts of the Soviet authorities to infiltrate them into nearly all major government agencies—usually in the position of vice-chairman. From this position, they could easily transmit Soviet views to the general public.[12] The leaders of the Soviet-Korean group were Hŏ Ka-i, Pak Ch'ang-ok, and Nam Il. Hŏ Ka-i was primarily in charge of building a new Communist party in North Korea. Until 1956, when they suffered a subtle form of erosion, the Soviet-Koreans, working with both direct and indirect support from the Soviet Union, played an important part in North Korean politics.[13]

The fifth group, or the Kapsan faction, was composed of Kim Il-sŏng and his small partisan bands who fought for Korean independence in southern Manchuria until they were forced by the Japanese to retreat into Soviet Siberia around 1941. The Soviet occupation forces brought them into North Korea along with the Soviet-Koreans.[14]

Kim Il-sŏng, the leader of the Kapsan group, was born on April 15, 1912, in a village near P'yŏngyang. Although his original name was Kim Sŏng-ju, he used the alias of Kim Il-sŏng, the name of a legendary hero of the Korean independent movement in Manchuria. Having moved to Manchuria at the age of 14, Kim led a small anti-Japanese guerrilla detachment in southern Manchuria from 1932 until his retreat into Soviet Siberia in 1941.[15] But the information on Kim's wartime activities is scanty indeed. Prior to 1945, Kim Il-sŏng had never participated in the Korean Communist movement and held no position in the party or its youth group.[16] However, it was the Kapsan faction under the leadership of Kim Il-sŏng that brought about the final consolidation of power within the Korean Communist groups.

ESTABLISHMENT OF THE DPRK AND THE KWP

Although the leaders of the Yenan and the two domestic groups were well-known and popular, the Soviet authorities preferred to depend upon the Soviet-Koreans and Kapsan group. Amidst the hectic postwar confusion and emotionalism, the Soviet occupation forces put forward Kim Il-sŏng as the most appropriate Communist leader of Korea. In the years following, the Soviet authorities in North Korea, whose military occupation lasted until December 1948, not only placed Kim in a position of prominence, but also provided him with every opportunity to establish himself at the helm of the regime and of the Korean Workers' Party.

Kim Il-sŏng reportedly returned to North Korea early in September 1945, at the age of thirty-three, in the uniform of a Red Army major. But he did not publicly appear until October 14, 1945, when Kim was introduced to the public at a citizen's rally in P'yŏngyang as a nationalist hero.[17] On October 10, 1945, at the Conference of the North Korean Five-Province Party Members and Activists, Kim Il-sŏng was elected as the first secretary of the North Korean Central Bureau of the Korean Communist Party. According to an official North Korean source, this was the first Korean Communist Party organization established on the principles of Marxism-Leninism and guided by "the true Communists."[18]

With the rise of Kim Il-sŏng as the head of the Communist Party, the Soviet authorities hastened their moves toward the creation of a strong, indigenous North Korean regime fashioned after the Soviet political system. The basic Moscow strategy for Sovietizing North Korea was the effective use of Korean personnel while keeping Soviet influence strictly behind the scenes. The Russians thus maintained "indirect" control without a military governing body of their own.[19]

In February 1946, the North Korean Provisional People's Committee, which became the highest administrative organ in North Korea, was established with Kim Il-sŏng as its chairman and Kim Tu-bong as its vice-chairman. A year later, the Supreme People's Assembly was inaugurated as the highest legislative body in North Korea. Though representative in appearance, it had no real power. The Assembly created an executive branch called the Central People's Committee which consisted of various ministries and bureaus. This North Korean governmental structure remained unchanged until 1948.[20]

While Kim Il-sŏng and the Soviet-Koreans steadily increased their power within the Communist Party, the influence of the domestic Communists was definitely on the decline. On August 28, 1946, the NPP of the Yenan faction merged with the Communist Party. This merger gave birth to *Puk Chosŏn Nodong-dang* (the North Korean Workers' Party, or NKWP). Kim Tu-bong, the leader of the Yenan faction, was elected to the chairmanship of the NKWP while Kim Il-sŏng was "relegated" to the vice-chairmanship along with Chu Nyŏng-ha, a relatively insignificant leader of the domestic faction. Hŏ Ka-i was named first secretary of the NKWP—the position controlling all the organizational and administrative functions.[21] Why Kim Il-sŏng was not chosen as chairman of the NKWP is not clear. He may have sought to avoid the antagonistic feelings of the Yenan and domestic factions and to disguise the fact that the union was an absorption, rather than a merger, of the NPP into the Communist Party.[22] Whatever the case, the election of Kim Tu-bong to the chairmanship did nothing to alter the actual power structure, since, regardless of the actual strength of the Yenan group, Kim Il-sŏng was still the principal link between the North Korean Communists and the Soviet military command, and no one could effectively challenge Kim Il-sŏng's position.

For Kim Il-sŏng, the merger of the two parties was a sound political tactic. While the Communist Party was based on peasants and workers, the NPP membership included many intellectuals. By merging these diverse elements into one political party, a unity among these classes was made possible. In effect, agreeing to the merger, the leaders of the Yenan faction delivered their organized strength to Kim Il-sŏng. They then gradually faded from the political scene. The merger also helped Kim Il-sŏng purge and finally defeat domestic faction rivals by 1948.[23]

On August 25, 1948, a so-called "national election" was held to form the Supreme People's Assembly. The Assembly, nominally representing all strata of the population, has acted as no more than a rubber stamp. Kim Tu-bong was elected chairman of the Assembly and served in that position until September 1957, when he was replaced by Ch'oe Yong-gŏn, a veteran of partisan campaigns in Manchuria.[24] Ch'oe held the chairmanship until December 1972. On September 8, 1948, the Assembly ratified the first constitution and proclaimed the establishment of the Democratic People's Republic of Korea (DPRK).[25] Kim Il-sŏng was named premier of the DPRK and, on September 10, his choice of cabinet members was approved by the Supreme People's Assembly. Pak Hŏn-yŏng, leader of the South Korean Workers' Party, was appointed vice-premier and minister of foreign affairs.[26] North Korea adopted a new constitution on December 27, 1972 at the first session of the Fifth Supreme People's Assembly. A day after the adoption of the new constitution, Kim Il-sŏng was "elected" as its first president of the DPRK.[27]On October 12, 1948, the Soviet Union recognized the North Korean government. Although Soviet troops were withdrawn from North Korea by the end of 1948, the Soviets still exercised control over North Korea through its embassy, advisory personnel, and the Soviet-Koreans holding key positions in the government and the ruling Communist Party.[28]

The most important prewar political development in North Korea was staged on June 24, 1949, when the NKWP and the South Korean Workers' Party merged into *Chosŏn Nodong-dang* (the Korean Workers' Party, or KWP). Prompted by the outlawing of the SKWP in South Korea in December 1948, the merger resulted in Kim Il-sŏng becoming chairman of the KWP Central Committee, with Pak Hŏn-yŏng sharing the vice-chairmanship with Hŏ Ka-i.[29] The creation of this unified Communist Party signified the ultimate victory of Kim Il-sŏng since, in effect, the merger eliminated Pak's own autonomous base of power. Kim Tu-bong, even though retaining membership in the Central Committee of the KWP, also definitely lost influence within the party. Thus, Kim Il-sŏng became the leader of both party and state—a process which in the Soviet Union was not completed by Stalin until 1941.[30]

Kim Il-sŏng's success was due not only to Russian aid but also to the successive failures of the "old" Communists during the three years following the liberation of Korea.[31] As noted earlier, the Korean Communist movement had been particularly characterized by factional strife. In this regard, the fact that Kim himself had not been involved in the preliberation Korean Communist movement worked distinctly to Kim's advantage since it allowed him to provide a common meeting ground for the various factions.[32] Finally, the capabilities of the man himself may well have been another important factor, a factor that should not be underrated. As Professor Chong-Sik Lee put it, "the factors that have distinguished Kim from his rivals have been his greater skill as a strategist and tactician, and his receipt of effective support at the opportune time."[33]

SOVIET-NORTH KOREAN RELATIONS, 1945-1950

While the precise extent of initial Soviet control yet remains to be revealed, it seems clear that North Korea was a veritable Soviet satellite prior to the outbreak of the Korean Conflict. Soviet control was effected by Soviet officers and advisers placed at almost all levels of North Korean governmental and economic structure.[34] Indeed, a State Department research mission which studied the Soviet system of control in North Korea concluded that North Korea, by 1950, was "already well advanced toward becoming a republic of the USSR."[35]

The agreement reached in March 1949 between Stalin and Kim Il-sŏng, for example, included all the "features of satellite treaties." In fact, the North Korean Communists were required to observe the following unwritten but implicit "articles of faith": (1) acceptance of the Soviet Union as a superior country and the fountainhead of wisdom; (2) acceptance of Soviet political and economic forms as the only means of achieving human progress; and (3) the grant to the Soviet Union of a monopolistic hold over the foreign intercourse of the country, to the exclusion of all influence considered inimical to the Soviet Union.[36]

The Soviets not only dictated the domestic and external policies of North Korea but also tried to Sovietize the North Koreans through intensive programs of cultural infiltration and economic integration. Russian cultural influence was evident on a large scale in language, art, dance, theater, movies, press, and radio. The study of Russian, for example, was made compulsory from the fifth grade up and a rigorous effort was made to promote the study of the language among the North Korean leaders.[37] Furthermore, to insure the compliance of the future leadership of North Korea with Soviet policies, the Soviet Union took steps to oversee the choice and direct the education of the

North Korean candidates for further study in Soviet schools. The nature of their training served as an additional means through which the Soviet Union hoped to perpetuate its control over the North Korean leadership.[38]

In developing their economy, the North Korean Communists undoubtedly sought assistance from Moscow, to which the Soviet Union responded with material and technical aid.[39] A formal agreement on mutual economic and cultural cooperation was signed in Moscow on March 17, 1949. The agreement called for the development of trade and cultural relations and provided for reciprocal most-favored-nation treatment for the exchange of technical specialists and for information on agriculture and industry.[40] By this agreement, the Soviet Union granted North Korea a loan of 212 million rubles (about $40 million) to be spent between 1949 and 1951 for the purchase of Soviet goods in excess of the agreed volume of barter trade.[41] This loan possibly covered arms purchases.[42]

However, to an increasing degree the resources and production capacity of North Korea were being drawn into the Soviet economic orbit, particularly the Soviet Far East. For instance, the expansion of heavy industry in North Korea was directed toward "meeting Soviet requirements."[43] To this end, Soviet authorities in North Korea played a dominant role in planning the direction of North Korean investment and in supervising industrial production and foreign trade.[44]

In the field of trade, volume between the Soviet Union and North Korea increased from 74 million rubles in 1946 to 265 million rubles in 1948. Trade with the Soviet Union in 1950 was to have expanded over 750 million rubles. This figure represented more than three-quarters of North Korea's total foreign trade.[45] One-third of this trade was, however, in military goods.[46]

Although the details of the trade between the two countries were closely guarded secrets, a number of sources indicated that the terms of trade between them were extremely unfavorable to North Korea. For example, North Korean commodities exported to the Soviet Union were sold at greatly reduced prices with various excuses, while the Soviet Union sold its goods to

North Korea at prices substantially higher than in the world market.[47] Some equipment removed by the Soviet Union from North Korea during 1945–1946 was "paid for" in military script and listed among North Korea's exports. Furthermore, in response to Soviet pressure, the North Korean regime concentrated its efforts on expanding both the production of certain commodities and the volume of exports to the Soviet Union.[48] As a State Department research mission in October 1950 aptly concluded, the economy of North Korea, "to an ever-increasing degree, was being integrated into the Soviet economic orbit."[49]

SINO-NORTH KOREAN RELATIONS, 1945–1950

Despite early expectations, the Chinese Communists took very little (if any) part in North Korean politics prior to the entry of the Chinese "People's Volunteers" into the Korean Conflict. To what extent Soviet efforts neutralized or contained Chinese Communist interests in North Korea is not clearly known. But it was obvious that the promotion of Chinese interests positively conflicted with Soviet control of North Korea. The Chinese Communists were not in a position to exercise influence in North Korea against Soviet wishes—primarily because of their internal situation.[50]

The Yenan returnees, through whom the Chinese Communists could exert their influence in North Korea, were not in a favorable position to exercise power in North Korean politics. The Soviet occupation authorities considered them to be "unreliable," and they found themselves becoming further suspected as members of a "Chinese clique." For example, Mu Chŏng, the military leader of the Yenan group, was censured at a KWP congress in 1949 for personal "heroism" and for "building within the party a clique of personal followers."[51]

Even after the Chinese Communists finally established the People's Republic of China (PRC) in October 1949, there was no significant expansion of Chinese influence in North Korea. It is noteworthy to point out that there was no comparable rise even in Chinese cultural influence in North Korea before the Korean

War.[52] Prior to the early 1950s, the two countries failed to exchange ambassadors, to negotiate formal and public treaties, and to set up the usual agencies of diplomatic intercourse. Nor was there any economic or cultural agreement between them up to 1953.[53] However, the outbreak of the Korean War and the subsequent entry of the Chinese troops into the conflict signalled the end of the Soviet Union's exclusive role in the direction of North Korean affairs and considerably increased Chinese influence. Let us turn now to the ways in which the Korean Conflict affected domestic as well as foreign affairs in North Korea.

DOMESTIC POLITICAL CONSOLIDATION AFTER THE KOREAN WAR

The Korean Conflict resulted in the strengthening of Communist control, particularly in regard to the position of the Kim Il-sŏng faction. The conflict provided Kim an excellent opportunity to consolidate his power. At the outbreak of the war, a "war committee" was created and Kim himself became its chairman. All citizens, political parties, and social organizations were obliged "to submit themselves completely to the decisions and directives of the war committee."[54] Under the control of this military administration, Kim eliminated two of the most important figures involved in factional politics, men whose ascension to power might have led to closer relations with Communist China or the Soviet Union.[55]

At the third plenum of the KWP Central Committee on December 4, 1950, Kim Il-sŏng blamed General Mu Chŏng, a prominent leader of the Yenan faction and a symbol of close collaboration with Peking, for the North Korean military defeat in October 1950, and accused him of disloyalty to the higher command during the conflict. Mu Chŏng was purged in December 1950 and, at Chinese request, transferred to China.[56] Kim Il-sŏng apparently intended to place all the blame for the North Korean defeat on Mu Chŏng in order to escape his own responsibility. He also probably realized that Mu Chŏng, who enjoyed great popularity with the Chinese "volunteers," was a serious political rival for power in North Korea. Indeed, Mu Chŏng, if unchecked at this time, might have become an important contender for leadership against Kim Il-sŏng.[57]

In November 1951, a Central Committee plenum censured Hŏ ka-i, the leader of the Soviet-Koreans, for "defective organizational works." Hŏ was reported to have committed suicide in March 1953 in order to avoid trial for his "crimes." Certainly the suicide of Hŏ Ka-i weakened the Soviet control system in North Korea.[58]

Immediately after the signing of the Armistice Agreement in July 1953, Pak Hŏn-yŏng and his followers were purged on the pretext that they were "American spies." They were also accused of failure to mobilize the South Koreans during the war and of planning a coup d'état against the Kim Il-sŏng leadership to establish a new revolutionary government to be headed by Pak Hŏn-yŏng.[59] Pak was reported to have been executed in December 1955,[60] probably as a scapegoat for the failure of the war. With Pak out of the way, the domestic faction was completely eliminated from North Korean politics.

This final stage of Kim's power consolidation was followed by the de-Stalinization movement, which began immediately after the Twentieth Congress of the Communist Party of the Soviet Union at which Nikita S. Khrushchev assailed Stalin as a "murdering paranoid."[61] During the August plenum of the KWP Central Committee in 1956, Ch'oe Ch'ang-ik of the Yenan faction and Pak Ch'ang-ok, who succeeded Hŏ Ka-i as leader of the Soviet-Koreans, had attacked Kim Il-sŏng openly for his "cult of personality," his "dictatorial style of leadership," and his exclusive emphasis on heavy industry leading to the neglect of popular needs.[62] Pak Ch'ang-ok reportedly wrote a letter to Khrushchev complaining that Kim Il-sŏng had neglected the Twentieth Congress decisions.[63]

This revolt against Kim Il-sŏng, later known as the August Incident, was obviously influenced by Khrushchev's de-Stalinization campaign. In fact, the Soviet representative in P'yŏngyang was sympathetic to their cause. Perhaps as a result of this, Soviet Ambassador Ivanov was recalled to Moscow at the request of P'yŏngyang, allegedly for interfering with domestic policies of North Korea.[64] This challenge against Kim's leadership was indeed the most serious one made after his assumption of the chairmanship of the KWP in 1949. If Kim Il-sŏng was not faced with a combined Sino-Soviet attempt to purge him, he was at least confronted with adversaries who had strong Chinese and Russian connections.

However, Kim and his followers outnumbered his critics and succeeded in expelling these "reactionary and antiparty elements" from the party. The Russian and Chinese responses to the incident were to send First Deputy Premier Anastas Mikoyan and Marshal P'eng Teh-huai to P'yŏngyang for an investigation. They apparently advised the P'yŏngyang regime that the August opposition should be treated as "comradely self-criticism of party policy," and that the party expulsions should be withdrawn. But their advice was not taken seriously by Kim's regime.[65] After the August Incident, Kim's leadership in North Korea became stronger than ever, and the idolization and deification of Kim Il-sŏng has increased in intensity.[66]

Following the August Incident, Kim Il-sŏng launched an intensive but rather gradual campaign against the Soviet and Yenan groups. All but a few of the Soviet-Koreans who were directly engaged in technical assistance to industry and military establishments were purged from the party and governmental hierarchies, and most of them chose to return to the Soviet Union. The moderating influence of the Soviet faction was thus practically eliminated. The anti-Yenan faction movement culminated in the ouster of Kim Tu-bong from the chairmanship of the Presidium of the Supreme People's Assembly on August 27, 1957, and his expulsion from the KWP in March 1958.[67] With the purge of Kim Tu-bong, the Yenan group was also eliminated as a political force in North Korea. Thus, Kim Il-sŏng had become by early 1958 the undisputed leader of the KWP and had secured a position comparable to that of Stalin in the Soviet Union after his purges in the 1930s.

Since then, Kim Il-sŏng has been party chief, president (premier until December 1972) and commander in chief of the North Korean armed forces. He has held, concurrently, the highest positions in both party and government longer than any other political leader in the post-World War II Communist world. Kim's authority today is absolute, his personality all pervading. The sole repository of power in North Korea is the KWP, which in turn is but an instrument of Kim Il-sŏng.[68]

THE GROWTH OF CHINESE INFLUENCE, 1950–1957

The most important change in North Korea's postwar international position was the increase of Chinese influence in North Korea. Peking's position in the international Communist movement was greatly enhanced as the result of Stalin's death in March 1953, and the consolidation of the Chinese Communists' hold on the mainland after they successfully established the People's Republic of China in October 1949. Several important factors tended to enhance Chinese influence in North Korea.

When the North Korean party-state was on the verge of extinction following the intervention of American and United Nations forces in the Korean Conflict, crucial aid came from the Chinese—not the Russians. The massive intervention of Chinese "People's Volunteers" (CPV) on the side of the North Koreans in November 1950 rescued the DPRK from total disaster. Even though there was some friction[69] in Sino-North Korean relations during and after the conflict, the North Koreans were favorably impressed by Chinese military assistance. In the words of *Jen-min Jih-pao*, the official organ of the Chinese Communist Party (CCP), the two countries built up "an unbreakable, militant friendship" that was "cemented by blood."[70]

The Soviet Union, by comparison, suffered in popular esteem because it had not given greater assistance to the North Korean war effort, especially when the Kim regime was on the verge of total disaster in October 1950. The Russians provided advice, fighter pilots, weapons and other military supplies, and relief goods. But the P'yŏngyang leadership apparently was not content. The North Koreans wanted the active participation of Soviet infantry divisions in the conflict, and they also hoped for direct retaliation by Soviet airpower against American attacks on the North.[71]

In addition to their contribution to the North Korean war effort, the Chinese troops provided the badly needed manpower for postwar rehabilitation. They are reported to have built hundreds of reservoirs, dams, dykes, roads, and houses, and repaired many demolished railway facilities.[72] According to a Chinese source, they "contributed nearly five million work-days to build, among other things, 4,107 bridges, five reservoirs, and 3,768 dykes with a total length of 346 kilometers."[73] In the first six months of 1958 alone, while the withdrawal of troops was in progress, the Chinese soldiers are reported to have contributed "1,300,000 man-days of work for the North Korean postwar recovery."[74] The timely Chinese voluntary service, which had been of immense help to North Korea in overcoming some of the pressing economic difficulties, certainly contributed to the growth of Chinese influence in North Korea.

It was also reported that the behavior of the Chinese "volunteers" toward the North Korean populace was notably better than that of the Soviet occupation army. Chinese troops established better rapport with the North Koreans than did the Russians.[75] This rapport was perhaps because of Mao Tse-tung's injunction to the Chinese soldiers in North Korea to "love the Korean Democratic People's Republic, the Korean People's Party, and the Korean people as your own government, party, and people—and treasure every mountain, stream, tree, and blade of grass the same."[76]

The Chinese economic assistance in North Korea's postwar economic recovery was very impressive. There is considerable evidence to suggest that during the Korean War Communist China extended several free grants amounting to about $75 million to North Korea.[77] The first Sino-North Korean economic agreement was the Treaty for Economic and Cultural Cooperation which was signed on November 23, 1953. The agreement declared that both countries "shall extend to each other all possible economic and technical aid, carry out the necessary economic and technical cooperation and endeavor to promote cultural exchange between the two countries."[78] A joint communiqué issued by the two governments at the conclusion of the pact announced that the PRC waived all war debts incurred by

North Korea from June 25, 1950, through December 31, 1953. China also granted North Korea eight billion *yuan* (approximately $320 million) to be used from 1954 to 1957.[79] The Chinese promised to use the money grant to give North Korea coal, cloth, cotton, grains, building material, agricultural tools, fishing boats, and "other daily necessities of the people." They also agreed to help the North Koreans rehabilitate their devastated railway system and supply locomotives and passenger and freight cars.[80] In 1955, according to a North Korean source,[81] the Chinese provided North Korea with transportation facilities, machine tools, coal, construction materials, locomotives and coaches, textile machines, cotton, textile goods, and paper. China's share in North Korea's total trade rose from 9 percent in 1955 to 27.3 percent in 1957.[82]

This extensive aid, particularly when China was launching its own First Five-Year Economic Plan for which all available resources were desperately needed, testifies to the open identification of China's national interest with the preservation and stabilization of the North Korean regime. It also clearly indicates that the Chinese had decided to undertake a share in underwriting the government of North Korea.

To what extent the Chinese Communists intended to reorient the North Korean regime during and after the war is not known. But, during the conflict, they seem to have made no serious effort to satellitize North Korea, perhaps because it would have been neither practical nor desirable. The Yenan group, through which Chinese control would have to be exercised, was strongest in the North Korean army. But its position was badly weakened by the catastrophic North Korean defeat in the autumn of 1950 and the subsequent purge of its leader, Mu Chŏng. The defeats suffered by the CPV in the spring of 1951 must have further weakened the Chinese capacity to establish control over the North Korean regime. Moreover, to have tried to replace Soviet influence with preponderant Chinese influence in North Korea would certainly have produced a serious controversy with the Soviet Union that the Chinese could hardly have afforded at that time.[83] Even after the truce in 1953, there was no evidence to suggest that the Chinese followed the Stalinist pattern in dealing with North Korea, even though the Chinese troops were in North Korea for nearly five years in sufficient numbers to enforce many of the desires China might have had.

The PRC's main motive in intervening in the Korean Conflict and granting extensive aid for the postwar economic recovery appears to have been to protect its own security by denying the United States the power to occupy North Korea. The Chinese Communist Party organ indicated this by declaring: "We hold that the economic recovery of every town and village of Korea and the growth of the Korean people's strength represent an additional safeguard to the Chinese people's security."[84] Thus, Peking's major interest in influencing P'yŏngyang's behavior was the cultivation of long-term goodwill rather than the establishment of direct control over the North Korean regime.

SOVIET-NORTH KOREAN RELATIONS, 1950–1957

North Korea's exclusive economic and military dependence upon the Soviet Union disappeared after the Korean Conflict, and China clearly emerged as the Soviet Union's principal rival in influencing North Korea. However, the primacy of Soviet influence in North Korea seems to have been maintained until P'yŏngyang's growing emulation of Chinese policies began in the summer of 1958.

The increase of Chinese influence did not result in the displacement of Soviet-oriented leaders by Chinese-oriented leaders. The purges of Hŏ Ka-i and Pak Ch'ang-ok were an obvious indication of weakening of Soviet control in North Korea.[85] But the Yenan group also suffered equal, if not greater, defeat in the factional struggles by the purges of Mu Chŏng, Ch'oe Ch'ang-ik, and Kim Tu-bong. The situation of North Korea, between the Soviet and Chinese "spheres," can also be explained by the composition of the KWP Central Committee membership. Of seventy-one members who were elected in April 1956, 65 percent could be classified as pro-Soviet, 21 percent as pro-Chinese, the remaining members leaning toward neither side. The Standing Committee of the KWP Central Committee consisted of eight pro-Soviet and three pro-Chinese members.[86] Soviet advisers also wielded greater influence in North Korea than did Chinese advisers.[87] This Soviet influence was particularly evident in the North Korean army, which ironically had only Soviet advisers even after the Korean Conflict.[88]

The North Korean regime consistently recognized the Soviet Union as the leader of the entire socialist camp and placed the Soviet Union ahead of China in its lists of contributions to North Korea. It did not formally accord to China a comparable position.[89] On the occasion of the fifth anniversary of the founding of the North Korean army in February 1953, for example, the North Korean leaders declared: "Basing itself upon advanced Soviet military science and the priceless battle experience of the Soviet army, the Korean People's Army has experienced great qualitative and quantitative development during the fatherland liberation war." The pronouncements credited the Chinese with having contributed "blood," "their finest sons and daughters," and "a fine spirit of proletarian internationalism."[90]

When North Korea launched its program for collectivizing the farming population between 1953 and 1957, the primary object of emulation appeared to be the experience of the Soviet Union. "Experience in agricultural collectivization in the Soviet Union," wrote Kim Il-sŏng for *Pravda* in October 1957, "becomes the guiding compass of our party's cooperative policies."[91] At the beginning of the First Five-Year Economic Plan (1957–1961), in industrial and institutional development, the North Korean Communists seem to have attempted, first of all, to follow the Soviet example.[92] Indeed, North Korean industry was rebuilt on the Soviet pattern. It is also noteworthy that, until 1958, North Korea followed the Soviet economic system more closely than that of China. North Korean emulation of Chinese domestic policies did not begin until after the summer of 1958.[93]

Soviet economic aid to North Korea was also significant. In September 1953, the Soviet Union granted one billion rubles (about $250 million) to North Korea. The grant was to be used between 1954 and 1956, the period coinciding with North Korea's Three-Year Economic Plan. North Korea's debts to the Soviet Union were scaled down substantially, and the Soviet

Union agreed to provide technical assistance.[94] In 1956, Moscow granted $75 million in economic aid.[95] Finally, between 1953 and 1956, the Soviet East European satellites threw in another 1,192.9 million rubles (approximately $298 million at the official exchange rate) (see Table 1).

Changes in North Korea's trade pattern showed the decline of Soviet preponderance and the rising importance of trade with Communist China. But, as of 1957, the Soviets had managed to stay well ahead in the game. In 1957, for example, the Soviet Union accounted for 57 percent of North Korea's total trade, while China's share was about 27 percent. The total trade volume of the East European satellites with North Korea in 1956 amounted to about $31 million.[96]

TABLE 1

GRANTS TO NORTH KOREA FOR POSTWAR RECONSTRUCTION FROM EAST EUROPEAN COUNTRIES, 1953–1958

Countries	Million Rubles
East Germany	545.4
Poland	362.0
Czechoslovakia	113.0
Hungary	32.5
Rumania	90.0
Bulgaria	50.0
Total	1,192.9

Source: Yoon T. Kuark, "North Korea's Industrial Development During the Post-War Period," in Scalapino, *North Korea Today,* p. 61; Philip Rudolph, "North Korea and the Path to Socialism," *Pacific Affairs,* vol. XXXII, no. 2 (June 1959), pp. 133–34.

SELF-RELIANT ECONOMY AND *CHUCH'E*[97]

Three years of war had not only hopelessly displaced North Korea's people, but also destroyed its industry. The damage by the war itself was estimated at approximately $3 billion.[98] Gross industrial production in 1953 was reported to be 36 percent of that in 1949. In the steel, coal, electric, cement, chemical, and fishing sectors of the economy, the drop in production varied from 60 percent to 93 percent.[99] The war had thus left the North Korean regime economically more dependent on the socialist bloc support than it was before the war.

As already noted, economic assistance from the socialist bloc contributed greatly to the recovery of the war-shattered economy of North Korea. During the period of the 1954–1956 three-year plan, North Korea received over $900 million in grants and credits from the Soviet Union, China, and the East European countries. During these years, North Korea made significant economic gains and thus succeeded in laying the foundation for peacetime economic development. The North Koreans claimed that the plan was fulfilled in two years and eight months.[100] By the end of 1955 North Korean industrial production was claimed to be 56 percent over the prewar (1949) level.[101] In consequence, P'yŏngyang launched (in 1957) the First Five-Year Plan to "further consolidate the economic foundation of socialism and to meet the main needs of the people for food, clothing, and housing."[102]

As the economic condition improved and foreign aid was reduced after the completion of the initial efforts for construction, the North Korean leaders began to place more emphasis on an "independent and self-reliant economy" as an essential aspect of the party's economic program. The proportion of foreign aid in the state revenue was 33.4 percent in 1954. After 1954 foreign aid decreased drastically, reaching only 4.5 percent of the total revenue in 1958.[103] This drop was due mainly to the fact that Soviet aid was not forthcoming, and the Chinese were not able to offer much assistance.

One of the significant postwar political developments in North Korea was the intensive campaign for "things Korean." In his report to the KWP Central Committee plenum on April 1, 1955, Kim Il-sŏng emphatically denounced the party members for their ignorance of "Korean history" and urged them to study how best to apply the principles of Marxism-Leninism to North Korea's actual situation rather than blindly emulating them.[104]

On December 28, 1955, before a group of propaganda and agitation workers, Kim Il-sŏng stressed the need for "firmly establishing *chuch'e*" and further declared: "Although certain people say that the Soviet way is best or that the Chinese way is best, have we not now reached the point where we can construct our own way?"[105]

The major factors that enabled the North Korean Communists to increasingly emphasize *chuch'e* in formulating domestic and foreign policies were: (1) the bitter memories of the Korean Conflict; (2) the postwar political consolidation; (3) the economic progress; (4) the possibility that Soviet and Chinese influence on North Korean decisions had reached a state of equilibrium; and (5) the growing conflict within the international Communist camp. However, it should be borne in mind that the North Korean regime could not afford to alienate either of the two neighbors, the PRC or the Soviet Union, for the cry of *chuch'e* alone.

NORTH KOREA AND THE GROWING SINO-SOVIET CONFLICT

The origins of the Sino-Soviet dispute might be traced back to the strained relationship between Imperial China and Imperial Russia and to the discords between Comintern and Chinese Communist policies in the 1920s. The Russians and Chinese share the longest frontier in the world, stretching over four thousand miles, and their border antagonism represents a continuation of disputes that are many centuries old. Further, there are immense differences between the essentially European Russian tradition and the completely Asian Chinese tradition.[106] However, the Twentieth Congress of the Communist Party of the Soviet Union (CPSU) in February 1956 represents the major turning point in Sino-Soviet relations in the post-Stalin era. The Twentieth Congress set the stage for several of the major elements of conflict that have since appeared. The major conflicting issues have been: (1) Khrushchev's denunciation of Stalin; (2) his emphasis on peaceful transition to Communism and on peaceful coexistence with the West as the "general line" of the international Communist movement—i.e., his policy of détente with the United States; (3) the permissible diversity of methods used in building socialism and Communism; and (4) the fundamental question of socialist camp leadership.[107]

The difference between Moscow and Peking on the de-Stalinization issue became apparent within a few months after the Twentieth Congress. The Chinese Communists objected to Khrushchev's all-out attack on Stalin.[108] There were three possible reasons. Peking's first purpose was probably to limit the attack to Stalin himself and to protect Mao from the possible charge that he was following in Stalin's footsteps. Limiting ⸂⸃ attack to Stalin was a reflection of Peking's felt need to defend its own adaptation of Stalinism to Chinese conditions. Like Stalin, Mao had pursued a policy of industrialization and rapid collectivization. Peking wished to ensure that Khrushchev's attack on Stalin did not lead to a widespread domestic reaction against "Maoism." The second aim of the CCP was to establish Peking as a source of doctrinal guidance for the entire Communist movement by opposing Khrushchev's de-Stalinization campaign. Finally, the Chinese resented Khrushchev's failure, in the campaign against Stalin, to consult Mao, who, after the death of Stalin, "considered himself the senior living Marxist-Leninist."[109]

The Pyŏngyang regime did not mention Stalin's name for some years. When the "cult-of-personality" issue was raised at the August 1956 plenum, Kim Il-sŏng's supporters claimed that collective leadership had always been practiced in North Korea and that the cult of personality had never existed.[110] For a brief period, the large portrait of Kim Il-sŏng was removed from the platform. Songs praising Kim were not sung. Delegates to the party congress abstained from praising Kim for his glorious accomplishments.[111] The KWP even took the step of including the policy of collective leadership in the party rule (Article 25).[112]

But the North Korean leaders have never disgraced the dead hero. The emphasis upon the principle of collective leadership must have satisfied Moscow. The policy was also one that would have been satisfactory to Peking because P'yŏngyang did not attack Stalin personally. In fact, de-Stalinization has never been practiced seriously in North Korea, and the movement was obviously distasteful to the Stalinist Kim Il-sŏng. Indeed, the handling of the de-Stalinization issue in North Korea was strikingly similar to that in China.[113]

At the Moscow Conference of November 1957, Kim Il-sŏng was able to be an eyewitness to the divergent strategic views presented by Mao Tse-tung and Khrushchev, although their differences were virtually unknown in the West at that time. In his speech at the conference, Kim did not mention any controversial issue. All the North Korean leader was required to do at the conference was to sign the Moscow Declaration.[114] Returning home from the conference, Kim Il-sŏng did not mention the new development to his party members. Neither did the organs of the KWP hint at this subject, nor did they carry as many reports as they did previously in other conferences. Rather, the North Korean regime renewed more vigorously than ever before the campaign for *chuch'e* and emphasized the unity of the international Communist movement.[115]

The steadily growing dispute in Sino-Soviet relations placed the P'yŏngyang regime in a serious dilemma. The Sino-Soviet conflict on various issues forced the North Korean leaders to choose between the two powers, Moscow and Peking, at a time when they could not afford to alienate either. The continuous support of both the Soviet Union and China was vital if the country was to develop further its scientific, military, and industrial potentials. P'yŏngyang thus tried to avoid total alignment with either Moscow or Peking and to maintain a good relationship with both nations. This situation placed the North Korean leaders in an awkward position in which they had to serve two "masters."

CHAPTER 2
NORTH KOREA IN THE GROWING SINO-SOVIET CONFLICT, 1958-1959

During the years 1958-1959 the Sino-Soviet conflict was carried on without either side making public charges against the other. During this period the P'yŏngyang regime attempted to maintain friendly relations with both the Soviet Union and China. Kim Il-sŏng's major concern seems to have been the rapid development of the North Korean economy, and regardless of how much P'yŏngyang stressed a self-reliant economy, the economic development of North Korea was in large part dependent upon foreign aid from Moscow and Peking. Thus, P'yŏngyang apparently intended to remain neutral in the early stage of the Sino-Soviet dispute.

Two important issues dominated the Sino-Soviet rift during this period. One was the appearance of China's "people's commune" and "Great Leap Forward" programs in the fall of 1958. The other was the Chinese attack on Khrushchev's "peaceful-coexistence" strategy for leading the socialist bloc and international Communism to a final global victory. These two Chinese policies constituted a serious challenge to the traditional position of Moscow as the undisputed leader and arbiter of doctrine within the Communist bloc. Let us turn now to North Korea's relationships with the PRC and the Soviet Union and P'yŏngyang's attitudes on the disputed issues in Sino-Soviet relations.

SINO-NORTH KOREAN RELATIONS, 1958-1959

Beginning early in 1958 the theme of Sino-North Korean friendship was greatly stressed through both North Korean and Chinese press and radio.[1] Exchange of high-ranking leaders between P'yŏngyang and Peking was unusually frequent,[2] and the statements made by the leaders were very warm and friendly. From February 14 to 21, 1958, Chou En-lai visited P'yŏngyang at the invitation of the North Korean government. Arriving at the P'yŏngyang airport, Chou stated that "Korea and China are friendly states united by blood. You helped us when we needed you. We came to your assistance when you were invaded by American imperialists."[3] As a result of Chou's visit, a Sino-North Korean joint communiqué was issued on February 19, 1958. Declaring that both sides held identical views on expansion and development of friendly relations between the two countries, the communiqué said:

> The two peoples had undertaken protracted joint struggles against aggression, through which, and particularly through the struggle against the aggression of United States imperialism, their traditional friendship was cemented and developed with the blood of their best sons and daughters. In order to promote their respective socialist construction the two countries have developed an extensive cooperation in the economic, cultural, scientific, technical, and other fields, and given each other brotherly assistance.[4]

In return, Kim Il-sŏng visited Peking, November 21-28 and December 2-10, 1958.[5] In his speech at the Peking rally, Kim declared that "the Korean people will treasure their friendship with the Chinese people and will do their utmost to strengthen and develop that friendship." Thanking the Chinese people for their aid in the difficult times, Kim emphasized that "the traditional friendship between the people of the two countries... has grown still stronger and has entered new and higher stages."[6] Before Kim and his delegates departed, Kim and Chou En-lai signed a joint statement expressing the complete unanimity of views of the two governments on the current international situation, their determination to further develop friendly cooperation, and to strengthen the solidarity of the socialist camp headed by the Soviet Union.[7]

On October 3, 1958, a Sino-North Korean Friendship Society was, for the first time, formed in Peking. The Society sought to strengthen and develop "the traditional friendship, solidarity, and cultural relations between the Chinese and Korean peoples."[8] Undoubtedly, there were friendly ties between the leaders of these two countries, even though the background of the North Korean leadership tended to give them a more decided pro-Moscow orientation. In his farewell speech to the Chinese "People's Volunteers" in October 1958, Kim Il-sŏng voiced P'yŏngyang's attitude on Sino-North Korean friendship in the following words:

> The blood you shed in this land will stay forever in the hearts of our people. The common struggle of the Korean people and the Chinese People's Volunteers in the past eight years has brought unprecedented strength and growth to the friendship and solidarity of the Korean and the Chinese people.[9]

The typical Chinese expression of Sino-North Korean friendship in this period was made by Kuo Mo-jo at the Peking rally on the occasion of a "Korean Day" celebration. He commented: "We, the peoples of China and Korea, are comrades-in-arms. Our unbreakable friendship is sealed in blood. The relationship between our two peoples is like lips and teeth and as close as flesh and blood."[10]

Economic and trade relations between North Korea and China increased greatly during this period. A long-term credit agreement was signed on September 27, 1958. Under this agreement, the Chinese extended to North Korea a credit of $25 million.[11] The P'yŏngyang regime was to purchase machinery for one textile mill and two paper bag plants for making cement containers. Payment was to begin in 1961, with goods delivered over a ten-year period.[12] By the same agreement, North Korea also established a joint project with the Chinese regime to build the 400,000-kilowatt Unbong hydroelectric power station on the Yalu River. Peking was to provide a long-term loan to P'yŏngyang to cover half of the expenses undertaken by the North Koreans in constructing the power station. The project was to be established on the principle of equal rights and joint stock.[13]

An agreement on scientific and technical cooperation was

signed by the two countries on December 31, 1957.[14] An additional protocol providing for the exchange of relevant data was signed by the Sino-North Korean Scientific and Technical Cooperation Committee in June 1959.[15] By these agreements, Chinese specialists and technicians helped the North Koreans in shipbuilding and cement and silk industries. Also, North Korean students were sent to China for technical training.[16] There were joint scientific and technical undertakings that included the harnessing of the Tuman River on the Sino-Korean border and fishing research in the Pacific.[17] In addition to these joint undertakings, an agreement signed in Peking on August 25, 1959, provided for joint development of their fishing industries in the Yellow Sea.[18]

A formal Sino-North Korean trade agreement was signed on May 15, 1958.[19] The volume of trade between them in 1958 was expected to be 50 percent larger than that in 1957 and eleven times what it was in 1954.[20] The protocol on exchange of goods between the two countries for 1959 was signed in Peking on November 19, 1958. Under the terms of this protocol, China was to send North Korea coal, rolled steel, cotton, cotton yarn, and sulphur. North Korea's exports were to include copper, zinc, fertilizers, high-speed steel, Korean ginseng, and seafoods. North Korea is also reported to have sent 400,000 tons of iron ore in 1958 to help Chinese steel production and to have sent increased shipments of explosives needed in China for mining purposes.[21]

Cultural cooperation between P'yŏngyang and Peking increased considerably in 1958–1959. A regular exchange of publications and films began in 1956. In 1958, the Chinese sent cinema and art delegations, soccer and volleyball teams, and a circus to North Korea. In return, North Korean cultural and film delegates and gymnastic and table tennis teams visited China.[22] A Sino-North Korean agreement on cultural cooperation for five years was signed on February 21, 1959. This agreement arranged for mutual visits by delegates in the fields of culture, education, science, public health, sports, and journalism. It also called for the exchange of students and senior researchers and the supplying of books, magazines, and other publications.[23] It is interesting to note, however, that Kim Il-sŏng called in January 1959 for the simplification of the language and the elimination of "unnecessary foreign words using Chinese characters."[24]

EMULATION OF THE CHINESE POLICIES, 1958–1959

The initiation of China's commune and Great Leap Forward policies in the summer of 1958 introduced a new element of discord into Sino-Soviet relations.[25] The Chinese claimed that the new programs were their own "creative applications of Marxism-Leninism" to the "special conditions" in China.[26] According to a *Hung Ch'i (Red Flag)* article entitled "Under the Banner of Chairman Mao," Mao Tse-tung was credited with discovering in the commune and Great Leap Forward programs a special road for leading China and Asian countries to the quick achievement of socialism and Communism.[27] The Chinese thus clearly implied that their new policies, not Soviet experiences, represented the most appropriate organizational model for all Asian countries building socialism. The Russians were slow to recognize the challenge that the Chinese programs represented. But when they did, they were firm in their rejection of them.

The P'yŏngyang regime, however, enthusiastically endorsed both programs. Echoing the Chinese statements, an editorial of *Nodong Shinmun* called the programs "an example of the creative application of Marxism-Leninism to the realities of their country," and praised the new Chinese policies as the great victory of the Chinese people.[28] Deviating further from its traditional role as a docile Soviet satellite, the North Korean regime embraced a series of Chinese economic policies in the summer and autumn of 1958. The North Korean leaders were apparently convinced that Chinese innovations actually promised solutions to North Korea's own pressing economic problems. In August 1958, Kim Il-sŏng told local administrative heads that North Korea intended to catch up with the Soviet Union by going beyond the Soviet experiments. Implying that he intended to adopt the Chinese policies, Kim said:

The Soviet economy is now highly developed and the Soviet people are living well. But we are now living in difficult conditions. In order to live well quickly we must go forward faster than others. Why should we adhere precisely to Soviet norms of production? Is it bad that Korea produce two while Russia produce one?[29]

In the summer of 1958, the P'yŏngyang regime began to model her economic policy after the Chinese example. North Korea launched a mass movement for construction of small industrial installations combining old and modern. This movement followed closely, both in time and method, China's mass line of industrialization.[30] At the September 1958 plenum of the KWP Central Committee, North Korea inaugurated the *Ch'ŏllima Undong* (Flying Horse Movement) and an agricultural collectivization program.[31] The Flying Horse Movement, which bore a striking resemblance to China's Great Leap Forward Movement, aimed at accelerating the pace of the North Korean economic development through intensive exploitation of human labor to a degree unknown in modern history.[32] Kim Il-sŏng urged the North Koreans to "rush forward like a flying horse" for the fulfillment of the First Five-Year Plan "one year and a half ahead of schedule."[33] According to Dong Jun Lee, who witnessed the development in North Korea until early 1959, the people were "forced to work like animals."[34] One of the important features of the Great Leap Forward emulated by the North Koreans was the attempt to raise the production of pig iron by manual methods through the construction of small local blast furnaces. This was related to an attempt to decentralize certain types of modern industry in order to use local resources effectively and to improve administration.[35] The North Korean leaders, however, insisted that their movement had been launched in December 1956, at a time when the Chinese were not yet considering such bold economic experimentation.[36] The Flying Horse Movement was discussed at the meeting of the KWP Central Committee in December 1956, but the movement was not actually launched until after the Chinese Great Leap Forward began in the summer of 1958.[37]

In October 1958, the Cabinet of Ministers of the DPRK decided to begin the amalgamation of agricultural cooperatives.[38] All cooperatives in each village were to be merged; the same individual was to be chairman of the village people's committee and the amalgamated cooperative. It was announced in November that 13,309 cooperative farms were merged into 3,880 political-economic units of township size. It was called *ri*—the lowest administrative unit. The average size of the cooperatives increased to approximately three hundred households from an average of seventy-nine before the reorganization.[39] Although there were some exceptions,[40] the North Korean Communists closely emulated many of the principal features of the Chinese commune.[41] In fact, the North Korean cooperatives were not operated very differently from the Chinese communes. The P'yŏngyang regime claimed that this "victory" of agricultural policy would bring "seven million tons of grain in the near future."[42]

When Kim Il-sŏng visited China in late November and early December 1958 he was able to view the commune and Great Leap Forward programs at first hand. During his extended tour, Kim passionately endorsed the new Chinese policies, which were, to a significant extent, also put into practice in North Korea. He asserted that North Korea and China were advancing to socialism and Communism with "flying leaps," and emphasized that "we will certainly pass on to our peasants the great results you have achieved from your commune movement."[43]

Returning home from China, Kim Il-sŏng reported to the North Koreans that the Chinese were achieving enormous success in their socialist construction. The Great Leap Forward Movement demonstrated "the great creative power of the 650 million Chinese people." He even predicted that China would overtake and outstrip Great Britain in the production of steel and other major industrial goods within the next few years.[44] He also pointed out that the people's commune movement had important meaning for the promotion of socialist construction and for the preparation for transformation to Communism in China.[45]

The Chinese claim for discovery of a special road for leading

Asian countries to the rapid achievement of socialism and Communism, and Kim Il-sŏng's subsequent acknowledgment of this claim, implicitly denied the validity of the Soviet model for the special problems of economic and social development in Asia. The Soviet leaders responded to this development with strong and unmistakable objections. In his report to the Twenty-first Congress of the CPSU, early in 1959, Khrushchev declared that "V. I. Lenin foresaw that the Soviet Union would exert chief influence on the entire course of world development by its economic construction." He also insisted that the transition to Communism was "a natural historic process which cannot be intentionally violated or bypassed." Thus, the progress would inevitably be long and gradual, and the only sure way of speeding the advent of Communism was to increase the production of material goods.[46] The Russians claimed that both Europe and Asia should follow the "correct" Soviet road.[47] Khrushchev was also reported to have told Senator Hubert H. Humphrey in December 1958 that communes were "old-fashioned" and "reactionary."[48] It was clear that the Soviet Union intended to determine the pace and order of bloc progress to Communism and that Khrushchev, not Mao Tse-tung, would solve any problems of Marxist-Leninist theory connected with the transition from socialism to Communism.

The Soviet counteroffensive was directed primarily at China. But many of its criticisms applied to North Korea as well. North Korea appeared to have acted upon the Soviet pressure. At the Twenty-first Congress of the CPSU, Kim Il-sŏng declared that North Korea was proceeding along the road to socialism with the "rich experience" accumulated by the CPSU and the Soviet people.[49] In his article contributed to *Pravda* on March 17, 1959, Kim Il-sŏng repeated his earlier statement that North Korea was adopting the "rich experience" of the Soviet Union in the matter of collectivization.[50]

However, P'yŏngyang continued to praise and imitate Peking's model of a more radical approach to the domestic construction of Communism. In the fall of 1959, the North Korean leaders once again spoke out vigorously in defense of China's economic programs and of the friendship between the two coun-

tries. At a mass rally to celebrate Communist China's tenth anniversary Kim Il-sŏng said that the Chinese people, guided by
the general line for building socialism, were sure to achieve new
and greater successes in the Great Leap Forward and commune
movements. The Great Leap Forward in China and the Flying
Horse Movement in North Korea both showed, Kim declared,
"the resolute fighting spirit, and the inexhaustible creativeness
in building a new life, of people who had liberated themselves
from exploitation and oppression and become masters of their
own destiny." No force, he concluded, could disrupt the friendship between the people of the two countries, whose combined
forces were invincible.[51] *Minju Chosŏn* also carried an editorial
that defended the Chinese economic policies.[52]

After the plenary session of the KWP Central Committee, in
December 1959, North Korea abruptly decided to slow down the
path of economic activity and to designate 1960 as a "buffer
year." According to a North Korean source, this decision was
made to correct deficiencies in agriculture and provide a needed
adjustment period for its economic-development programs.[53]
Throughout 1960 the North Korean leaders studiously dis-
avowed the Chinese commune as a model for North Korean
emulation, and they reduced the tempo in implementing the
Flying Horse Movement.[54]

One of the important reasons for this North Korean decision
was Soviet pressure on P'yŏngyang. In July 1959, in a speech in
Poland, Khrushchev made a direct attack on the whole concept
of the communes. Dismissing the communes with contempt, he
said that people who advocated them "had a poor idea of what
Communism is and how it is to be built."[55] At the Hungarian
Party Conference on December 1, 1959, Khrushchev again publicly launched an attack on China's commune and Great Leap
Forward programs. He characterized them as a "distortion of
the teaching of Marxism-Leninism on the building of socialism
and Communism."[56]

Even while imitating the Chinese communes, the North Koreans apparently tried to avoid offending their Russian comrades. For example, the vast scale of the Chinese commune was
not attempted. The average size of the amalgamated North Ko-

rean cooperatives was approximately three hundred households, which equaled that of the average Soviet *kolkhoz*. [57] They also retained the term "cooperative" (as did Russia), even though the Chinese adopted the term "commune" in July 1958. Thus, the North Korean Communists could justify their agrarian policy merely as an extension of the Soviet Union's experience with "high type cooperation." [58]

The North Korean leaders also appeared to have become disenchanted with Chinese programs as a solution to their own industrial and agricultural problems. In December 1959, Kim Il-sŏng complained that the economic progress in 1959 had revealed "many defects," such as "draining of rural manpower, declining steel production, and shortages of industrial raw materials, housing, and food." [59] In fact, North Korean grain output in 1959 dropped nearly 10 percent, instead of increasing 35 percent as anticipated. [60] In short, Chinese policies borrowed by the North Koreans had proved no more effective in solving the economic problems of North Korea than they had been in removing the economic difficulties of China.

The North Korean emulation of the Chinese policies did not proceed under Chinese military or political dictation, nor was it accompanied by the emergence of a new Chinese-oriented KWP leadership. This emulation began at the time when the CPV were being withdrawn. The withdrawal of the Chinese troops might have been initiated by the North Korean proposal of February 5, 1958, which requested the complete removal of "all foreign troops from Korea." [61] On February 7, Peking issued an official statement supporting the North Korean proposal, and the Chinese indicated that they were willing to negotiate the withdrawal of the Chinese troops with the P'yŏngyang regime. [62] The Soviet Union supported the P'yŏngyang proposal and the subsequent Chinese statement. [63] The Sino-North Korean joint communiqué, issued on February 19, 1958, at the time when Chou En-lai visited P'yŏngyang, revealed that the CPV would be completely withdrawn from North Korea before the end of 1958 and requested the United Nations forces to do likewise. The first stage of the withdrawal would be completed before April 30, 1958. [64] Moscow expressed its full support of the joint com-

muniqué.[65] The withdrawal of the Chinese troops from North
Korea was completed on October 26, 1958.[66]

The emulation of the Chinese policies did not in itself consti-
tute evidence of the emergence of a new Chinese-oriented KWP
leadership. As noted earlier, all the Yenan faction leaders were
completely eliminated from party life by early 1958. P'yŏngyang's imitation of the Chinese policies thus took place at a time
when Chinese influence was considerably reduced. There was
also no clear evidence that the adoption of the Chinese policies
meant a general rejection of Soviet experience.[67] The North
Korean leaders repeatedly made it clear that the Soviet Union
was heading the world-socialist camp. But they did not formally
accord China a comparable position in 1958–1959.[68]

What, then, was the main reason for North Korea's decision to
emulate the Chinese policies in spite of Moscow's objections?
The most plausible explanation appears to be that the P'yŏngyang leaders became convinced that Chinese innovations would
"work"—would enable North Korea to solve her own economic
problems. By early 1960, however, it appeared that the North
Korean regime aspired to a position of neutrality in the deepen-
ing Sino-Soviet controversy over the "correct" road to socialism
and Communism.

NORTH KOREAN-SOVIET RELATIONS,
1958–1959

Commemorating the establishment of the Soviet-North Korean Friendship Society in July 1958, *Nodong Shinmun*
editorialized on P'yŏngyang's attitude in the Soviet-North Korean relationship. The organ of the KWP stated that the North
Koreans "regard it as their sacred duty to unite around the
Soviet Union, learn from it, support it, and stand with it."[69] At
the Twenty-first Congress of the CPSU, Kim Il-sŏng praised the
Soviet Union for attaining great successes in the development of
economy, science and technology. The "rich experience" accumulated by the CPSU and the Soviet people in socialist and Communist construction, he continued, "always serves as a guide in

all our work."[70] The North Korean Communists repeatedly stated that the socialist camp should be united under the leadership of the CPSU.[71] This attitude toward Moscow prevailed generally in North Korea throughout 1958–1959.

At the same time, the North Korean leaders also stressed the policy of *chuch'e* by emphasizing the "creative application of Marxism-Leninism to the national peculiarities" of North Korea. They argued that the intrabloc relationship should be based on "principles of complete equality, respect for territorial integrity and independence, and noninterference in each other's national affairs."[72] Returning from the Twenty-first CPSU Congress, Kim Il-sŏng declared that "Solidarity centered on the Soviet Union has always been necessary." But "it does not mean that somebody is dominating somebody else; nor does it mean our submission to Moscow."[73] He would hardly have dared to make such a statement if the pre-1950 Soviet control system had existed in North Korea.

The Soviet Union rendered North Korea significant economic and technical aid to rehabilitate and expand the latter's industries. According to Kim Il-sŏng, "over twenty modern enterprises have been restored or newly built with Soviet help." They included such important enterprises as the P'yŏngyang textile mill, the Kim Ch'aek iron works, the Supung hydroelectric power station, the Hŭngnam fertilizer factory, and the Changjin steel foundry.[74] On March 17, 1959, an agreement was signed between the Soviet Union and North Korea. The agreement provided for technical assistance by the Soviet Union to North Korea in the construction of "a thermopower station with a generating capacity of 200,000 kilowatts, ammonium and chloride-vinyl factories, and flax spinning and woolen textile mills." The expansion of the Kim Ch'aek iron works and the P'yŏngyang silk mill was also involved. The assistance by the Soviet Union envisaged in the agreement amounted to about $125 million (500 million rubles). North Korea was to repay this amount to Moscow by means of commodity delivery through trade.[75]

By an agreement signed between the Soviet Union and North

Korea on September 7, 1959, the Soviet Union was to provide for technical assistance to North Korea "in constructing an atomic research reactor, a nuclear physics laboratory, an isotope laboratory, a betatron and a cobalt installation," in training North Korean cadres, and in other forms of technical cooperation in the "peaceful use" of atomic energy.[76] It is significant to note that this agreement came after Moscow unilaterally abrogated (in June 1959) the Sino-Soviet atomic agreement of October 1957, and refused to supply the Chinese with a sample of an atomic bomb and technical data concerning its manufacture.[77] The North Koreans hailed the Soviet offer,[78] and this certainly strengthened the Soviet-North Korean relationship.

A North Korean-Soviet trade protocol on mutual delivery of goods for 1958 was signed on January 9, 1958, on the basis of "the spirit of equality, mutual benefit, friendship and cooperation."[79] The important commodities that the Soviet Union exported to North Korea in 1958 included machines, electric locomotives, trucks, chemical products, and pipes. But total trade volume between the two countries in 1958 (420 million rubles) was less than that in 1957 (490 rubles), mainly because of a decline in North Korea's exports to the Soviet Union.[80]

An extended trade agreement and protocol on mutual delivery of goods for 1959 between P'yŏngyang and Moscow was signed on December 30, 1958. Total trade volume was expected to be increased in 1959 by more than 50 percent over that of 1958.[81] Under the agreement, the Soviet Union was to deliver to North Korea various types of industrial equipment, motor vehicles, road-building machinery, tractors, farm machinery, rolled ferrous metals, pipe, tin plate, cable items, oil products, chemical goods, rubber, and items for industrial use. North Korea would deliver to the Soviet Union ores and concentrates of nonferrous metals, lead zinc, high-speed steel, pig iron, cement, silk fabrics, and fruit.[82]

The North Korean-Soviet cultural cooperation program for 1959 was intended to further extend the contact between the two countries in the fields of culture, arts, broadcasting, education, science, public health, and sports.[83] The Soviet Union helped train North Korean cadres, and many North Korean students and workers were sent to the Soviet Union to receive training in the various fields.[84]

NORTH KOREA ON KHRUSHCHEV'S PEACEFUL COEXISTENCE POLICY

Khrushchev's speech at the Twentieth Congress of the CPSU introduced "new" Soviet foreign policy and global revolutionary strategy. He declared that peaceful coexistence was a "fundamental principle" of Soviet foreign policy, based on "our certainty of the victory" of Communism in peaceful competition. Modifying the Marxist-Leninist dogma that "wars are inevitable as long as capitalism survives," Khrushchev concluded that "war is no longer a fatalistic inevitability." Finally, he emphasized that there was an increasing possibility of a nonviolent transformation to socialism in a number of capitalist countries.[85]

Khrushchev reasoned that the victory of socialism could be achieved by peaceful competition with different social systems without having to resort to the real possibility of nuclear war. In his *Foreign Affairs* article, Khrushchev stated that "peaceful coexistence can and should develop into a peaceful competition for the purpose of satisfying man's needs in the best possible way."[86] "In our day," he continued, "there are only two ways: peaceful coexistence or the most destructive war in history. There is no third choice."[87]

It is highly doubtful that the Chinese Communists seriously accepted the new Soviet strategic outlook enunciated at the Twentieth Congress. As noted previously, Peking publicly disagreed with Moscow on the de-Stalinization issue immediately after the Twentieth Congress. But it was not until two years later, in 1958, that the Chinese attacked the Twentieth Congress line of peaceful coexistence. The Chinese argued that the limits Moscow imposed on herself and the bloc, because of the fear of all-out nuclear war, were too severe, and that the opportunities available as a result of Soviet military and economic power and Western weaknesses were not being sufficiently exploited.[88] They further accused Khrushchev of having excluded active revolutionary struggles of the oppressed peoples and subordinating them to the Soviet policy of peaceful coexistence.[89] Peking declared that "as long as imperialism remains, the people cannot avoid the threat of war."[90] On April 15, 1960, *Hung Ch'i* carried an article entitled "Long Live Leninism." Going beyond the usual official pronouncements assailing "opportunists" and "revisionists" like Tito, the article launched a public attack on the theoretical rationale of Khrushchev's foreign policy by reviving Leninist dicta on the inevitability of war, the intrinsically aggressive nature of imperialism, and the need for direct revolutionary action to promote international Communism.[91]

Contrary to the Chinese attack against the new Soviet strategic outlook since 1958, the North Korean regime supported Khrushchev's line of peaceful coexistence. From 1956 through 1959 the general tone of the official organs of P'yŏngyang was emphatically in favor of the new Soviet foreign policy. It was reported that the decisions of the Twentieth Congress of the CPSU were supported unanimously at the KWP Congress held in August 1956.[92] At the Moscow Conference of November 1957, Kim Il-sŏng is reported to have supported Khrushchev's idea of peaceful coexistence.[93] An editorial of *Nodong Shinmun*, published immediately after the Moscow Conference, praised Khrushchev's "peace-loving policy" as well as Russia's tremendous economic achievements. The editorial quoted a substantial part of Khrushchev's speech made at the conference, while ignoring Mao's speech completely.[94] At the Twenty-first Congress of the CPSU, Kim Il-sŏng said that the Twentieth Congress of the CPSU made contributions to the development of the international Communist movement and to the "strengthening of the world peace forces."[95] At the meeting of the Supreme People's Assembly on October 26, 1959, Nam Il, vice-premier and vice-chairman of the KWP Central Committee, declared that the "peace-loving foreign policy of the Great Soviet Union and the other socialist countries made a great progress toward the easing of the international tension."[96]

During the 1958 Taiwan Strait crisis, P'yŏngyang gave rather reserved support to Peking's actions and carefully avoided any direct involvement. This stance was perhaps due to Moscow's "lukewarm" and "noncommittal" attitude toward the Chinese intention to take over Taiwan and the offshore islands. Although the organs of the P'yŏngyang regime urged that the United States withdraw from the Taiwan Strait and insisted that "Taiwan and the offshore islands must be returned to the Chinese people,"[97] they conspicuously refrained from endorsing the Chinese attacks on the offshore islands and the Chinese intention to invade Taiwan. The official statement of North Korea on the crisis was issued only after Chou En-lai's statement of September 6, which expressed Peking's willingness to negotiate with the United States[98] and after subsequent Moscow appraisal of Chou's announcement.[99] The timing of the North Korean statement seems to be very important. Defending Peking's claim over Taiwan and the offshore islands, the official P'yŏngyang statement, which was issued on September 12, pledged that "the Korean people will always march together with the Chinese people in the struggle against the United States imperialists' war provocation" in the Far East and the world. The P'yŏngyang statement, however, was no more than a repetition of the statements of Chou and Moscow.[100]

The Sino-Soviet dispute over the peaceful-coexistence policy with the West was deepened further by Khrushchev's lengthy visit to the United States in September 1959. The visit ended with talks with President Dwight Eisenhower at Camp David; the joint declaration of September 27, which was on the whole optimistically phrased, also announced President Eisenhower's return visit to the Soviet Union in early 1960.[101] In a report that Khrushchev delivered to a mass meeting in Moscow he spoke favorably of President Eisenhower and extolled his "statesmanlike wisdom in judging the present international situations" and his "courage and determination."[102]

Peking flatly rejected the possibility of peaceful coexistence and doubted Washington's sincerity by saying that one could no more hope for the United States to relax than to expect "a cat to keep away from fish."[103] An editorial in *Jen-min Jih-pao,* entitled "Whence the Difference in Views," openly voiced disapproval of Khrushchev's policy of 1959:

Particularly around the time of the Camp David talks in September 1959, certain comrades of a fraternal party [the CPSU] put forward a series of erroneous views on many important issues relating to the international situation and the international Communist movement, views which departed from Marxism-Leninism... They portrayed the Camp David talks as a "new state," a "new era" in international relations.... They were especially ardent in lauding Dwight Eisenhower... as one who had "a sincere desire for peace," who "sincerely hopes to eliminate the state of cold war," and who "also worries about ensuring peace just as we do...."[104]

Contrary to Peking's attitude, P'yŏngyang's reaction to Khrushchev's visit to the United States was highly favorable. A *Minju Chosŏn* editorial of August 7 welcomed the official report on the forthcoming mutual visits of Premier Khrushchev and President Eisenhower. The editorial stated that the mutual visits were "a fruit of the sincere efforts of the Soviet Union for easing international tension... and a victory of the idea of peaceful coexistence among countries with different social systems."[105] On the eve of Khrushchev's departure for Washington, *Nodong Shinmun* carried an editorial entitled "Eternal Hope of Mankind: Peace!" The editorial described Khrushchev's trip to the United States in the following words:

Comrade Khrushchev's American visit will promote better understanding between the Soviet Union and the United States, end the cold war, and contribute to easing the international tensions.... We wholeheartedly support the Russian effort for the establishment of the peaceful world.[106]

Nodong Shinmun reported the activities of Khrushchev in the United States comprehensively. At the conclusion of the visit, the organ praised it as a "victory of the peace-loving policy of the Soviet Union."[107] It carried the full content of the Soviet-American joint communiqué,[108] and it declared that Khrushchev's speech on his return to Moscow signaled the end of the cold war.[109] At the sixth session of the Second Supreme

People's Assembly, Nam Il also praised Khrushchev's visit. He said that the visit brought up "the new prospect and encouragement to the strength of peace and easing of international tensions."[110] North Korea also supported the Soviet Union's nuclear test ban[111] and disarmament proposals.[112]

The Kim Il-sŏng regime spoke of the "peaceful unification of Korea" and endorsed the peaceful coexistence policy of the Soviet Union. At the same time, however, Kim was not ready to accept "peaceful coexistence" as a policy for North Korean-South Korean relations. The regime, instead, intensified hostility against the United States and the Republic of Korea and rejected the application of Khrushchev's new policy to the Korean situation. Kim Il-sŏng said there were some who extended the policy of peaceful coexistence of the two world camps into Korea and wrongly concluded that two separate Koreas could coexist. But the principle of peaceful coexistence was, he continued, impossible to apply to Korea, because "it is a view obstructing our efforts for unification."[113]

The North Korean leaders, particularly after late 1959, became increasingly uneasy about Khrushchev's formula of peaceful coexistence. North Korean commentary evidenced open skepticism of Khrushchev's contention that a growing number of Western leaders were sincere in their desire to reduce international tensions.[114] In October 1959, Khrushchev publicly cautioned the North Korean leaders against the use of force because "the United States is not seeking a military conflict in Korea."[115] Despite Khrushchev's warning, however, P'yŏngyang continued to accuse the United States of "planning war in Korea."[116]

On the other hand, the Chinese views on the Korean problem were very much in tune with those of the North Korean leaders. In January 1958, for example, Chou En-lai stated that he considered the continued presence of American forces in South Korea a major threat to peace in Asia, "a state of affairs which the Koreans and Chinese people cannot allow to continue."[117] This position clearly illustrated that Kim Il-sŏng shared with Mao Tse-tung a common hostility toward the United States as the power that blocked reunification of Korea under Kim and prevented Mao's absorption of Taiwan.

North Korean divergence from Khrushchev's foreign-policy pronouncements first came into light on September 12, 1959, when P'yŏngyang proclaimed its "full support" for Communist China in the Sino-Indian border dispute.[118] This was in contrast to a prior Soviet declaration of neutrality in this matter. The Soviet statement, which was issued on September 9, declared that "the Soviet Union is in friendly relations both with the Chinese People's Republic and the Republic of India."[119] It was, in fact, this Russian statement that first revealed to the outside world the existence of the Sino-Soviet dispute.

SUMMARY

From the discussion thus far, a few summarizing comments are in order. First of all, the trend of KWP policy decisions, at least since 1958, no longer makes it accurate to regard the North Korean regime as a pre-1950 type of Soviet puppet. Rather, Soviet and Chinese influence on North Korean decisions apparently had reached a state of equilibrium that permitted Kim Il-sŏng increased freedom of action to choose Chinese domestic policies. But this does not necessarily mean a rejection of Soviet experience or the displacement of the Soviet Union as the primary object of emulation. The P'yŏngyang regime was able to utilize the Sino-Soviet dispute to enlarge its scope of autonomous action. Denying blind imitation of both Peking and Moscow, the North Korean leaders insisted on "creative application of Marxism-Leninism" to the realities of North Korea.

Secondly, North Korea and China were both still in the stormy and hectic days of their respective revolutions. Thus, they shared similar views on the pattern of socialization, particularly economic policy. Both Kim Il-sŏng and Mao Tse-tung wanted hard-line economic and social programs in order to achieve rapid economic self-sufficiency, preferably with extensive Soviet aid, but, since that was not possible, by labor-intensive policies. They also shared a hostile attitude toward the United States.

They believed that United States "imperialism" was the main enemy because it blocked the reunification of Korea under Kim Il-sŏng and Mao's absorption of Taiwan. This anti-Americanism was undoubtedly an important factor in binding them together.

Finally, Kim Il-sŏng's major concern during this period was the development of the North Korean economy. The Five-Year Plan (1957–1961), which aimed to lay the foundation of socialist economy, was still in progress. Kim apparently realized that the success or failure of his economic plan depended heavily upon economic aid from the Soviet Union and China. Without extensive aid from both countries, North Korea would not have been able to carry out its economic goals. The P'yŏngyang regime was extremely careful to side with neither Peking nor Moscow in the growing Sino-Soviet conflict and tried to satisfy both the Chinese and Russians. Thus, North Korea was torn between the reality of needing economic and military assistance and the desire to maintain their more aggressive ideological line.

CHAPTER 3
P'YŎNGYANG'S NEUTRALISM
IN THE SINO-SOVIET RIFT,
1960–1961

The growing cleavage between Moscow and Peking erupted into the open in 1960. Although P'yŏngyang was ideologically closer to Peking than to Moscow, the North Korean Communists at first adopted a cautious neutral stance toward the Sino-Soviet dispute. They then sought to use the opportunity afforded by the conflict to enhance their independence and maneuverability. The wider the Sino-Soviet rift became, however, the more the North Korean regime showed an increasing support of the Chinese ideological line.

THE JUNE 1960 BUCHAREST CONFERENCE[1]

The Bucharest Conference in late June revealed for the first time to other bloc parties the fundamental nature and disruptive effect of the Sino-Soviet dispute. During this conference, the bitter debate between Khrushchev and P'eng Chen, chief Chinese delegate and then mayor of Peking, was for the first time witnessed by an international audience.[2] Khrushchev is reported to have attacked Mao Tse-tung personally and to have denounced him as an "ultraleftist, an ultradogmatist, [and] a left revisionist." Khrushchev compared Mao to Stalin, and he also told the Chinese that they knew nothing about modern war. P'eng is said to have reacted with an equally bitter attack on the Soviet Union and on Khrushchev personally. He reportedly accused Khrushchev of arranging the meeting solely to denounce China and undermine its prestige. He also said that the Chinese Communist Party did not at all trust Khrushchev's analysis of the international situation.[3] This violent debate between Khrushchev and P'eng was not disclosed to the outside world.

Khrushchev devoted a substantial part of his public speech at the conference to reassuring the delegates that Soviet foreign policy was based on the principle of peaceful coexistence among states. He laid great stress on the destructiveness of nuclear war, omitting any claim that only imperialism would be wiped out in the event of such a catastrophe. He cautioned that a local war would lead to a world nuclear conflict. He did not list the national-liberation movements as a factor making war less likely. Mentioning his trip to the United States for the meeting with President Eisenhower at Camp David, Khrushchev said that "all the peoples want peace, including the American nation. I did not doubt this before my trip to the United States and [I] became even more convinced of this after I had been there."[4] These statements obviously displeased the North Korean delegates.

On the other hand, P'eng Chen violently accused the United States of playing "the trick of faking peace while actually preparing for war." He warned that "the peoples of the world must never entertain any unrealistic illusions about imperialism, especially United States imperialism."[5] Indeed, the speeches made by the two Communist leaders were in striking contrast, especially in respect to the strategy of international Communist movement against the Western world. In short, Khrushchev emphasized the peaceful competition with the West, while China stressed a more militant approach to the international Communist movement.

All the East European parties at the Bucharest Conference supported the Soviet Union except Albania, which sided completely with the Chinese. The North Korean and North Vietnamese delegations, the only two remaining ruling Communist governments, remained neutral in their public speeches. The North Korean delegation was headed by Kim Ch'ang-man, a member of the Politburo and then vice-chairman of the KWP Central Committee. Kim's speech at the conference was in its general tone more sympathetic toward the Chinese views. He neither endorsed Khrushchev's peaceful coexistence policy nor mentioned that war could be prevented. Unlike all the East European (except Albanian) party leaders, Kim Ch'ang-man did not praise Khrushchev or the Soviet Union for promoting world peace. More than two-thirds of his speech was devoted to the harsh criticism of "American imperialism" and the Republic of Korea. Echoing P'eng Chen's speech, the North Korean delegate also charged that "American imperialists" were actually preparing for war in Korea. He strongly opposed revisionism, although he did not single out Yugoslavia at this occasion. Calling for strengthening the socialist camp, Kim concluded his speech with the statement that the Soviet Union was still heading the world socialist camp.[6]

No official organ of North Korea reported on the Sino-Soviet quarrel that occurred at the conference.[7] P'yŏngyang's communiqué on the Bucharest Conference was issued after a significant delay. The statement balanced a declaration of "full support of the peace-loving foreign policy of the CPSU based on Leninist principle of coexistence" with an immediate reminder that "United States imperialism," the "sworn enemy of the people," remained inherently aggressive.[8]

FROM THE BUCHAREST CONFERENCE TO THE MOSCOW CONFERENCE OF NOVEMBER 1960

Sino-Soviet relations continued to worsen after the Bucharest meeting. Throughout the summer increased Sino-Soviet polemics on both sides were coupled with extensive Soviet economic and propaganda sanctions against the Chinese, including the Soviet withdrawal of their technicians from China.[9] The North Korean response to these developments revealed grave apprehension over the growing rift in Sino-Soviet relations and a consequent desire to remain neutral.

In August 1960, marking the fifteenth anniversary of its liberation, the P'yŏngyang regime sought to portray its nonalignment unmistakably. The KWP organs praised Moscow for "sharing bitter and sweet" in helping to solve many complicated problems of North Korea's postwar rehabilitation program.[10] In his lengthy speech for the occasion, Kim Il-sŏng endorsed the Soviet foreign policy of peaceful coexistence. He commented:

> The Soviet Union and all the socialist states, standing firmly on the Leninist principle of the peaceful coexistence of countries

with different social systems, unflinchingly pursue a peace-loving foreign policy. The Korean people fully support the Soviet Union's firm position, peaceful initiatives and constant efforts, motivated by a desire to forestall the aggressive actions of the imperialists, to reduce tension and strengthen peace.[11]

In the same speech, Kim Il-sŏng launched a new propaganda drive for "peaceful unification" of Korea, in which he advocated the creation of a "Korean confederation." Such a confederation, he said, could be preceded by "a general election held throughout the North and South without any influence by foreign nations." Kim also suggested that "the two regimes take immediate steps to establish a supreme national committee," which would undertake economic and cultural exchanges.[12] This statement conformed nicely with the Soviet prescription of final victory through "peaceful competition," and Khrushchev specifically endorsed Kim's proposal in a September 23, 1960, address to the fifteenth session of the United Nations General Assembly.[13] The North Korean leaders expressed "great satisfaction over the support extended to the stand and proposal of the DPRK government" by Khrushchev at the United Nations for the solution of the Korean issue.[14] The Chinese also supported enthusiastically Kim's proposal.[15]

On the other hand, Kim Il-sŏng devoted a substantial part of his Liberation Day speech to the attack on the Republic of Korea and the United States. Kim revealed a continuing affinity for Peking's militant policy of unremitting struggle against the United States in Asia. Speaking at a Peking rally on the same occasion, Chou En-lai echoed Kim's speech by saying that "United States imperialism has become the most vicious enemy of the people of the whole world."[16]

The Third North Vietnamese Party Congress, in early September 1960, was, like the Rumanian Party Congress in June, dominated by the Sino-Soviet conflict. At the Hanoi meeting, the North Korean party, along with the North Vietnamese and Japanese parties, took a neutral position between the Russians and the Chinese. All the East European parties took clearly pro-Soviet positions except the Albanians who came out strongly in favor of the Chinese.[17]

In October 1960 Peking began to exert a number of pressures in order to consolidate its position in North Korea. First of all, Peking agreed to grant a loan of $105 million to finance deliveries of equipment and technical assistance for industrial development of North Korea.[18] Another friendly gesture from China toward North Korea came on the occasion of a joint celebration of the tenth anniversary of the CPV's entry into the Korean War. Peking dispatched an unusually large and high-ranking military good-will mission[19] to North Korea for the celebration. Ho Lung, a Politburo member and leader of the mission, stressed the close relationship, which was "sealed in blood" and "ever-lasting and unbreakable."[20] He attacked the "modern revisionists" for their "bitter envy and hatred of our countries' constructive achievements," their "vain attempt to isolate China" and their "vain attempt to sabotage . . . the friendship and unity" of China and North Korea.[21] More suggestions of a continuing struggle for influence in North Korea were made by General Yang Yung, another Chinese delegate, who stressed a special relationship between the PRC and North Korea:

> China and Korea are separated by only a river. They are as dependent on each other as the lips and the teeth. What is concerned with one of them is also concerned with the other.[22]

The Chinese apparently intended to utilize this occasion to draw North Korean support at the forthcoming Moscow Conference in November 1960.

These two Chinese offensives coincided with the cancellation of Khrushchev's scheduled visit to P'yŏngyang. On August 12, 1960, it was announced that, at the invitation of the North Korean government, Khrushchev would make his first visit to North Korea early in October 1960.[23] However, on October 11, he cancelled his trip to P'yŏngyang on the ground that his stay in the United States attending the fifteenth session of the United Nations General Assembly had been longer than anticipated.[24] Khrushchev might have intended to ask for P'yŏngyang's undivided support against China at the coming Moscow Conference and foresaw that his visit at the time was unlikely to get his request. Moscow's waiving of North Korea's debt of $190 million might have been intended to atone for the cancellation of Khrushchev's trip to P'yŏngyang. But there still remained an unfavorable reaction in North Korea.[25]

P'YŎNGYANG'S POSITION AT THE 1960 MOSCOW CONFERENCE

The Moscow Conference of eighty-one Communist parties opened in November 1960 and lasted several weeks. The conference was the most important gathering of its kind in the entire history of Communism. All but the parties of China, North Korea, Japan, Indonesia, and Italy were represented by their party first secretaries. The conference provided the first international forum for a direct confrontation of Russian and Chinese views. All the sessions were secret.[26]

The Moscow Conference was held to end the schism that had developed between China and the Soviet Union. Although the meeting resulted in some kind of modus vivendi between Moscow and Peking, Sino-Soviet and, even more, Soviet-Albanian relations deteriorated further after the meetings. In fact, the conference confirmed and deepened the rifts and feuds in Sino-Soviet relations.[27]

The Moscow Statement, published in *Pravda* on December 6, 1960, constituted a victory on points for the Soviet Union. "It was," Dr. Zagoria writes, "essentially a Soviet document in the sense that the Soviet grand strategy—aiming at the world-wide triumph of Communism without war—remained intact." However, the Chinese, although they did not succeed in establishing any of their principal points, succeeded in "qualifying and hardening certain Soviet theses . . . moving the manifesto further to the Left than it would have been if drafted by the Russians alone."[28] Therefore, it was not a decisive victory on the part of the Soviet Union, but rather a "collation" of Soviet and Chinese views. Most important of all, the statement demonstrated that "the Russians were no longer able unilaterally to dictate law for the entire international Communist movement."[29]

The Soviet leadership apparently realized that the CPSU was no longer the sole leader of the socialist bloc. North Korea also explicitly recognized China as co-leader of the Communist bloc following the Moscow Conference. By referring for the first time to "the socialist countries led by the Soviet Union and the Chinese People's Republic," the official organ of the KWP appeared to be announcing the arrival of a new stage in intrabloc relations.[30] Thus, the important result of the Moscow Conference would be the emergence of "polycentrism" as a reality within the international Communist movement.

The North Korean delegation to the Moscow Conference was headed by Kim Il, vice-chairman of the KWP and the closest lieutenant of Kim Il-sŏng. At the conference, Kim Il supported the Soviet Union on most policy issues and expressed organizational loyalty to Moscow. He also used the formula "the socialist camp headed by the Soviet Union." However, the use of this formula did not necessarily imply a pro-Khrushchev attitude.[31] On the other hand, Kim Il supported or at least indicated sympathy toward the Chinese on the issue of "modern revisionism," the euphemism that Peking had employed for Khrushchev's ideological line since 1958, and strongly upheld the struggle for national liberation in the colonial area. On the possibility of avoiding war, the North Korean delegate, along with the Chinese, Albanian, and North Vietnamese delegates, did not explicitly endorse the positive Soviet line on the issue.[32] Without reporting what had actually been discussed at the conference, *Nodong Shinmun* editorially praised the Moscow meeting and the statement.[33]

The fact that neither Kim Il-sŏng nor Mao Tse-tung attended the Moscow Summit Conference implies one or both of two possible assumptions. The North Korean leaders might have felt that the conference would be too risky for Kim Il-sŏng because he might be forced to take a stand one way or the other, a move that the P'yŏngyang regime could ill afford at that time. Or, the fact that Kim Il-sŏng and Mao Tse-tung were the only two ruling Communist party leaders in the bloc who did not attend the conference might indicate the existence of strong ideological bonds between Peking and P'yŏngyang.

Returning home from the Moscow Conference, Kim Il reportedly made a comprehensive report to the Central Committee of the KWP, and the Central Committee subsequently adopted a resolution. It endorsed the stand its delegation had taken at Moscow and emphasized national liberation struggle directed against "imperialism."[34]

The resolution criticized both "dogmatism," the term that the Soviet Union used in speaking of China, and revisionism. It dealt with dogmatism as purely an internal matter, a danger to the organizational effectiveness of the KWP, that had, however, been overcome. The resolution treated revisionism as a more serious threat, on both the international and the internal planes, and as a threat still in existence. Thus, it was necessary to "wage a struggle against even its slightest manifestation."[35]

During and immediately after the Moscow Conference, the North Korean position continued to adhere to neutralism. An editorial in *Nodong Shinmun* (December 7, 1960) clearly revealed North Korea's intention of remaining neutral in the Sino-Soviet conflict. The editorial attacked both revisionism and dogmatism and advanced its own independent policy. The editorial criticized dogmatism for clinging to existing formulas and theses, failing to see the developing concrete reality and appreciate it correctly according to one's own experience. Finally, it emphasized that each Communist party should shape its own policy independently on the basis of Marxist-Leninist principles.[36]

SOVIET-CHINESE COMPETITION OVER NORTH KOREA

From 1960 to the Twenty-second Congress of the CPSU in November 1961, there was a strong tug-of-war between the Soviet Union and China for North Korea's allegiance. As the Sino-Soviet conflict worsened after 1960, the Soviet leaders apparently intended to make sure that North Korea would side with them unreservedly in a decisive showdown with the Chinese. Moscow thus demonstrated a rare economic benevolence to the P'yŏngyang regime. On June 22, 1960, a commercial and navigation treaty provided for "further developing of trade relations between the two countries in the spirit of friendly cooperation and mutual assistance and on the basis of equality and mutual benefit."[37] On the fifteenth anniversary of the liberation of Korea in 1960, the Soviet Union opened an industrial-agricultural fair in P'yŏngyang, which reportedly drew one and a half million North Koreans.[38] At the end of the fair, Moscow presented P'yŏngyang with its investment in the construction of the exhibition halls and part of its exhibits.[39] On October 13, 1960, the Soviet Union agreed to exempt North Korea from repayment of past loans amounting to $190 millon (760 million rubles) and to defer repayment of another $35 million (140 million rubles).[40]

On December 24, 1960, the Soviet Union signed two more important agreements with North Korea. The first was an agreement concerning technical and scientific cooperation in building and expanding a series of industrial enterprises and power stations in North Korea during 1961-1967, the period that coincided with the forthcoming Seven-Year Economic Plan in North Korea. By this agreement, the Soviet Union was obligated to aid in expanding the Kim Ch'aek iron works to an annual production capacity of 2.8 million tons of steel and 2.3 million tons of rolled structural steel and to build two thermoelectric plants in Pukch'ang and P'yŏngyang with the generating capacity of 600,000 and 400,000 kilowatts respectively. The Soviet Union also agreed to construct an oil refinery plant with an annual capacity of two million metric tons and to provide the crude oil needed for its use. Since North Korea is entirely dependent upon foreign oil, the Soviet agreement to build and supply raw materials for an oil refinery appears to have been both a belated concession to North Korean need and an attempt to maintain a vital economic link. The agreement was also to provide technical assistance for the construction of such light industrial plants as textile and movie industries.[41]

The other treaty concerned the exchange of goods between the two countries during the 1961-1965 period. Under this agreement, the volume of trade would increase by more than 80 percent compared with the previous five years. P'yŏngyang was to supply nonferrous metal, steel alloy, machine tools, cement, leaf tobacco, and other goods. In return, Moscow would deliver equipment and machines of various kinds, oil products, rolled structural steel, chemical goods, and ferrous metal.[42] Implementing the economic aid agreement signed on August 4, 1956, the Soviet Union provided goods amounting to 85 million rubles to North Korea in 1963.[43]

On the other hand, China tried its best to compete with the Soviet Union for influence in North Korea. On May 23, 1960, an agreement on the Sino-Korean border river navigation cooperation was signed between the two countries in Peking.[44] In August 1960, Peking sent a locomotive and twenty-five rice transplanting machines.[45] On October 13, 1960, the Chinese agreed to provide a long term loan of $105 million (420 million rubles) to North Korea during the period of 1961–1964.[46] By the Sino-North Korean agreement, signed on October 13, 1960, Peking was obligated to help North Korea build industrial plants for the manufacture of rubber tires and radio communication instruments and a number of light industries for the production of consumer goods.[47] In March 1961, Peking signed a similar protocol with P'yŏngyang whereby it would provide whole sets of equipment and technical assistance, and factories for the manufacture of knitted goods and rubber products.[48] A protocol on the Sino-North Korean scientific and technical cooperation, signed on October 30, 1961, stipulated that China would furnish North Korea with blueprints for the manufacture of equipment for textile, chemical, and light industries. In addition, Communist China would also provide other technical data as well as agricultural seeds.[49] Coming at a time of stringency in China's own economic development program,[50] this extension of technical and material aid clearly indicated a new effort to compete with the Soviet Union for influence in North Korea.

P'YŎNGYANG'S SECURITY TREATIES WITH MOSCOW AND PEKING

On June 29, 1961, the North Korean delegation led by Kim Il-sŏng himself arrived in Moscow, some three weeks after the visit of President Sukarno of Indonesia and two days after that of North Vietnamese Premier Pham Van Dong.[51] Without prior public notice, on July 6, the Soviet Union and North Korea signed and published a treaty of "Friendship, Cooperation, and Mutual Assistance."[52] This took place only two days after General Park Chung Hee assumed sole power within the junta ruling South Korea.[53] This treaty was significant in the sense that North Korea had to wait until July 6, 1961, when the pressures of the Sino-Soviet split seemed to have overcome Soviet hesitance to sign such a treaty with a divided state like North Korea. A similar treaty had been signed between the Soviet Union and the PRC as early as February 14, 1950.[54]

During Kim's visit to Moscow, another agreement was signed between the two countries. Under the agreement, the Soviet Union would render additional economic and technical assistance to North Korea in the development of the metallurgy and mining industries, and in the construction of a television station. The Soviet Union agreed to speed up the deliveries of equipment for the thermopower stations which were being built with Soviet technical assistance. Moscow was also to provide goods and additional technical assistance for the development of North Korea's chemical industry during the 1962–1965 period.[55] Judging from the fact that the Central Committee of the KWP had been preparing for the Fourth Congress in September, to which the forthcoming Seven-Year Plan was to be presented, Kim's visit was also motivated by this new economic plan.[56]

From Moscow, Kim Il-sŏng proceeded to Peking where he received a noticeably warmer welcome.[57] In Peking, on July 11, Kim concluded a treaty of "Friendship, Cooperation, and Mutual Assistance" with China,[58] but he was not able to obtain additional economic aid as he did in Moscow. The treaty came into force on September 10, 1961.[59] The Moscow and Peking treaties were largely identical, especially in the four essential elements.

First, both treaties were emphatic with respect to mutual defense. Article 1 of the Moscow treaty stipulated that "in the event one of the undersigned parties is the object of an armed attack by any state or coalition of states and is thus in a state of war, the other undersigned party will immediately render military and other assistance with all the means at its disposal." Article 2 of the Peking treaty declared that "the contracting parties undertake jointly to adopt all measures to prevent aggression against either of the contracting parties by any state." "In the event of one of the contracting parties being subjected to the armed attack by any state or several states jointly and thus being involved in a state of war," it continued, "the other contracting party shall immediately render military and other assistance by all means at its disposal."

Second, both treaties put emphasis both on the economic and cultural ties and on the principles of sovereignty and equality. Article 4 of the Moscow treaty stipulated that the two contracting parties should undertake, in the spirit of friendship and cooperation and in accordance with the principles of equality, mutual respect for state sovereignty, territorial integrity and noninterference in each other's internal affairs, to develop and strengthen economic and cultural relations between the two countries. Article 5 of the Peking treaty stated that "the contracting parties, on the principles of mutual respect for sovereignty, noninterference in each other's internal affairs, equality and mutual benefit and in the spirit of friendly cooperation, will continue to render each other every possible economic and technical aid in the cause of socialist construction of the two countries."

Third, both treaties clearly implied that the P'yŏngyang regime should remain neutral in the Sino-Soviet dispute. Article 2 of the Moscow treaty stated that "each of the undersigned parties pledges not to conclude *any* alliance and not to participate in *any* coalition or to take *any* other action or measure directed against the other undersigned party [emphasis supplied]." Article 3 of the Peking treaty also stipulated that "neither of the contracting parties shall conclude *any* alliance directed against the other contracting party or take part in *any* bloc or in *any* action or measure directed against the other contracting party [emphasis supplied]." The important aspect of the above clauses is that both Moscow and Peking jointly accentuated P'yŏngyang's neutral position in the Sino-Soviet rift.

Fourth and finally, concerning the unification of Korea, both treaties held the same view that the unification should be realized on the basis of "peaceful and democratic lines and that such a solution accords exactly with the national interests of the Korean peoples and the aim of preserving peace in the Far East."

However, there were also differences in the two treaties. First of all, it is interesting to note the differences of emphasis in the preambles of the two treaties with the Soviet Union and Communist China. The Soviet preamble stated that both parties would follow the purposes and principles of the United Nations in preserving and strengthening peace and security in the Far East and in the world. But the preamble of the Peking treaty did not mention the United Nations. Rather, the Chinese text stressed that North Korea and China would jointly defend the safety of the peoples of the two countries, and maintain and secure peace in Asia and in the world. It also stated that Peking and P'yŏngyang believed that "the development and reinforcement of such relationships between the two countries are consistent with not only the basic interest of the peoples of the two countries but also with that of the peoples of all countries in the world." The Chinese preamble emphasized "the mutual respect for state sovereignty and territorial integrity, mutual nonaggression, noninterference in each other's internal affairs, [and] equality. . . ."

Secondly, the Peking treaty did not specify its duration. Article 7 states that "this agreement shall remain effective until the signatories shall agree upon its revision or termination." On the other hand, the Moscow treaty was to be effective only for ten years, although it could be renewed for another five years if neither of the signatories announced its wish to nullify the treaty one year before it expired. Either contracting party could thus terminate the treaty after ten years.

Finally, the joint communiqués issued in Moscow and Peking stand in contrast to each other. In the Peking communiqué,[60] Kim strongly attacked modern revisionism represented by the leading group of Yugoslavia and stressed his support for China's "just" stand on Taiwan. But the Moscow communiqué[61] did not mention anything about modern revisionism and, unlike the Peking statement, devoted a substantial part of the communiqué to the issue of peaceful coexistence. In the Moscow communiqué only, Kim stated that the Soviet Union "is the universally recognized vanguard of the world Communist movement." During Kim's trips to Moscow and Peking, both Khrushchev and Liu Shao-ch'i[62] must have pressed Kim to support either the Soviet Union or China as a price for the treaty, especially in the coming Twenty-second Congress of the CPSU in November 1961. But Kim took a middle-of-the-road line which, for the time being, seemed to be a safe path for the P'yŏngyang regime. Returning home from his extended tour, Kim Il-sŏng praised both Moscow and Peking in fairly equal terms. At the P'yŏngyang rally on July 15, 1961, Kim said:

> The Soviet Union and the Chinese People's Republic are our two great neighbors and closest fraternal countries. The Korean-Soviet friendship and Korean-Chinese friendship are immeasurably valuable to our people....[63]

THE FOURTH CONGRESS OF THE KWP

While the Soviet Union and China tried their best to woo the North Korean Communists, the Fourth Congress of the KWP was held at P'yŏngyang from September 11 to 18, 1961, more than five years after the Third Congress, which had been held in 1956. For the Fourth Congress, the Soviet Union sent F. L. Kozlov, a member of the Presidium and a Central Committee secretary, and Peking sent Teng Hsiao-p'ing, a member of the Standing Committee of the Politburo and the secretary-general of the CCP Central Committee. Thirty-two foreign delegates from the socialist bloc and other neutral countries attended the congress.[64]

The Fourth Congress was a "proud" one for the North Korean Communists. They had just "successfully completed" the Five-Year Plan and, at the meeting, announced a Seven-Year Economic Plan for 1961–1967.[65] According to Kim Il-sŏng's report to the congress, the main task of the plan was "to carry out an overall technical reconstruction and cultural revolution and rapidly improve the living standard of the people on the basis of the triumphant socialist system." During the seven years, Kim claimed that gross industrial output, rising annually on the average of 18 percent, would increase by more than 2.5 times that of 1960. The national income would also increase 2.7 times by the end of the plan.[66]

Certainly these practically unrealistic goals of the Seven-Year Plan could not be achieved without counting on heavy economic and technical assistance from the Soviet Union, China, and East European Communist countries. Kim Il-sŏng was well aware of the fact that, beginning in July 1960, Moscow had drastically reduced its economic aid to Peking and had withdrawn all the Soviet technicians from China, taking with them all the blueprints and essential spare parts. The Soviet Union had also reportedly put pressures on Peking to repay loans.[67] For Kim Il-sŏng these developments made it all the more imperative to remain nonaligned between Moscow and Peking so that both, whatever their differences, would honor their aid commitments to P'yŏngyang.

On the subject of the international Communist relations, Kim Il-sŏng's speech at the congress was carefully phrased and well balanced so as not to offend either the Soviet Union or China.[68] Praising the Soviet achievements, Kim stated that the successful building of Communism in the Soviet Union added to the might of the entire socialist camp, and he pledged to march "forward forever with the Soviet people in the struggle for the common cause."[69] Yet, he also made it clear that the P'yŏngyang regime supported unswervingly "the national liberation struggle of the oppressed nations." "The United States imperialists," he stressed (as usual), "are still occupying the southern half òf our country and have turned it into their military base." He thus reasoned that "peace does not come of its own accord; it must be won through the unflinching struggle of the people."[70]

In the same report, Kim Il-sŏng also attacked both revisionism and dogmatism. "Without a relentless struggle against revisionism and dogmatism," he declared, there could not be any genuine development of the Communist bloc. According to Kim, the contemporary revisionism represented by the Yugoslav leaders was "emasculating the revolutionary spirit of Marxism-Leninism" and undermining the socialist camp and the interna-

tional Communist movement from within. Dogmatism, like revisionism, was harmful to "the revolutionary work, and can become the chief danger at particular stages in the development of
individual parties." He concluded his report by calling for
adherence to the Moscow Statement of 1960 in order to achieve
the unity of the entire socialist camp and the solidarity of the
international movement.[71]

P'YŎNGYANG'S POSITION ON THE
TWENTY-SECOND CONGRESS OF THE CPSU

The most dramatic event of the Twenty-second Congress of
the CPSU in November 1961 was open disagreement between
Moscow and Peking over Albania.[72] Khrushchev openly attacked the Albanian party leadership, by whom he clearly meant
the Chinese Communist leadership as well, and aimed at the
expulsion of Albania from the Communist bloc.[73] Many ideological lines of the Albanian leaders coincided with those of the
Chinese, and the Albanian leadership unfailingly supported the
Chinese position in the Sino-Soviet rift. Khrushchev's attack on
the Albanian leaders provoked an angry retort from Chou En-
lai, the leader of the CCP delegation at the congress. Chou
declared that "it is un-Marxist to reveal our differences before
the enemies and to attack fraternal parties." He then departed
from Moscow in a huff at the very height of the congress, having earlier left a wreath on the tomb of Stalin.[74]

As Khrushchev had undoubtedly intended, his public attack
on Albania compelled each of the sixty-six Communist parties at
the congress to take its public stance on the Albanian question.
The position of each Communist party was thus made more
public than it had been at the 1960 Moscow meeting. The Albanian issue was the first one in the international Communist
movement that was put to a vote by the bloc parties. Officially
twenty-two countries,[75] including North Korea,[76] had neither
endorsed Khrushchev's condemnation of the Albanian leadership nor taken any position at all on the Soviet-Albanian controversy. The remaining forty-four parties in varying degrees
supported Moscow's position on Albania. The Russians carried

with them nearly all the parties in Europe, the Middle East, and South America, while the Chinese were tacitly supported by all the Asian parties with the exception of Outer Mongolia and Ceylon.[77]

On October 21, Kim Il-sŏng, representing the KWP, delivered an unusually brief speech to the congress. More than half of his time was spent in praising the Soviet achievement and in proclaiming gratitude for Soviet help. Kim noted that the "consolidation of unity with the CPSU is the duty of Communists of all countries and is a principle of proletarian internationalism." However, he neither criticized the Albanian party leadership nor did he belabor the evils of Stalinism (despite what must have been substantial Soviet pressure to do so). Kim also intentionally avoided the controversial issues of factionalism, peaceful coexistence, the de-Stalinization movement, and modern revisionism and dogmatism, which were actually the central theses of the congress, at which Kim was apparently placed in an extremely difficult position. His only recourse was to do his best to remain neutral in the worsening intrabloc conflict.[78]

On November 27, soon after his return from Moscow, Kim Il-sŏng reported on the Twenty-second Congress of the CPSU to the second enlarged plenum of the fourth KWP Central Committee. For the first time, he openly admitted to the Central Committee that there was real division in the international Communist movement, and his report was published in the various organs of the KWP. He frankly indicated that the Twenty-second Congress dealt extensively with the issues concerning de-Stalinization, Albanian leadership, and the world Communist movement.[79]

Kim's speech contained high praise of Soviet progress. "Today," he declared, "Communism no longer remains a mere ideal but is turning into reality in the Soviet Union." The new CPSU program and its fulfillment, he predicted, "will have a powerful impact on drawing hundreds of millions of people in the world over to the side of Communism." He also praised the Soviet Union for continuing to maintain peaceful coexistence with the countries of different social systems and for striving to solve international disputes by means of negotiations.[80]

On the de-Stalinization issue, Kim took a neutral position. His comments on this issue are worth quoting at length:

> At the congress much mention was made of the cult of Stalin's personality. . . . Stalin was the leader of the Communist Party of the Soviet Union for a long period, and his activities exerted great influence on the international Communist movement as a whole. Stalin's name is well known to the Communists and peoples of the world. But the members of the Communist Party of the Soviet Union themselves must know Stalin better than anyone else, and the question of how his activities and role are appraised in the Soviet Union is an internal affair of the Communist Party of the Soviet Union.[81]

Emphasizing that the question of antiparty factionalist elements was an entirely internal affair of the CPSU, Kim went on to state:

> We always consider that no party is entitled to interfere in any form in the internal life of the fraternal parties. This is one of the fundamental principles which all fraternal parties should abide by in their mutual relations. Therefore, the questions concerning Stalin and antiparty sectarians within the Communist Party of the Soviet Union have nothing to do with our party, nor can they become an object of discussion within our party. . . .[82]

He made it quite clear that the de-Stalinization issue would not be the subject of discussion in the KWP Central Committee meetings. The above passage also clearly meant that the KWP would not abide by Khrushchev's de-Stalinization campaign in North Korea. Indeed, North Korea has never experienced "de-Stalinization." "The adulation given him by all mass media," Dr. Scalapino writes, "exceeds even that given Mao; the cult of personality reigns supreme."[83]

Concerning the Albanian issue, the North Korean leader reported that the relationship between the Soviet Union and Albania was continuously deteriorating and, should the "abnormal" situation continue, grave damage would be caused to "the unity of the socialist camp" and to "the solidarity of the world

Communist movement." He then expressed his hope that a satis-factory solution to the Albanian question would be "achieved through enduring efforts to remove present disputes and dif-ferences of views and to attain mutual understanding."[84] Kim held to a strict neutral position by blaming neither Albania nor the Soviet Union for the complicated situation. In the same re-port to the KWP Central Committee, however, Kim Il-sŏng clearly hinted that he did not want interference from any frater-nal party (presumably the CPSU) in the internal affairs of the KWP.[85]

Kim's report to the KWP Central Committee indicated that he was leaning toward the Chinese ideological line even though he still tried to remain in the middle of the road by affirming his party's loyalty to the Soviet Union. Another indication of a pref-erence for the Chinese position was North Korea's attitude to-ward the Albanian leadership. North Korea reportedly sided with the Chinese line at meetings of the international Communist-front organizations.[86] It is also noteworthy that, after November 1961, Radio P'yŏngyang ceased to transmit Radio Moscow broadcasts in the Korean language.[87]

NORTH KOREAN-ALBANIAN RELATIONS

North Korea has been maintaining friendship and support for Albania, the only East European country which has consistently backed China in the Sino-Soviet dispute. In late November 1960, an unusually laudatory article in *Minju Chosŏn* asserted that "our two countries are very close to each other, like real brothers, because of common ideology and aims" and that "no force on earth can break the invincible friendship and solidarity between the Korean and Albanian peoples."[88] At the Fourth Congress of the Albanian Workers' Party held in February 1961, Pak Kŭm-ch'ŏl, leader of the North Korean delegation, was reported to have emphatically praised the "correct" leadership of the Al-banian party.[89] In April 1961, the P'yŏngyang regime entered into economic agreements with Albania.[90]

Even after Khrushchev denounced the Albanian leaders Enver Hoxha and Mehmet Shehu as false Marxists and vicious tyrants, fraternal greetings flowed to Albania from North Korea. On November 7, 1961, on the occasion of the twentieth anniversary of the founding of the Albanian Workers' Party (AWP), the North Korean Communists sent the Albanian party leaders a warm congratulatory message. The KWP praised its achievements and leadership, both in the war of liberation and in the tasks of socialist construction. "We firmly believe," the message concluded, "that the friendship and solidarity between the peoples of Albania and Korea will continue to develop and become stronger in the future."[91] On November 28, 1961, the North Korean Communists sent another warm message of congratulations to the Albanian leaders on the occasion of the seventeenth anniversary of the liberation of Albania. The P'yŏngyang leaders praised "the correct guidance" of the AWP and stressed that the friendly relationship between the two countries would be further consolidated and developed. The North Korean message also praised the Albanian people for having exposed and shattered at every step "all the provocative machinations of the imperialists and the Yugoslav revisionists."[92] On January 23, 1962, agreements on the exchange of commodities and on scientific and technical cooperation were signed between P'yŏngyang and Tirana.[93] The two countries also signed an agreement on cultural cooperation on March 30, 1962.[94] The North Korean position on Albania has not changed since then. Kim Il-sŏng's belief in the Soviet Union's concern for the interests of small Communist regimes was probably shaken by Khrushchev's treatment of Albania, particularly after the Twenty-second Congress of the CPSU.

SUMMARY

During the 1960–1961 period the North Korean regime tried to avoid explicit commitment either to the Soviet Union or China, mainly because of North Korea's desperate need for economic and military assistance from both Moscow and Peking. P'yŏngyang's neutral stance was perhaps "safe" ground for the North Korean Communists as it was for both Moscow and Peking, each of which presumably preferred to keep P'yŏngyang in the middle rather than openly allied with the other. At the same time, the North Koreans utilized the opportunity given by the Sino-Soviet rift. North Korea's security treaties with Moscow and Peking are good examples of the North Korean Communists adroitly reaping the advantages of being wooed by rival neighbors. This formal assurance of support in case of trouble with the West was not made possible until July 1961, mainly because of Moscow's hesitation to enter into such an agreement with North Korea. By the end of 1961 the North Korean regime was displaying an increasing support of the Chinese position on the issues in dispute. Let us turn to the year 1962, during which North Korea moved even closer to China in the ever-worsening conflict between Moscow and Peking.

CHAPTER 4
P'YŎNGYANG LEANS
TOWARD PEKING, 1962

Throughout 1962 the Soviet Union and China continued their respective campaigns for support in the Communist world. The North Korean Communists were being wooed ardently by Peking and responded warmly. As noted earlier, North Korea had by 1960 embraced some of the economic programs of the Chinese Communists and was leaning toward Peking on such issues as war of national liberation and modern revisionism. However, P'yŏngyang's pro-Chinese stance in the Sino-Soviet dispute did not become obvious until the fall of 1962. As Sino-Soviet relations clearly worsened then,[1] North Korean "neutralism" was put to new and strenuous tests. The immediate issues were the Sino-Indian border conflict and the Cuban missile crisis. During this period, Kim Il-sŏng also emphasized *chuch'e* to build up a self-reliant national economy,[2] while tightening up his ideological campaign within the North Korean party.

SOVIET-NORTH KOREAN RELATIONS, 1962

During 1962, the Soviet Union and North Korea used several occasions to reaffirm their friendship and alliance. In April, Moscow sent congratulatory messages on Kim Il-sŏng's fiftieth birthday.[3] On the first anniversary of the signing of the Soviet-North Korean treaty of "Friendship, Cooperation, and Mutual Assistance" in July, speeches made by the leaders of the two countries pledged continuous and unbreakable friendship and close mutual cooperation.[4] Celebrating the seventeenth anniversary of the Korean liberation in August, Moscow and P'yŏngyang exchanged cordial messages, emphasizing their "everlasting and immortal friendship."[5]

However, there was some indication of a certain "formalism"

and lack of spontaneity in the public communications flowing between Moscow and P'yŏngyang during this period. The vocabulary used in messages and speeches was more restrained than that characterizing Sino-North Korean exchanges. For instance, messages between Moscow and P'yŏngyang on the occasion of the first anniversary of the 1961 treaty were more formal than those exchanged between Peking and P'yŏngyang for the same occasion.[6] There was also a falling off in the kind of diplomatic contact represented by the exchange of special missions. In fact, during 1962, no high ranking delegation was exchanged between the Soviet Union and North Korea. A similar tendency was observable in North Korea's relations with the East European countries.

On the economic side, the scale of economic and scientific exchanges between the Soviet Union and North Korea was not increased in 1962. The only exception was in the field of trade between the two countries. North Korean imports from the Soviet Union had increased from 69 million rubles in 1961 to 73 million in 1962, and its exports to the Soviet Union had also increased from 71 million rubles to 79 million during the same period.[7] During 1962, five minor treaties or protocols were signed between Moscow and P'yŏngyang, while there were eight agreements between Peking and P'yŏngyang.[8] A protocol on the exchanges of commodities for 1962 between Moscow and P'yŏngyang was signed on February 26, 1962.[9] On May 8, 1962, North Korea and the Soviet Union signed an agreement on cultural and scientific cooperation and drew up a plan for further expanding the cultural relations and strengthening the friendship, unity, and solidarity between the peoples of the two countries. The plan envisaged a mutual exchange of song and dance ensembles of the North Korean and Soviet armies, cooperation in science, education, public health, rural economy, and radio and television, and meetings and friendship matches between sportsmen.[10]

As for implementation of existing agreements on scientific and technical cooperation and commodity exchanges, North Korean reports on semiannual protocols were exceedingly vague in 1962 as compared with 1961.[11] North Korean agreements on appropriate occasions, such as the anniversaries of their 1949 economic and cultural agreement[12] and their 1961 treaty with the Soviet Union,[13] supplied no significant details on the economic relationship. In short, there was a falling off in the economic relations between the Soviet Union and North Korea in 1962.

SINO-NORTH KOREAN RELATIONS, 1962

Sino-North Korean relations became closer and stronger, whether measured in terms of the outstanding exchanges of high level delegates, the expression of mutual support and close friendship, or cultural and economic cooperation. On April 23, the Chinese National People's Congress (CNPC) delegation, headed by P'eng Chen, vice-chairman of the Standing Committee of the CNPC, visited North Korea at the invitation of the Supreme People's Assembly (SPA) of the DPRK.[14] The public exchange of messages was used to testify to the "unbreakable" solidarity of the Sino-North Korean alliance. P'eng Chen declared that "rain or shine, the 650 million Chinese people will always stand by the fraternal Korean people, building socialism and defending peace in Asia and the world shoulder to shoulder."[15] In return, on June 15, 1962, a delegation of the Supreme People's Assembly of the DPRK headed by Pak Kŭm-ch'ŏl visited Peking.[16] Reporting on his Peking trip to the SPA, Pak repeatedly emphasized that "no force in the world can break Sino-Korean friendship sealed in blood" and experienced through the historical trials.[17]

On the occasion of the fiftieth birthday of Kim Il-sŏng, the Chinese Communist leaders extended a message of greetings to him. Praising Kim's creative application of "the universal truths of Marxism-Leninism to the realities of Korea" and his achievement of "brilliant successes," the message stressed the friendship of the two countries:

> The friendship between the Chinese and Korean peoples is sealed in blood, and the unity of the Chinese Communist Party and the Korean Workers' Party and of China and Korea is as strong as

steel. The steady growth of the friendship between the two countries is inseparable from the colossal efforts you have been making. The Chinese people are proud of having such a sincere
friend and extend to you their highest respects.[18]

The Chinese message of greetings to the North Korean leaders
on the occasion of the first anniversary of the 1961 Sino-North
Korean treaty also emphasized that "the Chinese people will
always cherish and make enduring efforts to strengthen unity
and friendship. The Chinese people will resolutely discharge all
their obligations in defense of their common cause."[19] On these
and other[20] occasions, the statements made by the Chinese and
North Korean leaders in this period were strikingly identical in
content and showed a growing identity of interests and an unusual intimacy of friendship between the two countries.

During 1962, China became an increasingly important
supplier of goods, technical information, and trained personnel
in a variety of fields, and with some degree of reciprocity. On
January 5, a Chinese trade delegation visited P'yŏngyang, where
an agreement on the exchange of commodities for 1962 was
signed.[21] On April 30, a cultural exchange program between the
two countries was signed in Peking.[22] A Sino-North Korean protocol was signed in Peking during the fifth meeting of the
Sino-North Korean Scientific and Technical Cooperation Committee, which was held from September 7 to 22. According to
the protocol, China would make arrangements for North Korean scientific and technical personnel to study and gain experience in China's metallurgical, chemical, machine-building, textile, and light-industry plants. North Korea would also make
arrangements for Chinese scientific and technical personnel to
study in North Korea's building industry and aquatic products
department, and would provide China with technical data
about the metallurgical, textile, and building industries.[23] In
October–November 1962, a North Korean trade delegation
visited Peking. On November 5, China and North Korea signed
a treaty of commerce and navigation. At the same time, the two
countries signed a trade agreement for the period 1963–1967.
According to the provisions of the agreement, during 1963–

1967, Peking would supply P'yŏngyang with materials needed for carrying out its Seven-Year Plan, including fuel, minerals, agricultural products, chemical products, ferrous metals, and complete sets of equipment. In return, North Korea would supply China with minerals, nonferrous metals, machinery and equipment, chemical products, sea products, and textiles.[24] Sino-North Korean trade relations were thus put on a long-term basis, adjusting to the duration of the North Korean Seven-Year Plan.

P'YŎNGYANG'S POSITION ON THE SINO-INDIAN BORDER DISPUTE

The first Sino-Indian border clash occurred in September 1959.[25] The Soviet Union took a neutral position on the 1959 crisis by stating that "the Soviet Union is in friendly relations both with the Chinese People's Republic and the Republic of India."[26] The massive Chinese attack, launched on October 20, 1962, crossed the McMahon line and penetrated further into Ladakh.[27] Peking insisted that the Chinese were victims of Indian aggression, which was planned by an Indian "reactionary" group "whose interests are closely connected with those of the imperialists."[28]

The initial Soviet reaction to the Chinese attack in October 1962 was mildly favorable to China,[29] but it satisfied neither the Indians[30] nor the Chinese.[31] The second Soviet editorial on November 5 marked Moscow's return to its 1959 position of neutrality.[32] Despite its official neutrality, Moscow continued to make friendly gestures toward India and supplied her with some helicopters and transport planes. The Soviet Union was also reportedly negotiating with India for a dozen MIG-fighters, with the first to be delivered to India in December 1962.[33] By supporting China's enemy, India, Moscow further worsened its relations with Peking.

On the issue of the Sino-Indian border dispute, North Korea stood firmly behind the Chinese from the very beginning. As early as September 1959, in contrast with a prior Soviet declaration of neutrality, P'yŏngyang proclaimed its "full support" of Peking.[34] In December 1961, the North Korean regime vociferously supported all details of the Chinese claims in the border crisis.[35] On September 26, 1962, P'yŏngyang accused India of making an "illegal intrusion into Chinese territory" and commented that "the reactionary circles of the Indians have risen against China, instigated and abetted by America."[36]

North Korea launched a vigorous campaign against the Nehru government after the intensified border struggle erupted on October 20, 1962. The North Koreans condemned the Indian government as a "reckless aggressor" and as a "reactionary force working with the American imperialists, helping them to use the Sino-Indian boundary dispute for their sinister purposes."[37] They also charged that the Indian ruling circles launched a large-scale attack against China in order to "whip up a new anti-China campaign" in India and to "ask the Western imperialists" for more aid.[38] On October 26, 1962, *Nodong Shinmun* carried an editorial that enthusiastically supported the statement of the PRC issued on October 24. The Chinese statement included a three-point proposal for the solution of the border conflict: (1) both sides would respect the whole Sino-Indian borderline under their actual control, as of November 7, 1959; (2) each would withdraw its armed forces twenty kilometers from this line; and (3) talks would be held between the prime ministers of the two countries.[39] Chou En-lai thanked the North Korean government and its people for upholding "justice" during the Sino-Indian border clashes by condemning the Indian "aggression" against China and supporting China's "defensive" action and the Chinese three-point proposals for a "peaceful" solution of the boundary question.[40] An editorial of *Nodong Shinmun* on November 22, 1962, again attributed the Sino-Indian border conflict to "the reckless scheme of the Indian reactionary circles to change the borderline by armed force."[41]

P'yŏngyang's attack on India was accompanied by its continuous insistence on peaceful negotiation as a means of settling the dispute. On November 23, 1962, an editorial of *Minju Chosŏn* urged that the Sino-Indian boundary issue should be solved by peaceful means.[42] The official North Korean statement on the border crisis, issued two days after the unilateral Chinese ceasefire on November 21, stressed that the Indian government should accept the Chinese "three-point offer" immediately and insisted that the border dispute should be settled by peaceful means.[43] On December 8, 1962, Kim Il-sŏng, in his letter to Chou En-lai, praised the "tireless Chinese endeavor" for the peaceful settlement of the crisis and reassured his support on the "legitimate" Chinese claims. Again Kim urged that the conflict should be solved by peaceful means.[44] In February 1963, the North Koreans insisted once more that India should immediately accept "the Chinese proposals and measures for the earliest possible peaceful settlement of the boundary question and that the two countries become again good neighbors."[45] Commenting on the Sino-Indian border dispute, the North Korean leaders conspicuously ignored the Soviet Union.

There were two possible reasons for P'yŏngyang's insistence on a peaceful settlement of the border dispute. For one thing, the North Korean Communists were still susceptible to Soviet pressure. For another, P'yŏngyang apparently did not intend to break "normal" relationships with India. In 1958, a North Korean trade agency had been established and began activities in India.[46] In 1961, North Korea and India had agreed to renew trade relations on a yearly basis. It had been announced in July 1962 that the trade treaty was extended until the end of 1963. In accordance with the agreement, North Korea was to supply India with chemical fertilizers, zinc, special steels, anthracite, and various industrial equipment in exchange for ferromanganese, leather products, vegetable oils, mica, and other goods.[47] In March 1962, North Korea and India had agreed to establish consular offices in both capitals.[48] As a strong indication of P'yŏngyang's intention to maintain relations with India, Kim Il-sŏng sent a congratulatory message to Prime Minister Nehru on the occasion of the thirteenth anniversary of the Republic of India, and Nehru returned Kim's message of greetings.[49]

P'YŎNGYANG'S REACTION TO THE CUBAN MISSILE CRISIS

In September 1962, the Soviet Union began placing medium-range missiles in Cuba. On October 22, President John Kennedy declared a "quarantine" on all "offensive weapons" entering Cuba. On October 28, after the United States pledged not to invade Cuba, Khrushchev agreed to the withdrawal of Soviet "offensive weapons" from the island.[50]

The Soviet "retreat" in the Cuban crisis caused an even more drastic deterioration in Sino-Soviet relations than had the Sino-Indian border clashes.[51] Moscow increasingly emphasized the overriding necessity of avoiding thermonuclear war and later claimed credit for its commitment to peace, which had been preserved thanks to the "calm, confident, wise voice of reason" of the Soviet leaders.[52] On the other hand, Peking stressed the aggressiveness of American "imperialism," Soviet "cowardice," and the absolute priority of support for the Cuban leaders and of revolutionary struggle over fear of war.[53] The Chinese accused the Soviets of "adventurism" for stationing the missiles in Cuba in the first place and of "capitulationism" for withdrawing them in the face of the American reaction. Peking also charged Khrushchev with having staged a "second Munich" at the cost of Cuban independence and the international Communist movement,[54] and condemned "modern revisionists" for "begging for peace before imperialism at the expense of the revolutionary people."[55]

Khrushchev's withdrawal of missiles from Cuba marked a turning point in North Korean foreign policy. The North Korean Communists took a strong and militant position on the Cuban crisis, as did the Chinese. They indirectly criticized Khrushchev's policy on Cuba as appeasement of "American imperialism," and urged "all friends of peace and socialism to stand firm and to force the American imperialists to take their ... hands off Cuba at once."[56]

On November 17, 1962, *Nodong Shinmun* challenged the Soviet leaders with an editorial entitled, "Let Us Heighten Even More the Revolutionary Banner of Marxism-Leninism." The article indirectly denounced the Soviet Union for having betrayed the Cuban and other revolutionary people, and echoed the Chinese denunciation that "by begging the imperialists a peace we will encourage the aggressive ambition of the imperialists rather than easing the international tensions." The KWP organ no longer identified the modern revisionists merely as Titoists. It accused modern revisionists of "unhesitatingly pursuing . . . their various policies of slandering and dividing the socialist countries and of plotting to overthrow the socialist governments and parties." Therefore, all the Marxist-Leninists should always be "on the alert against all the subversive activities of these re-visionists, and struggle to smash them into smithereens."[57] Al-though the editorial did not identify the modern revisionist movement with Khrushchev or Moscow specifically, it was obvi-ous that Khrushchev himself was being brought under attack. The article was a first clear public challenge to Khrushchev's peaceful-coexistence doctrine and to the "modern revisionism" of the Soviet leadership.

Another editorial in the same publication stated that there should not be any activity harmful to any member of the socialist camp, nor should there be any "double-faced behavior." It fur-ther insisted that the Soviet withdrawal of her missiles from Cuba was unwise and that the United States would never give up its attempts at aggression against Cuba.[58] This was again an im-plicit criticism of Khrushchev's policy.

In the wake of the Cuban crisis it became increasingly clear that the Soviet Union did not want another showdown with the United States over Latin America. In spite of the United States government's refusal to take up negotiations with Castro, the Soviet Union was constantly urging him to settle his difficulties with the United States.[59] The North Korean leaders thus may have felt that Moscow wished to have the Cuban issue settled at any price, even that of capitulation and the dismantling of the socialist regime. Moscow's "adventurism" and "capitulationism" in the Cuban crisis may also have provoked the P'yŏngyang leadership to recall the bitter memory of the Korean War. For the P'yŏngyang Communists, it was perhaps Soviet "adven-turism" that had launched the Korean Conflict; and it was also Soviet "capitulation" that had almost cost the existence of Kim's regime when the Soviets were faced with the "unexpected" chal-lenge from the United States. Indeed, it was the Chinese inter-vention, not Soviet intervention, that had saved that regime from total disaster. Furthermore, a North Korean military delegation had visited Moscow in November–December 1962 to seek more military aid, apparently without avail.[60] It is not unlikely that the North Korean leaders had begun to question the Soviet Union as a reliable ally in case of emergency.

THE SELF-RELIANT NATIONAL ECONOMY

Throughout 1962 North Korean statements about economic progress increasingly stressed the necessity and desirability of self-reliance in executing the Seven-Year Plan and had more clearly defined their goal as economic self-sufficiency.[61] At the third plenary session of the Central Committee of the KWP, Kim Il-sŏng launched a strong campaign against modern revisionism and emphasized *chuch'e* and the spirit of self-reliance.[62] In a policy speech at the first session of the Third Supreme People's Assembly, Kim Il-sŏng stressed once again the necessity of developing an independent, self-supporting economic foundation in North Korea.[63]

From early 1962 on, the Soviet Union apparently began to apply economic pressure to North Korea in order to isolate it from China[64] and to urge the P'yŏngyang leaders to drop the policy of self-reliance.[65] Moscow may have asked North Korea to join the Council of Economic Mutual Assistance (CEMA), the Communist counterpart of the European Common Market, in order to integrate the North Korean economy more closely into that of the Soviet Union. In the summer of 1962, Khrushchev planned to reorganize the CEMA into a political and economic core of the Communist camp, including Yugoslavia.[66] At the June (6–7) 1962 meeting, Mongolia was admitted to the CEMA as a full member on June 7,[67] while Albania was expelled from it.[68] The Chinese, who refused to send observers to the 1962 meetings, were reportedly offered (but refused) full membership.[69] North Korea (along with China and North Vietnam) retained observer status[70] and was absent from the 1962 meetings.[71]

The Soviet leaders had told the North Koreans that they should fulfill their obligation to the overall economy of the socialist camp on the basis of "division of labor" and "specialization within the socialist family." But North Korea refused to participate in CEMA's "socialist division of labor" and stressed the need for economic self-reliance at home.[72] The official party history of the KWP noted critically that "modern revisionists [the Soviet leaders] opposed the development of an independent, self-supporting economy by negating the principle of self-reliance." The party history also stated that "they [modern revisionists] insisted on the development of an integrated economy [with the Soviet Union]."[73]

North Korea took the step of raising self-reliance to the level of a "correct" international revolutionary principle. "Only by building an independent national economy," they argued, "can we mutually fill economic needs among fraternal countries [and] more effectively carry on cooperation and division of labor with these countries and contribute to strengthening the might of the socialist camp."[74] Justifying independence in national planning as basic to the proper international division of labor in the Communist bloc, Kŭlloja asserted:

> Dealing with the international division of labor, it is necessary first of all to take the economic construction of each country as the prerequisite.... This condition is all the more necessary because the purpose of international division of labor does not end in itself but in its stimulation and promotion of the economic growth of each country. Therefore, if we do not ... develop an independent national economy, we shall continue to be a great burden to the various fraternal countries....[75]

P'yŏngyang's emphasis on self-reliance in 1962 was a clear indication of North Korean determination to continue an "independent" course with or without Soviet aid. At the fifth plenary session of the Central Committee of the KWP, the North Koreans modified the Seven-Year Plan so as to strengthen the national economy and defense simultaneously.[76] As 1962 came to a close, they were seemingly giving up the hope of getting economic and military aid from Russia. Their slogan became "all-out fight against the modern revisionism and all-out effort for self-reliance."

THE EAST EUROPEAN COMMUNIST
PARTY CONGRESSES[77]

The Twelfth Congress of the Communist Party of Czecho-slovakia was held from December 4 to 8, 1962. On December 7, Yi Chu-yŏn, vice-premier and head of the North Korean delegation to the congress, went on record in defense of "unity," proclaiming his party's solidarity with the Chinese Communist Party. The North Korean delegate criticized the Soviet leaders indirectly under the name of a "certain comrade":

> A certain comrade attacks unilaterally the Chinese Communist Party and the fraternal Chinese people in a manner which cannot be considered comradely at the party congress of a single country, which was not an international meeting. This will weaken our solidarity, and cannot but bring a great loss to the joint achievement of the international working class.[78]

According to *Peking Review* of December 1962, the Czechs and others attacked the North Koreans for supporting the Chinese.[79] North Korea also reportedly sided with the Chinese at the Congress of the Bulgarian Communist Party held in November 1962.[80]

These and other overt deviations of P'yŏngyang from the Moscow policy line could not be ignored by the Russians for long. At the Sixth Congress of the East German Communist Party, held in East Berlin in January 1963, Yi Hyo-sun, leader of the KWP, was refused time to make a scheduled speech, with the excuse that there was no time. The North Korean delegation reportedly submitted its speech in written form, but even that was not conveyed in full to the delegates attending the congress.[81] All the Asian delegates except the Mongolian and Japanese were refused time to speak.[82] This was an event without precedent in post-1945 Communist history. Presumably the primary purpose of this affront was to prevent the North Korean delegate from defending the Chinese and attacking the Soviet Union.

However, Yi Hyo-sun's intended speech was published in *Nodong Shinmun* on January 22, 1963. It stressed Chinese policy lines of unanimity through consultations, modern revisionism as the main danger, and avoidance of public discussion of differences among the socialist states. It also stated that "unilateral criticism has been made against the Chinese Communist party," something that is "just what our enemies want and hail."[83]

An angry editorial of *Nodong Shinmun,* published on January 30, 1963, came out in further defense of the Chinese line by stating that "to unilaterally attack and to try to isolate the Chinese Communist Party, which holds an important place in our socialist camp, endangers the unity of the socialist camp and inflicts grave losses on the common cause of peace and socialism." "Therefore, our party," the editorial continued, "opposed the unilateral attack on the Chinese Communist Party in order to defend the solidarity of the socialist camp."[84] The North Koreans were further outraged by the fact that the East German Party Congress not only allowed "the revisionist Tito clique" to openly slander the Chinese party but also hailed and responded to this slander enthusiastically.

The editorial also emphasized that "all fraternal parties are independent and equal; they shape their policy independently according to the principles of Marxism-Leninism and according to their own specific conditions." There should not be any larger and smaller countries. "Precisely for this reason," it argued, "no party should interfere in the internal affairs of other fraternal parties or exert pressure on them, force their unilateral will upon them and slander them."[85] This is clearly indicative of considerable pressure being brought to bear upon the P'yŏngyang regime by the Soviet Union.

Evidently these and other disciplinary measures, designed to bring the North Korean regime into the Soviet fold, apparently had quite the opposite effect. Chinese Communist organs during this period made it clear that the Chinese regarded North Korea, along with most other Asian Communist parties, as being firmly on their side, and the North Korean Communists did nothing to deny this assumption. By the beginning of 1963 the P'yŏngyang regime had clearly shifted away from its neutral position and toward the Chinese side in the Sino-Soviet conflict.

CHAPTER 5
P'YŎNGYANG SIDES WITH PEKING IN THE SINO-SOVIET RIFT, 1963–1964

From the beginning of 1963 to the fall of Khrushchev in October 1964 the North Korean regime took a position virtually identical to that taken by the Chinese on all of the burning issues in the Sino-Soviet dispute. Without attacking "dogmatism," the term with which China was usually identified by the Soviet leaders, the North Koreans unreservedly continued to criticize "modern revisionism." Modern revisionists were no longer confined to Titoists; Khrushchev himself was being brought under attack. Thus, P'yŏngyang became the boldest and most open ally of Peking in Asia. During the same period, the North Korean leaders called for an all-out effort toward "self-reliance" and the construction of an independent national economy. They repeatedly stated that "no country is ensured firm political independence and complete equality and sovereignty in international relations unless it is equipped with an independent national economy."[1]

SINO-NORTH KOREAN RELATIONS

The friendly Sino-North Korean relationship during the 1963–1964 period was clearly shown by the outstanding exchanges of high-level delegates and their public speeches. In 1963 alone, twenty-two various official delegations were exchanged between Peking and P'yŏngyang, and a similar number of exchanges were also registered in 1964.[2]

The close relationship between the two countries was highlighted by Ch'oe Yong-gŏn's visit to Peking from June 5 to 23, 1963, at the invitation of Liu Shao-ch'i, chairman of the PRC and the vice-chairman of the Central Committee of the CCP.[3] Commenting on Ch'oe's trip to Peking, *Nodong Shinmun* declared editorially that the North Korean people would tighten in every way the "traditional" friendship with the Chinese people, their close "neighbor," "brother," and *"reliable* ally," and would "march together with the great Chinese people under any circumstances."[4] During his stay in Peking, Ch'oe had generated much "good will" by his appeals for "national liberation" and a "decisive struggle against revisionism," and by his reminiscences about Chinese-North Korean collaboration in the Korean War.[5] At the rally in Peking, on June 8, Ch'oe Yong-gŏn said that the North Korean people "under the leadership of *your* party" would go forward with the Chinese people "sharing life, death and adversity [emphasis supplied]." Peking radio in its Russian service later accommodatingly (probably by the request of P'yŏngyang) reported Ch'oe as saying "the" party, and substituted "joy" for "death."[6]

On June 23, 1963, Liu Shao-ch'i and Ch'oe Yong-gŏn issued a joint communiqué in Peking expressing complete agreement on the question of further consolidating and developing friendship, unity, mutual assistance and cooperation between the two parties and the two countries and "on important questions concerning the current international situation and the international Communist movement."[7] Both sides agreed completely on the issue of peaceful coexistence:

> It is absolutely impermissible to reduce one-sidedly the foreign policy of the socialist countries to peaceful coexistence, to interpret peaceful coexistence as consisting merely of ideological struggle and economic competition, and to forget that peaceful coexistence will be out of the question if no resolute struggle is waged on all fronts against the imperialist policies of agression and war.[8]

In the communiqué, Liu Shao-ch'i praised the KWP and Kim Il-sŏng for "creatively applying the universal truth" of Marxism-Leninism to the practice of the revolution in North Korea and for formulating "a correct line and correct policies." He also stressed that the North Korean people were "unswervingly pursuing the policy of relying on their efforts in building the foundation of their independent national economy." This policy displayed fully "the Korean people's revolutionary spirit of both patriotism and internationalism." On the other hand, Ch'oe Yong-gŏn agreed with the Chinese on all the issues which were essential parts of the controversy between Moscow and Peking, including China's Great Leap Forward and commune policies, the Sino-Indian border dispute, the Cuban crisis, the Taiwan problem, the national liberation struggle in Asia, Africa and Latin America and the opposition to Russia's call for a world Communist parties conference.[9] Without naming Khrushchev directly, Ch'oe Yong-gŏn accused the Soviet leaders of putting economic pressure on the P'yŏngyang regime. "To oppose the construction of a self-supporting national economy in other countries or to exert economic pressure upon another country under this or that excuse," he said, "not only runs diametrically counter to the principles of proletarian internationalism but is a harmful act impeding the normal development of the world socialist economic system . . . and weakening the unity of the socialist countries."[10] The communiqué made a severe attack on "modern revisionists," which was obviously directed against Titoists as well as the Soviet leaders.[11]

The Peking statement also emphasized that socialist countries should base their mutual relations on the principles of complete equality, respect for each other's territorial integrity, independence and sovereignty, and noninterference in each other's internal affairs. "It is absolutely impermissible," it continued, "on the pretext of mutual assistance, to impair the independence and sovereignty of another country and interfere in its internal affairs."[12]

The communiqué also mentioned the forthcoming "Sino-Soviet bilateral meeting." It stated that North Korea and China "sincerely hope that the talks between the Chinese and Soviet parties will yield positive results and prepare the necessary conditions for the convocation of the international meeting of fraternal parties."[13] After his return to P'yŏngyang, Ch'oe praised the achievements of the PRC in unusually strong terms and indirectly attacked the Soviet Union for applying economic pressure on the North Korean regime, as well as attacking the Soviet policy of trying to extend the ideological differences between the socialist parties even to the relations of state.[14] In return for Ch'oe Yong-gŏn's visit to Peking, Liu Shao-ch'i visited P'yŏngyang on September 14–28, 1963.[15]

Between the exchanges of the two visits, on July 5, 1963, the Sino-Soviet bilateral conference was opened in Moscow to explore chances for a reconciliation of their differences. The meeting was "suspended" on July 20, however, upon the motion of the Chinese delegation headed by Teng Hsiao-p'ing, without any conclusion having been reached.[16]

With the failure of the Moscow meeting, Khrushchev, in an apparent change of tactics, planned a conference of world Communist parties at which he intended to excommunicate China. In the meantime, China made a great effort to bring the North Korean regime over to its side. It is not known to what extent North Korea responded favorably to Peking's overtures, but the Peking leadership must have persuaded the North Koreans to develop a united front against the Soviet leadership.[17]

Liu Shao-ch'i visited North Korea from September 14 to 28, 1963.[18] The KWP organ welcomed Liu with an editorial entitled "The Korean and Chinese Peoples are Comrades-in-Arms Tied with Indestructible Bonds."[19] At a rally in P'yŏngyang, Liu Shao-ch'i delivered a lengthy speech after remarks by Ch'oe Yong-gŏn and Kang Hui-won. In his address, Liu attacked the modern revisionists who sided with the imperialists' policy of nuclear blackmail[20] and who opposed revolutionary struggle. He also criticized the Soviet leaders for opposing the line of the self-reliant national economy:

> They [the Soviet leaders] are wrapping themselves in an attractive cloak in order to profit at the expense of others, and to bring the economically underdeveloped socialist countries under their political control. In their opinion, the other fraternal countries only have the duty to make sacrifices to serve their interests, and no right to develop an independent national economy. Their po-

sition is either or both of great-power chauvinism and national egoism.[21]

He concluded his speech with the statement that "China and Korea are allies as close to each other as lips are to teeth. The people of the two countries are sworn brothers who share their fate through thick and thin."[22]

During his visit, Liu met with Kim Il-sŏng and Ch'oe Yong-gŏn for a series of conferences on important problems of mutual interest.[23] At the talks both sides reaffirmed that the joint statement of June 1963 between Ch'oe and Liu was "entirely correct" and was of "great significance,"[24] and reportedly reached "a complete identity of views on all questions."[25] Unlike Ch'oe's visit to Peking, however, there was no official joint statement at the end of Liu's visit. There may have been a difference between Peking and P'yŏngyang concerning the future strategy against the Soviet Union. Since the failure of the Sino-Soviet Moscow Conference in July and the conclusion of the limited nuclear test-ban treaty,[26] the Sino-Soviet clash reached the point at which they began to accuse each other directly by name and a number of Chinese diplomats and students were expelled from the Soviet Union. Under these circumstances, Liu Shao-ch'i may have asked the North Korean leaders to lay down an ultimate demand to Moscow in the form of a joint communiqué. It should be remembered that the P'yŏngyang regime had not yet denounced Khrushchev or the Soviet Union directly by name and that the P'yŏngyang regime maintained a "moderate" rather than an "extreme" anti-Soviet position. Therefore, it is not inconceivable that the lack of a joint declaration was due to P'yŏngyang's reluctance to go to the extreme with the Chinese position.[27]

Nonetheless, the warmth of Chinese-North Korean relations after Liu's visit continued to increase. This was clearly attested to by the tone of Kim Il-sŏng's greetings to Mao on his seventieth birthday. He praised Mao as a "leader of the great Chinese people, outstanding figure of the international Communist and working class movement and close friend of the Korean people."

Kim also stated that Mao applied "the universal truth of Marxism-Leninism" creatively, concluding with: "You [Mao Tse-tung] have made a great contribution to the defense of the purity of Marxism-Leninism against imperialism and re-visionism."[28]

P'YŎNGYANG'S REACTION TO THE NUCLEAR TEST-BAN TREATY

On July 15, 1963, the Anglo-American-Soviet nuclear test-ban negotiations opened in Moscow, culminating in the nuclear test-ban treaty signed on July 25.[29] The Chinese repeatedly told the Russians that they would not be willing to adhere to a test-ban treaty and urged the Soviet leaders not to sign such an agreement.[30] After the treaty was signed, the Chinese launched a bitter attack on the treaty and refused to accept the American and Russian view that the treaty was a step on the road to nuclear disarmament. The Chinese viewed the treaty as simply an excuse for the Soviet leaders not to share their nuclear weapons with the Chinese. Denouncing the treaty as a "big fraud to fool the peoples of the world," the Chinese argued that it was merely an expression of the dangerous and disturbing détente developing between the United States and the Soviet Union, designed to enable the two nuclear powers to dominate the world.[31] In trying to counteract the effect of their refusal to sign the test-ban treaty, on July 31, 1963, the Chinese called for total nuclear disarmament.[32]

North Korea sided with Communist China in refusing to sign the test-ban treaty, which the North Korean Communists called an American "plot" to spread the falsehood that international tensions would be alleviated and to divorce the masses from the antiimperialist struggle. The true aim of the treaty was, they argued, "to obstruct China and other socialist countries from possessing nuclear weapons and to weaken the defense capabilities of the socialist camp."[33] P'yŏngyang then demanded the total test-ban treaty that Peking had proposed on July 31 in lieu of the limited one.[34]

On October 11, 1963, an editorial of *Nodong Shinmun* again

attacked the nuclear test-ban treaty as an imperialist "plot" to monopolize nuclear weapons, describing the treaty as "practically meaningless."[35] The North Koreans also indirectly accused the Soviet leaders of being afraid of the national revolution and of taking "the path of unprincipled concession and compromise in subservience to the nuclear blackmail policy of the American imperialists."[36] On December 6, 1963, the KWP organ carried still another editorial against the test-ban treaty.[37]

P'YŎNGYANG'S WORSENING RELATIONS WITH MOSCOW

From the beginning of 1963, Soviet-North Korean relations continuously deteriorated. On May 27, 1963, an editorial in *Nodong Shinmun,* entitled "The True Character of the Renegade of Marxism-Leninism," attacked Tito's revisionism, but the attack was actually directed equally against the Soviet Union itself. The editorial argued that the policy of positive peaceful coexistence was totally "un-Marxian" and that "the revisionists deny the cardinal principle that imperialism and its policies are the source of war and aggression." The peaceful coexistence policy, it continued, denied the class struggle in the domestic and international spheres. Shortly after Khrushchev's visit to Belgrade in August 1963, *Nodong Shinmun* lashed out at him, declaring that "of late, some people [Khrushchev] are even trying to draw the Tito clique, a group of dirty renegades, into the socialist camp and the ranks of the international Communist movement, saying that it has now corrected its 'mistakes'" of the past and become Marxist and Leninist again. "No arbitrary or unilateral declaration" could cover the crimes and true colors of the Tito clique, nor could "comradely treatment reform the renegade," the KWP organ declared.[39]

In 1963, the Korean edition of the Soviet-sponsored theoretical journal *Problems of Peace and Socialism* was discontinued.[40] In the fall of 1963, the North Koreans criticized the Soviet Academy of Sciences' *World History* as being "extremely regrettable and unbearable" in the way it had minimized the Korean historical contribution and played down the role of Kim Il-sŏng's guerrillas.[41] In a lengthy article, three historians at Kim Il-sŏng University challenged the description of Korea in *World History*. They said:

> There are grave errors which are incompatible with . . . basic requirements of the Marxist-Leninist historiography, and there are many distortions, falsifications and fabrications which came from the prejudice and ignorance of the authors with regard to the history of Korea.[42]

The North Korean relationship with the Soviet Union reached a new low following the publication of a long (nearly 30,000-word) editorial entitled "Let Us Defend the Socialist Camp," which appeared in *Nodong Shinmun* in October 1963.[43] From the beginning, the editorial declared, the Soviet leaders had been guilty of "isolating and expelling socialist countries by developing an ideological dispute to affect state relationships." "To be frank," the editorial asked, "how can one talk about the socialist camp if China . . . is excluded?" This purely rhetorical question was apparently directed against Khrushchev's attempt to call a conference of world Communist parties during which he intended to expel China.

The editorial also stressed the necessity of recognizing the changing nature of international Communism. No matter how large or how developed a nation might be, the editorial argued, one country could not represent or act on behalf of the entire socialist camp that encompasses thirteen states, nor could it dictate the course of world revolution. It urged, instead, that the equality of fraternal parties should be respected and that the notion of hierarchical order should be eliminated from the socialist camp. It would be neither possible nor desirable for any one country to control another from the center. The anachronistic idea of "backward Asia" and "the idea of superior nation and inferior nation" should be discarded, because "all these are arrogant attitudes of insulting the fraternal parties and acts of chauvinism."[44]

The North Koreans complained that the Soviet Union used, or attempted to use, its economic and military assistance as a bait to interfere with the internal affairs and economic planning of

North Korea. Economic assistance, the editorial declared, should not be used as a means of controlling the internal politics of other parties. The party organ also accused the Soviet Union of "revoking unilaterally their agreements with fraternal countries" and suspending almost all economic as well as technical cooperation.[45]

The editorial then specifically pointed out a number of instances of Soviet interference in the domestic politics and policies of North Korea. It stated that "in the past some comrades [the Soviet leaders] neither understood nor supported the socialist construction of our party." Nonetheless, they opposed North Korea's emphasis on heavy industry and its attempt to construct a self-supporting economy. Calling the Five-Year Plan (1957–1961) an "illusion," they insisted that North Korea did not need to construct a machine-building industry and that the speed of North Korea's agricultural cooperativization was too fast. The KWP organ attacked the idea of a "united economy of the socialist camp," the philosophy of the CEMA, as an endeavor to eliminate the economic independence of various states. Adoption of Soviet policies, the editorial charged, would have caused heavy damage both in agriculture and industry. Soviet interference, it continued, even extended to supervision of methods of studying Communist party history and the Russian language, and to inspection of how well Soviet films were shown.[46]

Concerning the de-Stalinization movement, the editorial declared that "it is all the more impermissible to try to force the antipersonality cult" campaign on other socialist parties. It claimed that the Soviet Union had even schemed to "overthrow the party leadership of the countries," obviously implying China and North Korea. Here the editorial seemed to refer to the attempt by Ch'oe Ch'ang-ik and Pak Ch'ang-ok to overthrow the leadership of Kim Il-sŏng in 1956, following the de-Stalinization campaign in the Soviet Union.[47]

"The relationship among the imperialist countries," the editorial argued, "is that of rule and subjugation, in which larger countries interfere in the domestic affairs of smaller countries, force their will on the latter, and demand unilateral respect and obedience on the part of the latter. Outwardly, imperialist countries speak of 'goodwill' and 'solidarity,' but behind the scenes they engage in subversive activities against each other."[48] With this accusation, the North Koreans went so far as to call the Soviet policy "imperialism." It should be noted, however, that even here the North Koreans made no direct reference to the Soviet Union and, in sharp contrast to criticisms made by Peking, the North Koreans avoided personal abuse of Soviet leaders. However, it is quite clear that the criticism was directed against Khrushchev and the Soviet Union.

There were possibly two immediate reasons for these harsh attacks against the Soviet Union at this time. First, during Ch'oe's visit to Peking in June and Liu's visit to P'yŏngyang in September, the North Koreans apparently asked substantial economic help from China in return for their support in the Sino-Soviet conflict, and the Chinese met P'yŏngyang's demand fairly well. It is reported that China signed (sometime in 1963) a five-year economic-cooperation pact with North Korea, which contained a provision that P'yŏngyang would support Peking more vocally.[49] Since aid from Moscow was completely cut off, the P'yŏngyang regime desperately needed more extensive Chinese assistance to compensate for that loss.

Second, the Soviet Union might have intended to exclude North Korea from the socialist camp. According to the 1963 edition of the *International Yearbook of Politics and Economics,* published by the Moscow Institute of World Economy and International Relations, the Soviet Union went so far as to exclude North Korea, Communist China, and Albania from the family of socialist countries. The yearbook was printed in the period of September 12 through September 24, at the very time that the Russians were beginning their verbal offensive to excommunicate Peking.[50] It is thus significant to note that it was just a little over a month later, on October 28, 1963, that the North Koreans published the extremely bitter *Nodong Shinmun* editorial.

NORTH KOREA'S INTERNATIONAL ECONOMIC RELATIONS

Although it is not clearly known to what extent Chinese assistance to North Korea was increased during the 1963–1964 period, China became the country's most important supplier of commodities, technical information, and technicians. As noted, sometime in 1963, China reportedly signed a five-year economic-cooperation pact with North Korea.[51] On June 10, 1963, a protocol on the implementation of the scientific-cooperation agreement for 1963 was signed between the PRC and DPRK academies of sciences.[52] At the conclusion of the sixth meeting of the Sino-North Korean Committee for Scientific and Technical Cooperation on June 21, 1963, a protocol on scientific and technical cooperation was signed between the two countries. The protocol stipulated that Peking and P'yŏngyang would exchange scientific and technical workers for specific investigation and practical work, and exchange scientific and technical data.[53] A protocol on commodity exchange for 1964 between the two countries was signed in P'yŏngyang on October 14, 1963. Under the agreement, North Korea would deliver to China machine tools, pig iron, and other mineral ores, various kinds of metal and alloy steel, cement, carbide and other chemical industrial products, and indigenous products. China would supply North Korea with coking coal and other minerals, crude oil, alloy iron, seamless pipe, various kinds of structural steel, tires, raw rubber, and various chemical reagents. The protocol envisaged a significant growth in trade between the two countries in 1964 compared with that of 1963.[54] But the important fact is that Chinese exports to North Korea did not include any heavy machinery or equipment.

Data on Sino-North Korean trade are very scant. Judging from increasing diplomatic and economic contacts between the two countries, however, there seemed to be a considerable increase in the Sino-North Korean trade volume. Another significant agreement in 1963 was the Sino-North Korean joint project of cooperation in exploiting and utilizing the Yalu and Tuman rivers. This agreement was signed in November 1963 for only one year, 1964.[55]

There were six economic- and technical-cooperation agreements between North Korea and China during 1964. These were as follows: (1) an agreement on technical aid signed on May 9; (2) a protocol on maritime transport signed on June 10; (3) a protocol on cooperation on railways signed on September 12; (4)

a protocol on the exchange of goods for 1965 signed on September 24; (5) a protocol on scientific and technical cooperation signed on October 27; and (6) an agreement on radio and television signed on December 25.[56]

As the North Korean pronouncements put North Korea firmly on the side of China in the Sino-Soviet dispute, the economic pressure from the Soviet Union mounted accordingly. Although Moscow renewed its treaties and agreements of economic, scientific, technical, and cultural cooperation with North Korea,[57] the Russians withdrew their technicians, cut economic aid drastically,[58] and refused military cooperation completely.[59] A significant downward trend was also observed in trade between the Soviet Union and North Korea. In short, economic relations between the two countries, affected by the ideological dispute and the decline of party and state relations,[60] dropped to the freezing point.

Soviet trade volume with North Korea increased from 94.5 million rubles in 1956 to 152 million rubles in 1962. This amounted to an average annual increase in the trade volume of about 10 million rubles. The increase of the trade volume between 1962 and 1963 was only 1.2 million rubles. The trade volume from 1963 to 1964, for the first time since the Soviet-North Korean economic relations began in 1945, dropped about 6 million rubles. The trade balance also changed from −5.5 million to +2 million rubles in favor of North Korea (see Table 2).[61] This indicates that Soviet export to North Korea declined considerably from 1963 to 1964, in spite of the fact that North Korea desperately needed the Soviet industrial equipment and goods for economic development. Overall, Soviet trade with Asian Communist countries decreased by some 40 percent from 1959 to 1962 and concurrently increased by 20 percent with the East European bloc countries. There was also a significant downward trend in the trade between the East European countries and North Korea (see Table 3).[62] By applying increasing economic pressure to North Korea, Moscow apparently tried to isolate P'yŏngyang from other socialist countries.

While trade volume with the Soviet Union and East European countries decreased, the North Koreans gradually built up their

TABLE 2

SOVIET TRADE WITH NORTH KOREA AND CHINA, 1956–1964

(Unit: Millions of Rubles)

		1956	1960	1961	1962	1963	1964
North Korea	Volume	94.5	102.7	140.0	152.0	153.2	147.2
	Balance	+2.3	−31.7	+2.0	+6.0	−5.5	+2.0
China	Volume	1,347.5	1,498.7	. .	. .	540.2	404.2
	Balance	−28.1	−27.9	. .	. .	−203.2	−161.1

Sources: Ernst Kux, "East Europe's Relations with Asian Communist Countries," in Kurt London, ed., *Eastern Europe in Transition* (Baltimore: Johns Hopkins University Press, 1966), p. 292; V. Wolpert, "Turns in North Korea Trade," *Far Eastern Economic Review*, no. 143 (February 13, 1964), p. 386.

TABLE 3

EAST EUROPEAN TRADE WITH NORTH KOREA, 1956–1964

		1956	1958	1960	1962	1963	1964
Albania	Volume	..	..	..	22.7	61.0	..
(Million Lek)	Balance	..	..	..	−2.5	−7.5	..
Bulgaria	Volume	0.5	..	2.0	2.0	2.8	..
(Million Lew)	Balance	+0.5	..	−0.2	−0.8	+1.8	..
Czechoslovakia	Volume	96.0	..	110.0	..	61.0	84.0
(Million Korunas)	Balance	+84.0	..	+58.0	..	−17.0	−22.0
East Germany	Volume	39.9[a]	..	39.1	..	27.0	19.7
(Voluta-Mark)	Balance	+26.5	..	+0.5	..	+3.6	+1.9
Hungary	Volume	48.0	..	92.4	..	50.0	43.0
(Deviza-Forint)	Balance	+43.0	..	+1.0	..	+13.7	−1.0
Poland	Volume	31.0	..	12.9	..	33.0	31.4
(Million Zloty)	Balance	+31.0	..	−2.1	..	+2.2	+1.4
Rumania	Volume	..	21.3	49.6	27.7	63.5	66.1
(Million Lei)	Balance	..	+16.9	+14.2	−7.7	−9.7	+0.1

[a]Million rubles.

Sources: Kux, "East Europe's Relations," pp. 291–95; Wolpert, "North Korea Trade," p. 386; *Far Eastern Economic Review: 1965 Yearbook*, p. 233.

economic relations with such non-Communist countries as Japan, West Germany, Great Britain, France, the Netherlands, and Austria.[63] Though no official figures were available, there were indications that by 1964 North Korea's and China's trade volumes with non-Communist countries began to surpass those with East European countries.[64]

As shown in Table 4, North Korea's trade with Japan increased rapidly. The 1964 trade volume between Japan and North Korea was more than twice that of the 1963 volume. In 1961 Japan accounted for 30 percent of North Korea's total imports from the non-Communist countries and 59.9 percent of her total exports.[65] North Korea's major import items from Japan consisted of heavy industrial and chemical products. For instance, 49.5 percent of the total goods imported from Japan in 1962 consisted of metal products (including steel pipe, alloys, and wire rope), followed by textiles such as nylon fishing net (13.1 percent), machines such as broadcasting equipment (12.2 percent), and chemical products such as plastic materials. The composition of import items remained similar in 1963 and 1964.[66] By 1968 North Korean exports to Japan had reached a total of $34 million, and imports from Japan totalled $20.7 million.[67]

In order not to depend exclusively on Japan in their trade with the "capitalist world," North Korea was anxious to develop trade with the West European countries (see Table 5).[68] North Korean trade missions particularly sought to buy from the West European nations heavy industrial equipment and whole plants on long-term credit arrangements.[69] Thus, in the fall of 1963, the North Koreans placed an order in Holland for a chemical fertilizer plant.[70] While West German imports from North Korea increased from DM 103,000 during the first ten months of 1962 to 1,045,000 during the same period of 1963, exports to North Korea dropped from DM 2,014,000 to 50,000 over the same period.[71] In 1964, however, a private West German firm concluded an agreement to export equipment for a steam-powered generating plant. The North Koreans also negotiated to buy from Austria a steel plant and heavy industrial equipment valued in the neighborhood of $50 million, and bought equip-

TABLE 4

NORTH KOREAN TRADE WITH JAPAN, 1961–1974

(Unit: Million Dollars)

	1961	1962	1963	1964	1965	1966	1967	1968	1970	1971	1972	1973	1974
North Korean Exports	3.5	4.6	9.4	20.2	14.7	22.7	29.6	34.0	34.4	30.0	38.3	72.2	108.8
North Korean Imports	4.5	4.9	5.3	11.2	16.5	5.0	6.4	20.7	23.4	28.6	93.4	99.6	251.9
Trade Balance	−1.0	−0.3	+4.1	−9.0	−1.8	+17.7	+23.2	+13.3	+11.0	+1.4	−55.1	−27.4	−143.1

Sources: Data for 1961–1965 were taken from: Soon Sung Cho, "Japan's Two Koreas Policy and the Problems of Korean Unification," *Asian Survey*, vol. VII (October 1967), pp. 712–14: *Far Eastern Economic Review: 1965 Yearbook*, p. 233; Wolpert, "North Korea Trade," p. 387. For slightly different figures on the trade volume between Japan and North Korea, see James W. Morley, *Japan and Korea: America's Allies in the Pacific* (New York: Walker and Co., 1965), p. 139. Data for 1966–74 come from: United Nations, *Yearbook of International Trade Statistics 1974*, p. 501; Lee and Wellington, "North Korea's Trade with the West: 1950–1968," *Journal of Korean Affairs*, vol. 1, no. 1 (April 1971), p. 27; *Far Eastern Economic Review: 1968 Yearbook*, p. 256.

ment and plants from France and Italy.[72] A British businessman, N. A. Hornstein, who visited P'yŏngyang in 1963, had placed orders valued at about $10 million in North Korea. Britain's trade with North Korea increased steadily, as shown in Table 6.

The total value of North Korea's trade with the non-Communist countries was of course relatively small. The important fact is, however, that North Korea had no choice but to seek to buy heavy industrial equipment and whole plants from

TABLE 5

NORTH KOREAN TRADE WITH THE NON-COMMUNIST COUNTRIES EXCEPT JAPAN, 1963–1968
(Unit: Million Dollars)

	1963	1964	1965	1966	1967	1968
North Korean Exports	1.3	0.6	5.5	4.0	5.5	11.1
North Korean Imports	1.7	6.7	18.8	18.2	20.8	20.9
Trade Balance	−0.4	−6.1	−13.3	−14.2	−15.3	−9.8

Source: Lee and Wellington, "North Korea's Trade with the West: 1956–1968," p. 27.

TABLE 6

NORTH KOREAN TRADE WITH GREAT BRITAIN, 1961–1963
(Unit: Pound)

	1961[a]	1962[a]	1963[a]
Great Britain's Imports	5,389	58	206,455
Great Britain's Exports	19,262	15,520	21,826

[a]The trade volumes are only the first eleven months of each year.
Source: *Far Eastern Economic Review: 1965 Yearbook,* p. 233.

the non-Communist countries. These materials were desperately
needed for North Korea to carry out her Seven-Year Plan,
which stressed the establishment of heavy industry, but she was
apparently unable to buy them from the Soviet Union and East
European countries. Although economic contacts between Peking and P'yŏngyang were very active, it is obvious that at that
time China simply could not supply the equipment and plants
that were necessary for North Korea's economic development.
In sum, the Soviet economic "boycott" on North Korea forced
the latter to attempt to purchase heavy industrial equipment in a
number of non-Communist countries.

P'YŏNGYANG ATTACKS MOSCOW BY NAME

Continuing pressures were placed on the North Korean leadership by the Soviet Union in order to isolate the P'yŏngyang
regime from other socialist countries; however, the Soviet pressures served only to push North Korea closer to Peking. A
lengthy editorial in *Nodong Shinmun* (January 27, 1964), which
was widely quoted in Chinese and Japanese Communist publications, accused the "modern revisionists" and "certain people"
(meaning Khrushchev) of dissuading the Afro-Asian and Latin
American peoples from waging national liberation struggles by
their insistent advocacy of a "peaceful-coexistence" strategy. The
editorial declared that this strategy would lead to the "ideological disarmament" of revolutionary movements. The North Koreans denied that the emergence of nuclear weapons had
changed the nature of war and that, in a nuclear age, local revolutionary wars and insurrections posed a serious problem of
escalation to nuclear war. This was an explicit challenge to
Khrushchev's policy on peaceful coexistence and revolutionary
struggles. "Marxist-Leninists unjustly expelled from certain parties," the editorial concluded, would be justified in building up
their own rival party organizations.[73] The tone of the official
voice of P'yŏngyang was becoming bitter toward the Soviet
Union and its leaders, and accurately reflected Peking's attitudes.

According to a March 3, 1964, report in the French daily *Le*

Monde, "North Korea had stopped the retransmission of Moscow radio broadcasts in Korea; shut down 'friendship societies'; recalled a large number of North Korean students in the Soviet Union for reeducation courses designated to combat 'revisionist tendencies'; and forbidden the showing of Soviet documentary films."[74]

On July 27, 1964, the KWP followed up with an article condemning the Soviet attack on the Japanese Communist Party. Endorsing the Japanese Communist Party, which also launched a sharp attack on the CPSU, the article declared that "they [the Soviet leaders] have been hurling calumnies and slanders at the Japanese Communist Party on a large scale and openly trying to split this party from within. . . . We see in those who oppose the Japanese Communist Party the casehardened great-nation chauvinist act." Furthermore, the article went on:

> As is known to everybody, these people [the Soviet leaders], spreading their wrong views, try to force all others to blindly follow them . . . and plot against those parties which do not obey them. We have already had a bitter experience of such an act of these people. They accuse others of having started polemics after they themselves provoked open polemics, and they condemn others as splittists while they themselves are resorting to splitting machination.[75]

In an editorial of *Nodong Shinmun* on August 31, 1964, the North Koreans, following the Chinese by one day, blasted Moscow's plan for a world conference of Communist parties which was to be convened on December 15. For the first time, the North Korean regime *directly* attacked the Soviet Union by name in the editorial:

> . . . that the Communist Party of the Soviet Union recently abruptly and unilaterally demanded the convocation of an international conference of fraternal parties and a preparatory conference for it. There certainly is some other purpose in hastily convening an international conference under the current complicated circumstances, and such a conference will eventually become one for division.[76]

The North Koreans charged that the Soviet Union intended to use such a conference to impose uniformity in the bloc, and "to pass judgement on other parties." They also accused the Soviet leaders of trying to isolate certain socialist parties (clearly meaning North Korea, China, and Albania) from the socialist camp. P'yŏngyang explicitly refused to participate in such a conference and defended the Chinese "splitting" policies.[77] Until August 31, 1964, the quarrel had been in progress without a single direct reference to the Soviet Union or Khrushchev, though the North Korean attacks had obviously been directed against the Soviet Union in general and Khrushchev in particular.

ASIAN ECONOMIC SEMINAR AT P'YŎNGYANG

The climax of the deterioration of the Soviet-North Korean relationship was reached on the occasion of the Second Asian Economic Seminar held in P'yŏngyang from June 16 to June 23, 1964. The seminar was arranged and completely controlled by China and North Korea. The conference was attended by seven out of eight member countries of the Standing Secretariat of the Asian Economic Conference[78] and by observers from twenty-eight countries.[79] The Soviet Union and India were excluded.

In his opening congratulatory speech, Ch'oe Yong-gŏn emphasized the principle of equality among the fraternal countries and an independent national economy built by mobilizing mainly the strength of one's own people and the resources of one's own country on the principle of self-reliance.[80] "Only those countries which have independent national economies," he elaborated, "can proceed to the international arena as full-fledged independent states enjoying equal rights with other countries of the world."[81]

The most bitter criticism of Moscow during the seminar came from Mme. Theja Gunawardhana, chairman of the Asian Economic Bureau and head of the Ceylon delegation, and from Nan Han-chen, head of the Chinese delegation. The former declared that the prophesy that disarmament would lead to peace and economic progress was "neocolonialism in a different form."[82] The Chinese delegate charged that the movement of the peoples (meaning the Soviet leaders) for peace and for general and complete disarmament was "allegedly aimed at creating an illusion among the Afro-Asian peoples."[83] Criticizing Soviet aid as being great-power chauvinist and national egoist in nature, Nan Han-chen continued to denounce the Soviet Union:

> ... there are often cases in which they [the Soviet leaders] have no respect for the independence and sovereignty of the Asian and African countries, and flagrantly interfere in the internal affairs of these countries.... [They] demand that some of these countries become their suppliers of raw materials and even control economic lifelines of other countries.... In order to impose on other people their revisionist line of not opposing imperialism and not waging revolutionary struggles, they have even gone so far as to cancel aid, withdraw experts, and tear off contracts as means of applying pressure.[84]

At the closing session, the seminar adopted the so-called P'yŏngyang Declaration, which emphasized that the building of an independent national economy by relying on its own efforts was one of the constructive revolutionary tasks in each nation's achievement of political independence. "The construction of an independent national economy does not exclude economic cooperation among the nations, but rather it promotes their mutual support and cooperation." Yet, economic cooperation and mutual assistance must be based on the principles of complete equality, mutual benefit, respect for sovereignty, and noninterference in another's internal affairs. In addition, the declaration severely attacked "imperialism and colonialism," but, unlike the Chinese pronouncements, did not mention "modern revisionists."[85]

The Soviet Union reacted with a strong attack on the seminar. Under the title "In Whose Interest?," *Pravda*, on August 18, 1964, denounced the conference in general and China in particular. Although Moscow did not name North Korea in its attack, the Soviet attack was directed against P'yŏngyang as well. *Pravda* called Mme. Gunawardhana a noted "Trotskyite" with a pro-Peking bias.[86]

The *Pravda* article pointed out that the seminar was convened

hastily and illegally and that the Soviet Union and India were
not invited to attend. While "world-famous progressive scholars
of the Asian countries were not invited to the seminar," it
charged, "many people who were invited were ignorant of economics" and were "obedient to the will of the Peking leaders."
The speeches made by the organizers were not factual, consisting merely of a "superabundance of filth, malice, and slander."
"Vicious slander against the socialist countries and the Soviet
Union" was the "purpose" and "contribution" of the P'yŏngyang
seminar's organizers. The seminar was "guided by interests far
removed from the economic problems of the Asian countries,"
and it sought to "split the Asian and African movements."[87]

Moscow also charged that the principle of self-reliance on
which much emphasis was placed in the conference was a theory
of "schismatics" and "exclusivism." Arguing that one could not
deny the constructive aid given by the Soviet Union to the
peoples of the developing countries of Asia, the article took as
examples of Soviet aid the P'yŏngyang textile combine and the
Hŭngnam fertilizer plant that the seminar participants had
seen.[88]

Counterattacking *Pravda* for its criticism on the Asian Economic Seminar, *Nodong Shinmun,* on September 7, 1964, carried
a lengthy editorial entitled "Why Do They [the Russians] Condemn the Success of the P'yŏngyang Economic Seminar?" The
editorial was extremely provocative from the very beginning.
The KWP organ proclaimed: "What a striking coincidence of
the Voice of *Pravda* with the Voice of America! . . . What a slight-
ing attitude of contempt and arrogance this is! . . . What over-
bearing, insolent, and shameless nonsense it is!"[89]

The editorial declared that the *Pravda* article was "full of
groundless denunciations, falsifications, and fabrications from
beginning to end." The Soviet leaders, the editorial charged,
were in the habit of thinking that they were entitled to decide
and order anything in other countries. The Soviet leaders argued that liberated people could not rely on their own efforts or
build an independent national economy, and they suggested
that the Afro-Asian countries should rely on economic cooperation with and assistance from the "most advanced socialist coun-

try." This meant "nothing but to tell us to live on other's charity" and entrust the destiny of their nations to a "most advanced individual socialist country."[90]

In the last half of the editorial, the North Koreans exposed all the "brutal" activities of the Soviet Union that had not been made public previously. The editorial argued that Soviet aid to North Korea was "ineffective and ungrateful." It criticized the Soviet Union for harshly exploiting North Korea on the pretext of giving economic aid. "By accepting Soviet aid," it stated, "we faced exploitation and interference in our internal affairs."[91]

The editorial admitted that the Soviet people contributed to the reconstruction of some parts of the P'yŏngyang textile mill and the Hŭngnam fertilizer plant, which *Pravda* had mentioned boastingly as examples of the Soviet aid to North Korea. But it accused the Soviet Union of charging much higher prices for its equipment, stainless-steel plates, and other materials, while paying far lower prices for the valuable North Korean raw materials than the international market price. The party organ also revealed that the Soviet Union took away from North Korea "scores of tons of gold bullion" and rare minerals.[92] Indeed, this was the strongest and most open attack on the Soviet leadership that P'yŏngyang had ever made.

In the meantime, North Korea initiated a series of active diplomatic moves, particularly toward neutral countries. In 1963, the P'yŏngyang regime established diplomatic relations with Uganda, Yemen, the United Arab Republic, and Algeria,[93] and, in 1964, with Indonesia, Mauritania, Cambodia, the Congo (Brazzaville), Ghana, and Tanzania (1965).[94] In 1964 alone, North Korean delegations of one sort or another visited Ghana and Guinea in March, Cambodia and Ceylon in April–May, and the Congo (Brazzaville) and Indonesia in September. And in November a large goodwill mission headed by Ch'oe Yong-gŏn travelled to the United Arab Republic, Algeria, Mali, Guinea, and Cambodia. An Indonesian military delegation came to P'yŏngyang in September, together with a parliamentary delegation from Ceylon, an "educational and cultural" delegation from Mali, an economic delegation from Algeria, and a "friendship and cultural" delegation from Yemen. President Modibo Keita of Mali and a parliamentary delegation from the Congo (Brazzaville) also visited North Korea in October, and Sukarno came to P'yŏngyang on November 1.[95] During this period, Chinese prestige was greatly heightened among the Asian Communist parties by the successful detonation of its first atomic bomb in October 1964.[96] Correspondingly, Russia's prestige among the Asian Communist parties declined to its lowest point.

THE MOTIVATIONS OF THE
PEKING-P'YŎNGYANG AXIS

What were the fundamental factors that drew the North Korean Communists closer to the Chinese?[97] Perhaps most important were the facts that the North Korean and Chinese Communist revolutions occurred at roughly the same time and that their respective leaders shared a similar world outlook. The leaders of both countries represented a first-generation revolutionary elite and were profoundly dissatisfied with world conditions, highly nationalistic, and extremely hostile toward the West. Kim Il-sŏng accordingly disagreed with Khrushchev's insistence on peaceful coexistence with the United States. The Soviet Union's "retreat" in the 1962 Cuban crisis evidently gave the North Korean leaders even more reason to question Moscow's seeming willingness to "sacrifice" the interests of other Communist countries in the interest of its own policy of peaceful coexistence with Washington. On the other hand, Peking's more militant line appeared more closely attuned to P'yŏngyang's interests. The North Koreans apparently believed that Peking's hard line offered more protection from the United States and was the more likely in the long run to bring about Korean unification on Communist terms. In fact, the Chinese Communists wholly endorsed North Korea's political and territorial ambitions. Furthermore, the Communists in Peking and P'yŏngyang shared common animosities and complaints against the United States, which alone "obstructs" the unification of their respective countries by the presence of its forces in the Republic of Korea and in the Taiwan Straits. This attitude toward the United States was one of the important factors that bound them together.

Both China and North Korea are still in the militant Stalinist stage of Communist revolution. In this stage, tensions abroad served both regimes as a necessary excuse for imposing maximum mobilization and the stringent policies that are required of the population if rapid industrialization is to proceed. External tension is also necessary to divert the public's attention away from the dissatisfactions and grievances generated by living conditions of austerity and hardship and to justify harsh internal controls. The North Korean and Chinese leaders have thus been constantly exhorting their people to greater productive effort to strengthen their countries in order to deter the "American imperialism" that is forever threatening peace in Asia and the world.

Closely related to the timing-of-revolution factor was Kim Il-sŏng's opposition to Khrushchev's de-Stalinization campaign. The whole cast of North Korean officials was (and is) hard-nosed Stalinist in make-up, and North Korea was modeled after the Stalinist system and is still practicing Stalinist policies under Kim Il-sŏng's one-man dictatorship. Thus, North Korea cannot afford to practice de-Stalinization, nor can it afford to repudiate the cult of personality, for to do either would jeopardize Kim's own dictatorial leadership. In fact, the most serious challenge to his leadership came soon after Khrushchev's famous secret speech at the Twentieth Congress of the CPSU in February 1956. Kim's internal opponents were charging him with the cult of personality and other crimes of a Stalinist character. China has not been practicing de-Stalinization either. Instead, the idolization and deification of both Kim Il-sŏng and Mao Tse-tung have steadily increased in intensity since 1956. By 1960 the cults of Mao and Kim were reportedly bidding to surpass the highest stage ever reached in the worship of Stalin in the Soviet Union.[98]

Also related to the stage-of-revolution factor are the two countries' similar attitudes toward economic development. Both North Korea and China are striving to emerge from economic backwardness and both have placed first priority on the construction of heavy industry. As discussed earlier, North Korea's agricultural and industrial policies closely paralleled China's commune system and her Great Leap Forward Movement. The Soviet leaders had been critical of North Korea's emphasis on heavy industry and had attempted to slow down its rural collectivization program. The North Korean leadership was also possibly disappointed by the limited amount of Soviet aid, particularly after the late 1950s. North Korea's stress on independence and a self-reliant national economy during the early 1960s was a strong indication of their dissatisfaction with Soviet aid. On the other hand, Peking's economic assistance to North Korea was "generous" considering the major economic difficulties that beset mainland China. And the Chinese aid, though very limited, reportedly suited the conditions and needs of North Korea.[99]

Another factor involved in the Peking-P'yŏngyang tie was the nationalistic resentment of the North Korean leadership against Soviet "big-power chauvinism" and Khrushchev's interference in P'yŏngyang's internal affairs. As clearly indicated in two editorials in *Nodong Shinmun*,[100] Khrushchev's excessive efforts to exert control over North Korean policy helped to push Kim Il-sŏng closer to China, which appeared to P'yŏngyang, at least for the moment, to be a "staunch champion" of the right of the small Asian Communist countries to national independence.

In addition, the Russians had been relatively insensitive to Asian needs, lending only begrudging assistance. The North Koreans also have bitter memories of the unfortunate behavior of Soviet troops during the period of occupation from 1945 to 1948. At the time of the Korean Conflict, however, Chinese troops established a somewhat better rapport with the North Koreans.[101] Moreover, the North Korean Communists were aware of the fact that it was the Chinese, not the Russians, who had risked their lives to save the P'yŏngyang regime from total disaster during the Korean Conflict. The repeated emphasis upon phrases such as "our friendship has been forged and tested in blood" suggest that this act was not forgotten by either the Chinese or the North Koreans. Especially after the military coup in the Republic of Korea in 1961 and the Russian retreat in the Cuban crisis in 1962, some Communist leaders in P'yŏngyang may well have suspected that such help might one day be needed again.

Finally, the cultural affinity between North Korea and China could also be an important factor. While P'yŏngyang and Peking share an ancient common civilization, the cultural link between North Korea and the Soviet Union has never been close. North Korea borders both with China and the Soviet Union. Yet by far the longest frontier is held in common with the Chinese, through which influence readily filters. In short, apart from their geographic propinquity and cultural affinity, North Korea's alignment with China was mainly based upon a coincidence of the two regimes' immediate practical interests and needs.

CHAPTER 6
P'YŎNGYANG LEANS
TOWARD MOSCOW AFTER
KHRUSHCHEV'S FALL

On October 14, 1964, Nikita Khrushchev was succeeded by
Leonid Brezhnev and Alexei Kosygin as, respectively, first secretary and chairman of the USSR Council of Ministers. The new
leadership in Moscow provided an opportunity for the P'yŏngyang leadership to reestablish closer economic and political ties
with Moscow and with the Communist countries of East Europe.
It also opened the way for a resumption of Soviet military aid to
North Korea which had been completely cut off during the last
years of the Khrushchev regime. Meanwhile, the North Korean
Communists were cautiously moving away from their solid and
uncritical alignment with Peking. The staunch antirevisionism
that had characterized North Korean statements and publications gave way to increasingly frequent warnings about the dangers of "left opportunism," "dogmatism," and "sectarianism."[1]
But the North Korean leaders continued to favor China's militant strategy for the world Communist movement and shared its
hostility toward the United States. Perhaps the most important
change in P'yŏngyang's policy following Khrushchev's ouster,
however, was North Korea's independent posture in its dealings
with Peking and Moscow.

KHRUSHCHEV'S OUSTER AND
SINO-SOVIET RELATIONS

The new Soviet leaders turned away from Khrushchev's collision course with Peking and stressed as priority goals of Soviet
foreign policy the reestablishment of unity within the Communist camp. Although they could hardly have expected
genuine reconciliation, what the Brezhnev-Kosygin team wanted
from the Chinese Communists was détente in Sino-Soviet rela-

tions and cooperation on such foreign policy issues as Vietnam. Accordingly, direct Soviet polemics against the Chinese ceased, and Peking stopped its open polemics against the Soviets; this seemed to be a unilateral Soviet initiative reciprocated by the Chinese.[2] The new Soviet leadership even stated that it would resume economic and technical aid to China.[3] Yet the primary concern of Khrushchev's successors was to gain domestic popularity, which they could get only by further liberalization at home and détente abroad. This was not, however, what the Chinese wanted.

The forty-seventh October Revolution celebrations held in Moscow in November 1964 demonstrated that the substantive Sino-Soviet differences remained as great as ever. An indication of this was the fact that Moscow invited both a Yugoslav government and party delegation and the pro-Soviet Japanese Communists to the celebrations but failed to invite an Albanian representative. In his speech on November 6, Brezhnev emphasized the production of consumer goods over heavy industry, reaffirmed the validity of the Twentieth Congress of the CPSU,[4] reiterated the Soviet peaceful-coexistence line, specially endorsed the partial nuclear test-ban treaty, and called for an international Communist conference to serve "cohesion" and "unity."[5] Thus, whereas Khrushchev's successors objected to some of his tactics against Peking, they were not willing to change the fundamental policies that Khrushchev had initiated.

Chou En-lai, who headed the Chinese delegation to the anniversary,[6] made his continued disapproval of Soviet policies publicly known in Moscow. He refused to welcome the Yugoslav delegation and laid a wreath on Stalin's tomb as he had in 1961. Following Albania's severe criticism of the new Soviet leadership, Peking once again attacked Moscow openly. In a *Hung Ch'i* editorial (November 21, 1964), the Chinese Communists maintained that Khrushchev's fall was inevitable because of the Soviet moves against Peking and his revisionist policies. The editorial concluded with an implacable announcement that the struggle against "Khrushchevism without Khrushchev" would be waged to the bitter end.[7]

The growing strain between Moscow and Peking had been

aggravated since the "Consultative Meeting" held in Moscow in March 1965. Attended by nineteen Communist parties,[8] the meeting was originally planned by Khrushchev to convene on December 15, 1964. Avoiding Khrushchev's tough line, in which he intended to excommunicate China, the CPSU Central Committee resolution urged "joint actions" in the struggle against "imperialist aggression," "collective efforts to improve relations among the parties, the use of bilateral and multilateral meetings and other forms of party intercourse, [and] the cessation of open polemics."[9] The appeal for "united action" and the proposals for preparation of a new world party conference were flatly rejected by the Chinese.[10]

The tension between the two countries came to a new head on November 11, 1965, when the Chinese published the *Hung Ch'i–Jen-min Jih-pao* joint editorial entitled "Reputation of the New Leaders of the Communist Party of the Soviet Union." The editorial stated that "capitalism is restored in Soviet society." Peking also accused Moscow of giving insufficient aid to North Vietnam and of using the call for "united action" as a "smoke screen" to cover Soviet-American collusion.[11] The Chinese proclaimed their intention to draw a "clear line of demarcation" both politically and organizationally between themselves and the modern revisionists.[12] Since then, the open polemics between Moscow and Peking have continued.

SOVIET-NORTH KOREAN RELATIONS, OCTOBER 1964–1965

The overthrow of Khrushchev was the beginning of a move to alleviate the extremely deteriorated relationship between the Soviet Union and North Korea. P'yŏngyang radio broadcast a brief report on Khrushchev's "resignation" and his successors.[13] Kim Il-sŏng sent a congratulatory message to the new Soviet leaders, calling for the further "strengthening of the traditional solidarity between the Soviet Union and Korea."[14] Accordingly, the North Koreans ceased their direct anti-Moscow polemics, and P'yŏngyang's references to revisionism became considerably milder and fewer in number after Khrushchev's ouster.[15] Thereafter, North Korea constantly stressed the need for "unity" in the socialist camp. As rulers of half of a divided country, and as a people in constant fear of conflict with the United States, the North Korean Communists apparently wanted above all to maintain unity among the socialist countries.

A strong anti-Soviet statement made by the North Koreans immediately following Khrushchev's fall appeared in a *Nodong Shinmun* editorial on December 3, 1964. The editorial argued that the fundamental differences within the international Communist movement were: (1) whether the Communist countries would wage a struggle against the imperialist countries and their policies; (2) whether they would support the revolutionary struggles for national liberation; and (3) whether they would defend the unity of the socialist camp and the solidarity of the international Communist movement.[16] The P'yŏngyang leaders then claimed that "in the past period" the revisionists were "prettifying and embellishing imperialism" and were seeking "unprincipled compromise with the imperialists."[17] But even this criticism referred only indirectly to Soviet attempts to compromise with the United States during the Khrushchev era and was not a direct attack on the new Soviet leadership.

The discreet but determined efforts of the Brezhnev-Kosygin team to reassert Soviet influence in North Korea were coupled with P'yŏngyang's interest in normalizing its relations with the Soviet Union. The first contact between the North Korean and the new Soviet leadership was made at the forty-seventh October Revolution anniversary celebrations in Moscow on November 7, 1964. The North Korean delegation, which included two vice-chairmen of the KWP Central Committee, Kim Il and Kim Ch'ang-man, spent eight days in Moscow during which talks were held on the high party level. Although the result of the conference is not known, they apparently reached a modus vivendi for the normalization of relations between the two countries, and an invitation was extended to Premier Kosygin to visit North Korea.[18]

On February 11, 1965, a Soviet delegation led by Kosygin came to P'yŏngyang, via Hanoi and Peking, with the stated purpose of contributing actively to "strengthening the traditional friendship between the peoples of Korea and the Soviet Union." Kosygin received warm greetings of welcome from the KWP organ, which stated that "the visit of the Soviet delegation will no doubt strengthen the bond between the two countries and its people; and the people of Korea welcome their visit wholeheartedly."[19] In his speech at a P'yŏngyang rally that honored him enthusiastically Kosygin stated:

> ... the Soviet people are the friends of the Korean people, and our delegation has arrived in fraternal Korea with one goal—to strengthen cooperation between our parties and our countries. The fraternal, militant friendship of the Soviet and Korean peoples has been tempered in our common struggle.[20]

During his stay in North Korea, from February 11 to 14, Kosygin had a series of talks with Kim Il-sŏng and other KWP leaders. It was also reported that on February 13 the North Korean minister of defense, General Kim Ch'ang-bong, and Chief Air Marshal K. A. Vershinin had a lengthy discussion on military matters. The talks probably paved the way for the forthcoming Soviet-North Korean military negotiations held in Moscow three months later.[21]

At the conclusion of the Kosygin trip to P'yŏngyang, a joint communiqué, signed by Kosygin and Kim Il-sŏng, was issued on February 14.[22] The communiqué emphasized that the Soviet-North Korean treaty of friendship, cooperation, and mutual aid "unites the two countries with firm and close bonds of brotherhood" and reaffirmed its validity. Pledging full support of North Korea's independent position, Kosygin declared that the Soviet Union would support "the Korean people's struggle for the peaceful unification of Korea," the liberation of Taiwan, and the revolutionary struggle for national liberation. The joint communiqué concluded with the following statement:

> The two sides are deeply satisfied with the results of the talks that were held and feel that the visit of the Soviet delegation ... will undoubtedly promote the further strengthening of fraternal ties, cooperation and friendship between the Union of Soviet Socialist

Republics and the Korean People's Democratic Republic and will contribute to the strengthening of the unity and solidarity of the socialist camp and the international Communist movement.[23]

In his departure speech Kosygin maintained that in the course of the talks with the North Korean leaders the two countries shared identical views on the basic political problems.[24] Kim Il-sŏng, in his reply to Kosygin's speech, declared that "the meeting and exchange of views between us on this occasion has enabled us to understand each other better and has contributed to the friendship and solidarity between the Korean and Soviet peoples."[25]

After his return to Moscow, Kosygin made a televised speech about his trip to North Korea, praising its economic progress and describing it as "a developed industrial and agricultural state."[26] Reiterating that his trip to North Korea contributed to "the strengthening of the unity between our countries," Kosygin declared:

> Soviet-Korean friendship developed and gained strength during the difficult years of war trials and in the years of peaceful construction. We are confident that the peoples of our countries will fight together for socialism and Communism, against the aggressive aspirations of the imperialists.[27]

The tone of Kosygin's speeches in P'yŏngyang and Moscow clearly indicated Moscow's willingness to pay a price to bring a member of the Chinese camp back into the Soviet fold. It can be assumed, therefore, that the Soviet Union apparently consented in principle to the resumption of military assistance and to an increase of economic aid to the North Korean regime, as well as to the immediate cessation of Soviet interference in North Korean internal affairs.

Following the Kosygin visit to P'yŏngyang, the North Korean regime gradually discontinued publication of Chinese policy statements critical of the Soviet Union and publicly praised the Soviet Union.[28] Although the North Koreans joined the Chinese in boycotting the Moscow meeting of Communist parties in March 1965, P'yŏngyang, in contrast to Peking's angry polemics against the meeting, withheld all comment.[29] Indeed, this is in striking contrast to North Korea's August 31, 1964, attack against the meeting.[30] North Korea also did not comment on the March 1965 student demonstration in Moscow in protest against the American bombing of North Vietnamese targets. Peking protested vehemently against what it called the brutality of Soviet troops and police, claiming that many Asian students who participated in the demonstration were injured and hospitalized.[31]

In his speech on the occasion of the twentieth anniversary of Korean liberation, Kim Il, vice-chairman of the KWP Central Committee, praised the Soviet Union for its contribution to the liberation of Korea from Japan, while conspicuously ignoring the Chinese contribution. He also mildly criticized both modern revisionism and dogmatism.[32] On the same occasion, the North Korean ambassador in Moscow, Kim Pyŏng-jik, stressed the strengthening and developing relations of friendship, cooperation, and solidarity with the Soviet people. He also expressed his country's gratitude to the Soviet army and people for "freeing our people from the yoke of Japanese imperialism. . . ."[33]

At the same time, the Soviet Union paid much more attention to the anniversary celebration of Korean liberation than she had done in previous years. In 1964, the Russians merely held a briefly reported commemorative meeting in Moscow and did not send any delegation to P'yŏngyang. In 1965, however, they held two meetings in Moscow which were well reported in *Pravda* and sent a delegation to P'yŏngyang led by A. N. Shelepin, a member of the Presidium and secretary of the CPSU Central Committee and vice-chairman of the USSR Council of Ministers.[34] By contrast, Peking sent only minor officials to the occasion in P'yŏngyang.[35]

Shelepin was warmly received during his visit and, for his part, had high praise for North Korea. In his speech at the Hamhŭng rally he stressed "the inviolable friendship of the Soviet and Korean peoples" and stated that the Soviet party advocated "the full equality of fraternal parties, for their comradely cooperation and their inviolable rights to determine for themselves the forms and methods of the struggle for socialism in their own countries." "The family of Communists is," he continued, "mighty . . . in its mutual respect and in the complete equality and independence of each of its national detachments."[36] This statement was apparently a deliberate attempt to dispel North Korean fears of the kinds of Soviet interference that had allegedly pushed the North Koreans into the Chinese camp. He concluded his speech by stating that "we are convinced that Soviet-Korean friendship . . . will continue to develop and grow stronger."

During 1965 the official Soviet presses emphatically praised the North Korean leaders and the KWP and stressed the "strong and indestructible" friendship with North Korea.[37] As noted earlier, in 1965 very few anti-Soviet articles appeared in the organs of the KWP; indeed, an increasing number of articles friendly to the Soviet Union appeared in these publications. It was indeed a striking contrast to the *Nodong Shinmun* editorials of 1963 and 1964. Thus, the Soviet Union's effort to reestablish its influence in Asia and to entice the North Korean Communists to loosen their ties with Peking appeared to be enjoying a measure of success. By the end of September 1965, Brezhnev, in his speech at the CPSU Central Committee plenum, was able to claim that "interstate and interparty contacts" between the Soviet Union and North Korea had been considerably strengthened.[38]

SOVIET-NORTH KOREAN ECONOMIC AND MILITARY RELATIONS, 1965

The willingness of the North Korean leadership to disengage the country from its complete alignment with Communist China can be understood from the effects of that alliance on North Korea's economic life. Kim Il-sŏng himself, in his 1965 New Year's day message, indicated that North Korea had to spend more to increase her "defense capacity" and thereby had slowed down her economic development.[39] Announcing the extension of the Seven-Year Plan for three more years, the North Korean leaders confirmed in October 1966 that they were not able to fulfill the goal of the economic plan because of excessive expenses for the military budget.[40] The decline of North Korea's trade with Japan immediately after the South Korean-Japanese normalization treaty in June 1965 further accelerated P'yŏngyang's need for economic relations with Moscow[41] (see Table 4). There appeared to be a direct relation between "normalization" of Japan's relations with South Korea and consequent deterioration of relations with North Korea.[42] Chinese aid, no matter how generous it might be, was not enough to compensate for the loss of Soviet economic and military assistance. The figures supplied by Kim Il on estimated industrial production clearly explained P'yŏngyang's economic difficulties as a result of the deteriorated relationship with Moscow (see Table 7).

The Kosygin delegation's visit to North Korea in February 1965 probably led to the stepping up of economic and technical cooperation between the two countries. The various agreements, though minor ones, were more speedily signed than in the immediately preceding years. In December 1964 the Soviets sold North Korea some commercial airplanes.[43] On March 3, 1965, a North Korean delegation visited the Soviet Union to solve the problem of oil supply, which was one of the most pressing problems in North Korea.[44] In March the Russians and North Koreans signed a cultural and scientific exchange agreement in P'yŏngyang. An agreement on the program for the Soviet-North Korean Friendship Association and one on technical and scientific cooperation were signed, respectively, in April and May of 1965.[45]

Several trade agreements signed in 1965 between Moscow and P'yŏngyang reportedly provided an increase in the trade volume over 1964. According to Moscow radio (July 1966), the Soviet Union doubled its North Korean exports for machinery and electric instruments in 1965. East European-North Korean economic relations also improved considerably, and they exchanged friendly greetings, cultural delegations, and economic missions. Observers from North Korea began to participate more regularly in the meetings of CEMA Commissions.[46]

However, the first stage of Soviet economic aid to North Korea since October 1964 was in large part the resumption of the interrupted economic and technical supplies without signing a major new economic agreement. Soviet economic and techni-

TABLE 7

ESTIMATED INDUSTRIAL PRODUCTION IN 1961, 1966 AND 1967

	1961 [a]	1966 [b]	1967 [c]
Electric Power (billion KWH)	9.7	12.5	17.0
Coal (million tons)	12.0	20.0	25.0
Pig and Granulated Iron (million tons)	0.96	1.5	2.5
Steel (million tons)	0.79	1.3	2.3
Cement (million tons)	2.4	2.5	4.3
Chemical Fertilizer (million tons)	0.7	. .	1.7

[a]Kim Il-sŏng's estimates for 1961, as presented in his report to the Fourth Party Congress on September 11, 1961.

[b]Kim Il's report to the KWP Conference on October 10, 1966.

[c]Target figures for 1967.

Sources: *Documents of the Fourth Congress of the Workers' Party of Korea* (P'yŏngyang: Foreign Languages Publishing House, 1961), pp. 168–81; Kim Il-sŏng, "Central Committee Reports," *Nodong Shinmun*, September 12, 1961; North Korean radio broadcast, October 10, 1966; Kim Il, "On the Immediate Tasks of Socialist Economic Construction," *Nodong Shinmun*, October 11, 1966; *Control Figures for the Seven-Year Plan (1961–1967) for the Development of the National Economy of the DPRK* (P'yŏngyang: Foreign Languages Publishing House, 1961), p. 5, cited in Kun, "North Korea," p. 49.

cal aid to North Korea was never completely interrupted during
the 1962–1964 period, and a small number of Soviet experts
remained in North Korea even after party relations came to a
breaking point.[47] Soviet technicians simply returned to North
Korea and picked up where they had left off. The Soviet assistance for the expansion of the P'yŏngyang thermoelectric plant
and Kim Ch'aek refinery and other construction projects were
resumed. *Pravda* maintained that during the previous years the
Soviet Union aided North Korea in building over forty industrial enterprises and projects and 2,500 sets of scientific-
technical documentation.[48]

Soviet military aid was of much greater immediate significance
for the North Korean regime than was economic aid. Since
Khrushchev completely cut off Soviet military aid to North
Korea during the last years of his regime, North Korea's defense
capabilities were seriously impaired. Militarily, the P'yŏngyang
regime remained almost entirely dependent on the Soviet Union
because its armed forces were equipped with Russian planes,
tanks, artillery, and so on. For instance, the Soviet-supplied
MIG-fighters were almost grounded because of a lack of jet fuel
and spare parts. China was incapable of providing military assistance in amounts adequate to North Korean needs,[49] especially
after the development of internal crisis in China with the Cultural Revolution.This circumstance apparently played an important role in influencing the Kim Il-sŏng leadership to reassess its
relations with the Soviet Union.

There were two important developments in Asia during 1965
that may have contributed to bringing North Korea closer to the
Soviet side. The first was the beginning of American bombing of
North Vietnamese targets on February 7, 1965. This apparently
alarmed the North Korean leaders. Kim Il-sŏng issued an "Order of Special Warning" to meet contingencies.[50] The Soviet
Union stood tough toward the United States and gave prompt
verbal support to Hanoi's angry outburst against the American
air strike on North Vietnam. On February 8, the Soviet government issued a statement declaring that "the Soviet Union will be
forced, together with its allies and friends, to take further measures to safeguard the security and strengthen the defense capability of the Democratic Republic of Vietnam." Moscow also

agreed to provide North Vietnam with additional Soviet military aid including antiaircraft missiles.[51] Meanwhile, P'yŏngyang might have been disillusioned with Peking's failure to react more positively to the gradual expansion of the American military effort in Vietnam.

The second event that helped bring North Korea closer to the Soviet Union was the signing of the Treaty on Basic Relations and other agreements between the Republic of Korea and Japan on June 22, 1965. The treaty and other agreements were ratified by the National Assembly of the Republic of Korea on August 14, 1965, and by the National Diet of Japan on December 11, 1965.[52] The North Korean leaders considered the treaty a first step by "American imperialists" to organize a "Northeast Asian Treaty Organization."[53] They pronounced the treaty "null and void" and claimed that North Korea would never recognize the agreement.[54] These developments might have convinced P'yŏngyang that in the future only Soviet military support with Moscow's nuclear protection would provide an effective deterrent to American power in case North Korea were again to become embroiled with the United States.

As early as the Kosygin visit to North Korea in February 1965 separate negotiations on military matters were taking place between the two countries. Possibly as a reward for the noticeably changed attitudes of the P'yŏngyang regime toward the Soviet Union, a Soviet-North Korean military agreement was signed, in Moscow on May 31, 1965, whereby the Soviet Union would provide military assistance to further strengthen the "defense potential" of North Korea.[55] The Soviet military assistance to North Korea was aimed primarily at strengthening the North Korean air force by supplying jet fuel, spare parts, and antiaircraft missiles.[56] It was also reported that the Soviet Union supplied the P'yŏngyang regime with a limited number of MIG-21's.[57] At the same time, Soviet military academies resumed the training of North Korean military personnel.[58]

SINO-NORTH KOREAN RELATIONS, 1965

North Korea's rapprochement with the Soviet Union had an immediate cooling effect upon Sino-North Korean relations.

Their first attack on the Chinese came in an editorial appearing in *Nodong Shinmun* on December 3, 1964, in which North Korea openly expressed their opposition to dogmatism. Implying that North Korea was under pressure from China to follow the latter's "dogmatic line," the editorial declared:

> It is necessary to resolutely do away with stubborness in following the outmoded line which has gone bankrupt in the face of living reality, and in compelling others to follow that line too. Prejudices or subjective views must not be obstinately clung to. The important thing is to assess the development of the events cool-headedly and scientifically, and to seek unity in the actual struggle.[59]

The KWP organ also stressed that unity and solidarity "are utterly incompatible with great power chauvinist arbitrariness and with the blindness of dogmatists." "For the sake of unity and solidarity," the editorial continued, "we must put a complete end to the interfering and splitting attitudes in the internal questions of fraternal parties and countries."[60] This criticism was obviously directed against the Chinese rather than against the Russians.

According to a report published in *The Indian Express* (New Delhi) on July 20, 1965, a North Korean embassy official revealed that China claimed a hundred square miles of North Korean territory near Mt. Paektu as "compensation" for its aid during the Korean Conflict.[61] It is conjectured that the Chinese Communists intended to reopen the Sino-North Korean boundary dispute as retaliation to P'yŏngyang's disengagement from the Chinese fold.

On the occasion of the twentieth anniversary of the Korean liberation, China sent P'yŏngyang an exceptionally low-ranking delegation headed by Wu Hsin-yu, who was not even a Central Committee member.[62] The Albanians did not send any delegation at all,[63] and the Chinese congratulatory messages of 1965 were visibly less enthusiastic than those of 1964. At the same time, the *Nodong Shinmun* editorial marking the occasion was conspicuous for its omission of any reference to China. While offering high praise of the Soviet Union, the editorial was silent on both North Korea's friendship with China and its indebted-

ness to the latter for help in the Korean War.[64] The North
Korean leaders as a whole also tended to omit any mention of
China in their speeches, and European Communists returning
from the celebrations were reported to have received a more
"fraternal" welcome than the Chinese.[65] North Korea reportedly
did not even send its delegation to the celebrations of the six-
teenth anniversary of the founding of the People's Republic of
China in Peking in October 1965.[66]

As to the cultural and economic relationships between Peking
and P'yŏngyang, there were no significant activities between
the two apart from several agreements during the 1965–1966
period. In 1965, an agreement on cooperation in public health
work (November 9), a protocol on railway cooperation (November 18), and a protocol on exchange of goods for 1966
(December 14) were signed between the two countries.[67] During
1966, six agreements between Peking and P'yŏngyang were concluded: (1) a protocol on the 1966–1967 plan for cultural cooperation signed on February 25; (2) a protocol on scientific and
technical cooperation signed on July 5; (3) an agreement on
animal diseases; (4) a protocol on cooperation between
Academies of Sciences; (5) a protocol on exchange of goods for
1967 signed on December 3; and (6) an agreement on radio and
television cooperation signed on December 30.[68]

There were possibly two immediate reasons for the slowdown
of Sino-North Korean economic and cultural activities. They
were, first of all, P'yŏngyang's rapprochement with Moscow and,
secondly, the internal chaos in China caused by the "Great Proletarian Cultural Revolution" and its Red Guard movement. In
fact, Peking was no longer in a position to help North Korea
economically at this time.

The North Koreans were, however, careful to remain cordial
to the Chinese. On the occasion of the fourth anniversary celebrations of the Sino-North Korean friendship treaty of 1961, for
example, the North Korean Communists emphasized their
warm friendship with the Chinese, which had "been sealed in
blood in the long-drawn arduous revolutionary struggle against
enemies."[69] At the Rumanian Communist Party Congress held
at Agerpres on July 21, 1965, Kim Ch'ang-man, head of the

North Korean delegation to the congress, reportedly took a neutral attitude in the Sino-Soviet conflict.[70] The P'yŏngyang leaders also supported Peking's position on the Indo-Pakistani conflict and the Indonesian crisis in 1965.[71]

Furthermore, the North Korean leaders made it clear that they continued to favor China's militant strategy on the world Communist movement, especially on such issues as "American imperialism" and modern revisionism.[72] Less than four weeks after the publication of the *Hung Ch'i–Jen-min Jih-pao* joint editorial, which repudiated the new Soviet leaders,[73] North Korea published an editorial in *Nodong Shinmun* that was entitled "Let Us Develop Antiimperialist Movement by Concentrating All Revolutionary Powers." In the editorial, the North Koreans did not echo the specific Chinese charges against the Soviet leaders, but they gave ideological support to Peking by emphasizing that they would strongly oppose revisionism and peaceful coexistence. The North Koreans also warned that some groups "may talk about antiimperialism but actually cooperate with the imperialists."[74] Jeno Fock, who led a Hungarian delegation to North Korea in 1965, clearly observed the North Korean leaders' ideological line on these issues. In an interview after his return to Budapest, Fock said: "We disagreed on a great many questions, namely the well-known contentious issues of the international Communist movement. On several questions our stands are different . . . [from those of North Korea]."[75]

The new Soviet leaders were much more patient than Khrushchev. They did not retaliate against the North Koreans' disagreement on some ideological issues through economic means nor did they counterattack through their presses. The Russians were apparently willing to settle for P'yŏngyang's friendly relationship with Moscow and its organizational neutrality, combined with ideological support for the Chinese in the world Communist movement.

MOSCOW-P'YŎNGYANG RELATIONS AFTER THE TWENTY-THIRD CPSU CONGRESS

The Twenty-third Congress of the CPSU was a major turning point in North Korean relations with the Soviet Union and

Communist China. In March–April 1966, a North Korean delegation led by Ch'oe Yong-gŏn attended the congress,[76] while the Chinese Communists publicly refused to send their delegates.[77] In his speech to the congress, Ch'oe stressed that the friendship and cooperation existing between North Korea and the Soviet Union "will develop in the interests of the peoples of our countries, the socialist camp, and the international Communist movement." He also praised Soviet economic achievements and endorsed the line that the Soviet people "are now striving to build the material-technical base of Communism." Yet, the North Korean delegate did not mention China in his speech, and he did not touch upon any controversial ideological issues directly related to the Sino-Soviet dispute.[78]

Leonid Brezhnev, in his report to the Twenty-third Congress, declared that the CPSU and the Soviet people "fully support the fraternal Korean people, who are struggling against American imperialism for the unification of Korea." He reportedly drew "strong applause" from the delegates when he praised North Korea. On the other hand, Brezhnev pointed out that Soviet relations with the Communist Party of China and the Albanian Workers' Party "unfortunately remain unsatisfactory."[79] A. J. Pelse, a member of the Politburo of the CPSU Central Committee, in his speech at the forty-ninth anniversary of the October Revolution, emphatically declared that "the working people of the Soviet Union are deeply satisfied with the successful development of fraternal relations with ... the Korean People's Democratic Republic...."[80] Throughout 1966, the Soviet party organs carried an increasing number of friendly articles on North Korea.[81]

The North Korean regime, for the first time, endorsed the Soviet call for a "united-front action" in support of North Vietnam in a communiqué issued at the end of a visit by the Japanese Communist Party delegation in March 1966.[82] This was a direct confrontation with Peking's stand in the international Communist movement. After the Twenty-third CPSU Congress, the North Korean regime sent delegations to all the congresses held by East European Communist parties and the Mongolian Party in 1966.[83]

In March 1966, the Russians sent a huge trade mission to

North Korea and opened a well-advertised exhibition of Soviet consumer goods in P'yŏngyang.[84] In June 1966, a new agreement on economic and technical cooperation for 1967–1970 and a protocol on fisheries cooperation were signed between North Korea and the Soviet Union. In the agreement, the Soviet Union agreed to assist North Korea in building or enlarging hot and cold rolling mills at the Kim Ch'aek steel plants, a large oil refinery, a thermal electric station in Pukchŏng, an ammonia factory, and a number of other unspecified projects.[85]

An agreement on reciprocal commodities exchanges between Moscow and P'yŏngyang in 1967–1970 was signed in June 1966. The two countries agreed to expand trade considerably during the four-year period and emphasized that the agreement would be "greatly conducive to successfully developing the national economy" of both countries. According to the agreement, Russia would substantially increase deliveries to North Korea of machinery and equipment, chemicals, fuel, tires, consumer goods, and various raw materials. North Korea would reciprocate with increased shipments of ferrous rolled metals, alloy steel, nonmetallic minerals, building materials, light industrial articles, and nonferrous metals.[86] It was disclosed that the projected trade volume between Moscow and P'yŏngyang in 1967 would surpass the 1966 volume.[87] By the end of 1966 the Soviet Union had sent North Korea more than twelve official missions for cultural and economic exchanges alone.[88]

From February 13 to March 3, 1967, Kim Il, vice-chairman of the KWP Central Committee, visited Moscow as the head of a delegation. There Kim Il and K. T. Mazurov, member of the Politburo of the CPSU Central Committee and first vice-chairman of the USSR Council of Ministers, signed agreements on economic, scientific and technical cooperation, on reciprocal goods deliveries for 1967, and on cooperation for the further strengthening of North Korea's military power.[89]

In late May 1967, Vladimir Novikov, deputy premier of the Soviet Union, paid a good-will visit to North Korea. While there, the Soviet visitor emphasized the "rapidly expanding economic cooperation" between P'yŏngyang and Moscow and other socialist countries, and he expressed satisfaction at the growing

Soviet-North Korean relations "not only in the economic sphere but also in the realms of party, social, cultural, and other activities." He also assured the North Korean leaders that the Soviet Union would do "all in their power" to promote Soviet-North Korean relations on the basis of the principles of Marxism-Leninism and proletarian internationalism.[90]

A North Korean economic delegation, headed by Vice-Premier Yi Chu-yŏn, visited the Soviet Union in October 1967. On October 16, North Korea and the Soviet Union agreed to establish an economic and scientific-technical consultative commission with the "aim of further developing the relations of cooperation between the two countries,"[91] and on October 23, the two countries signed a protocol on trade between Moscow and P'yŏngyang for 1968. The trade protocol provided for a "substantial growth" of Soviet-North Korean trade in 1968. The Soviet Union was to deliver to North Korea machine-tool, power and ship equipment, diesel locomotives, motor vehicles, instruments, means of communication, petroleum products, metals, steel pipe, industrial rubber products, chemical products, and so on. In return, North Korea would deliver to the Soviet Union metal-cutting tools, electric motors, pig iron, rolled ferrous metals, building materials, nonmetallic minerals, and other raw materials.[92]

The Soviet Union also signed an agreement of cooperation in the construction of enterprises and installations in North Korea. Under this agreement, the Soviet Union was to supply sets of equipment and give technical assistance in the reconstruction and construction of several enterprises and installations of the coal and electric equipment industries, and rail transportation.[93] Moscow and P'yŏngyang expressed the belief that the agreements would contribute to the further strengthening of the "traditional relations of friendship and cooperation between the two countries."[94]

P'yŏngyang's friendly relations with Moscow were further demonstrated by a few more developments in the latter part of 1967. When the Soviet Union celebrated the fiftieth anniversary of the October Revolution, North Korea sent a delegation headed by Ch'oe Yong-gŏn, the number two man in the KWP hierarchy.[95] In addition, Soviet Foreign Minister Andrei A. Gromyko made a strong appeal for the admission of North Korea and East Germany at the Twenty-second session of the U.N. General Assembly, September 22.[96]

According to *The New York Times,* the Soviet Union stepped up military assistance to North Korea as a device for improving relations with P'yŏngyang and offsetting China's influence. The nature and extent of Soviet arms deliveries were described by the *Times* as follows:

> In the last 12 months . . . Moscow has provided more than half of North Korea's 500 military jet aircraft. The North Korean air force is estimated to include 21 MIG-21, 350 MIG-17 and 80 MIG-15 fighters plus 80 IL-28 bombers. . . . North Korea is said to have 500 air-defense missiles.
>
> The North Korean army of 350,000 to 400,000 is equipped almost exclusively with Soviet equipment, including medium tanks, and the North Korean navy is said to have two Soviet W-class submarines, four Komar-type guided-missile ships, forty motor torpedo boats and two coastal defense complexes with Soviet radar and shore-to-ship missiles.[97]

When the North Korean navy seized the American intelligence ship *Pueblo* on January 23, 1968, Moscow expressed its support of the North Korean action the following day. Peking's support came on January 28, after North Korea had publicly demanded that all socialist countries indicate their approval.[98] In August 1968, North Korea promptly supported the Soviet-led invasion against Czechoslovakia, while Peking condemned the invasion as a "shameless act" and a "fascist crime."[99] North Korea's reaction to the event appears to have been dictated by its need to preserve Moscow's good will toward P'yŏngyang.

P'YŎNGYANG'S WORSENING RELATIONS WITH PEKING

The new North Korean policies caused rapidly deteriorating relations between P'yŏngyang and Peking, especially after the Twenty-third Congress of the CPSU. The North Koreans re-

jected the Chinese insistence on drawing "a clear line of demarcation" between themselves and the followers of the CPSU.[100]
Instead, they urged that the Chinese join Moscow's call for
"united action" in support of North Vietnam. In fact, the mili-
tancy of North Korean policy on a "united front" far exceeded
what the Soviet and European Communist regimes proclaimed.[101] Arguing that "joint action" in the struggle against
"American imperialism" did not conflict with the struggle
against revisionism, the P'yŏngyang regime declared that difficulties between Communist parties should be shelved for the
time being in order to form the international antiimperialist
joint action and to present a united front.[102] The uncompromis-
ing Chinese attitude toward "united action" and the CCP's growing inflexibility on ideological issues might be important factors
contributing to the deterioration of the relationship between
Peking and P'yŏngyang.

Although neither the Russians nor the Chinese escaped criticism, an editorial of *Nodong Shinmun,* on August 12, 1966,
leveled a much heavier attack on Chinese party policy and its
divisive effects upon the Communist world.[103] The editorial specifically attacked "dogmatism" for hewing to the letter of Marx-
ism without taking into account the changing situation in the
world. "The dogmatists criticized our party's policy of educating
old intellectuals and remolding them as 'leading the party toward the right,'" the KWP organ stated. "By resolutely rejecting
all erroneous contentions and obstructionist machinations of the
dogmatists and flunkeys," the editorial continued, "our party
could successfully push ahead with revolution and construction." In this criticism, the North Korean leaders clearly implied
that there was Chinese pressure on P'yŏngyang because of its
attitudes toward Moscow. Emphasizing that in international relations the North Korean party waged the struggle against
modern revisionism from an independent stand in accordance
with its own judgment, the North Koreans also flatly refuted the
argument that P'yŏngyang had followed Peking's ideological
line.[104]

The possibility of a purge of pro-Chinese elements within the
KWP was clearly implied in the editorial's attack on "ideological

survivals of flunkeyism in our party."[105] At the fourteenth plenum of the KWP Central Committee, which was opened on October 5, 1966,[106] Kim Ch'ang-man, a member of the Politburo and vice-chairman of the KWP Central Committee and vice-premier, was removed from his positions. Kim, the only remaining well-known leader of the Chinese faction,[107] was the likely man to oppose Kim Il-sŏng's new policies. Although it is not known whether he actually revolted against those policies, Kim was indeed a victim of a new approach to Moscow and Peking.

P'yŏngyang's harshest attack on the Chinese appeared in an editorial of *Nodong Shinmun* on September 15, 1966.[108] This editorial was carried in full by *Pravda* under the title, "Antirevolutionary Theories of 'Left' Opportunists."[109] Most important of all, North Korea's opinion of the Cultural Revolution in China was manifest in the article. Ostensibly attacking "Trotskyism," the KWP organ pointed out that the major departure and basis of the position of Trotsky's "left-wing" opportunism was the theory of "permanent revolution." Trotskyism was also an anti-revolutionary theory denying the possibility of the victory of the socialist revolution and of the building of socialism in one country. The Trotskyites, the editorial continued, opposed any improvement in the material and cultural life of the population on the ground that it would supposedly cause the danger of the restoration of capitalism. The Trotskyites categorically opposed any combination of violent and nonviolent methods in the revolutionary struggle, and favored only "offensive and reckless rebellion."[110] The North Korean leaders were apparently alarmed by the violence of China's Cultural Revolution, which they did not want to follow. However, P'yŏngyang refrained from commenting on the Cultural Revolution in explicit terms.

The same editorial of the KWP organ also made clear reference to the subversive actions of the Chinese against the North Korean regime and other socialist countries. The crimes of the Trotskyites, it declared, were their schismatic and subversive activities to undermine the party of the working class and the international Communist movement. The editorial further denounced their involvement in factional and splitting activities in foreign parties.[111] Overall, this editorial was North Korea's official denunciation of China.

In his report to the KWP Conference on October 5, 1966, Kim Il-sŏng criticized Chinese intervention in the internal affairs of the KWP and the Japanese Communist Party. He also urged that "every socialist country should dispatch volunteers to Vietnam to defend the southeastern outpost of the socialist camp and preserve peace in Asia and the world."[112] Though he warned against weakening the struggle against modern revisionism, which was "on the decline," Kim made his major attack on "left opportunism," an obvious assault on the Chinese ideological line. Said Kim Il-sŏng: "Left opportunism takes no heed of the changed realities, and recites individual propositions of Marxism-Leninism in a dogmatic manner, and leads people to the extremist action under superrevolutionary slogans."[113]

On the other hand, the Chinese began to retaliate against P'yŏngyang's pro-Soviet attitude and its criticism of Peking. The CCP representative to the national conference of the pro-Chinese New Zealand Communist Party criticized Ch'oe Yong-gŏn's appraisal of the Soviet economic achievements at the Twenty-third Congress of the CPSU as a "prettification" of the Soviet leaders.[114]

A direct Chinese attack against the North Korean leadership came at the peak of the hectic days of the Cultural Revolution. Although official relations between China and North Korea remained "cordial," in mid-January 1967 Peking's Red Guard posted reports of political disturbances in North Korea. Some Peking wall-posters reported that anti-Kim Il-sŏng campaigns had erupted in various parts of North Korea,[115] while others called for the removal of Kim Il-sŏng. The Chinese even rumored that Kim had been overthrown by a coup d'état.[116]

On January 27, 1967, the North Korean news agency angrily denied the Chinese charges and bitterly criticized the Chinese. P'yŏngyang's official statement said:

> False propaganda has been conducted recently in various parts of China, including Peking, in . . . newspapers . . . leaflets, to the ef-

fect that some kind of a "coup" has allegedly taken place in our country, and that this has created an atmosphere of political turmoil.[117]

The Chinese charges, the news agency continued, were "an absolute lie, without any foundation whatever. This is nothing but intolerable slander against the party, government, people and people's army of our party." But subsequent posters appearing in China continued the attack, calling Kim Il-sŏng a "fat revisionist" and a "disciple of Khrushchev." During the period, the North Korean leaders were desperately trying to build a strong wall by which they could stop the waves of the Red Guard movement from China.

The steady deterioration of P'yŏngyang-Peking relations was further evidenced by the slowdown of economic and cultural activities and the absence of contacts between the two countries. Throughout the 1965–1968 period, China and North Korea failed to exchange delegations at national-day celebrations. P'yŏngyang did not send a representative to the CCP's Ninth Party Congress in April 1969.

In March and again in December 1968, there were reports that the Chinese-North Korean border was closed from the Chinese side. Also, military clashes between the two countries occurred in late 1967, in December 1968, and again in March 1969, over the ownership of Mt. Paektu at the disputed border.[118]

North Korea's pro-Moscow policy did not mean the exchange of one partner for another, nor did it mean the conversion of the P'yŏngyang regime to the Soviet ideological line. During the period, North Korea was extremely reluctant to join Moscow's anti-China campaign and consistently refused to associate itself with a Soviet-led scheme to expel China from the world Communist movement. Further, the North Korean leaders made it clear that they continued to favor China's militant stance on the world Communist movement, especially on such issues as "American imperialism" and modern revisionism.[119] In February 1968, North Korea rejected the Soviet invitation to attend the Budapest Conference of world Communist parties, joining

China on the absentee list. This rejection came even after Boris N. Ponomarev had visited P'yŏngyang in an effort to persuade North Korea to attend the meeting.[120]

INDEPENDENCE FROM BOTH MOSCOW
AND PEKING?

Despite its friendly and close relations with the Soviet Union, the North Korean regime made clear the limits of P'yŏngyang's swing toward Moscow. On December 3, 1964, P'yŏngyang attacked both dogmatism and revisionism and stressed the equality and independence of all the socialist countries.[121] In a speech on an Indonesia visit in April 1965, Kim Il-sŏng emphasized P'yŏngyang's independent position in its attitude toward the Communist bloc. In the struggle against revisionism and dogmatism, he said, the KWP acted strictly on the basis of its own judgment and conviction and in conformity with its own policy of *chuch'e*.[122] At the twentieth anniversary celebrations of the KWP on October 10, 1965, Kim Il-sŏng again stated his intention to maintain an "independent and principled stand," that is, independent both of China and of Russia.[123]

North Korea's most forthright statement of "independence" of both Chinese and Soviet leadership came on the occasion of the twenty-first anniversary celebration of its liberation from Japan. At the time, *Nodong Shinmun* carried an editorial entitled "Let Us Defend Independence."[124] The North Korean Communist press claimed that P'yŏngyang, not Peking nor Moscow, was the best judge of how Communist doctrine should be applied to North Korea's problems. "The Communists," the editorial declared, "should always do their own thinking and act independently, maintaining their own identity."[125]

The KWP organ then laid emphasis on political and economic independence. "There can be no superior party or inferior party, nor a party that gives guidance and a party that receives guidance," it declared. Arguing that there "is no privileged party" in the Communist bloc, the editorial stressed the principles of complete equality, sovereignty, noninterference in each other's internal affairs, and mutual respect. The prerequisite of solidarity among the Communist countries is political independence. The North Koreans continued to emphasize a self-reliant national economy. Without economic independence, they argued, no country or party could achieve political independence.[126]

At the conference of KWP representatives on October 5, 1966, Kim Il-sŏng officially confirmed the *Nodong Shinmun* editorial of August 1966 when he said that he would maintain an independent posture in the international Communist movement. Although his party maintained a close relationship with other "fraternal" parties, he declared, the KWP would not follow any other party's ideological line or policy without discrimination. The socialist parties that maintain an independent position, he claimed, should not be referred to as "neutralist, eclectic, opportunist, and the like."[127]

By October 1966, Kim Il-sŏng tightened his ruling oligarchy by removing both the Chinese and Soviet factions from the center of power. The purge of Kim Ch'ang-man in October 1966 coincided with the demotion of Nam Il, vice-premier and equally well-known leader of the Soviet faction. Nam Il was not included in either the five-man Presidium of the Political Committee or the eleven-man Secretariat of the KWP Central Committee. Althouth he was allowed to retain the title of vice-premier, his main job was to be in the powerless railroad business as the minister of railroads.[128]

In his lengthy speech to the Fourth Supreme People's Assembly of the DPRK on December 16, 1967, Kim Il-sŏng emphasized the "revolutionary spirit of independence, self-sustenance, and self-defense in all fields of state activites." He then said, "As a full-fledged independent state, our country now determines all its lines and policies independently and exercises complete equality and sovereignty in its foreign relations."[129]

North Korea adopted once again a neutralist policy in the Sino-Soviet rift as a necessary step to safeguard its "independence." Several factors may be described as the immediate reasons for the "success" of P'yŏngyang's policy. First of all, the present leadership in Moscow had shown itself willing and even eager to furnish economic and military assistance without demanding ideological and political conformity from P'yŏng-yang.[130] Another factor was that North Korea, unlike North Vietnam, was not so immediately dependent on both Moscow and Peking economically as well as militarily. Finally, there were no longer any powerful pro-Chinese or pro-Soviet factions within the North Korean party whom the Chinese or Russian Communists might manipulate against the Kim leadership.

SUMMARY

The overthrow of Khrushchev marked the beginning of a move to improve the badly deteriorated relationship between the Soviet Union and North Korea. North Korea sought friendly and close relations with the Kremlin for economic, military, and other pragmatic reasons, while, at the same time, intending to continue to maintain its ties with Peking. P'yŏngyang's interest in normalizing its relations with Moscow was coupled with the discreet but determined efforts of the Brezhnev-Kosygin team to reassert Soviet influence in North Korea. As P'yŏngyang's relationship with Moscow was improving considerably, North Korea's relationship with the PRC was somewhat cooling off.

North Korea's friendly attitude toward the Soviet Union did not mean exchanging one big brother for another. Rather, P'yŏngyang's policy simply reflected a realistic reassessment of North Korea's changing national interest. The North Korean Communists, like the North Vietnamese and Japanese parties, clearly indicated that they would put their own interests before allegiance to the Soviet line or to the "dogmatic" Chinese version of Marxism-Leninism. The North Koreans' primary aim was to fulfill the country's economic plan by the end of the 1960s and to strengthen their military capabilities without having to sacrifice political independence either to Moscow or to Peking. Thus, North Korea's over-all posture in the Sino-Soviet dispute during 1965–1968 was, as Professor Byung Chul Koh has summed it up, "one of neutrality—not neutrality pure and simple but with a slight slant in favor of Moscow."[131]

CHAPTER 7
P'YŎNGYANG'S
NEW RELATIONS WITH PEKING:
"LIPS AND TEETH" AGAIN?

Friendly relations between North Korea and China were restored after the Ninth Congress of the CCP in April 1969, which marked the end of the most intense phase of the Cultural Revolution. As the Cultural Revolution in China drew to a close at the end of 1969, Peking apparently decided to relax its policy of self-imposed isolation and attempted to reestablish normal political relations with selected countries, including North Korea. The North Korean Communists once again seemed to feel that they had leaned too far in one direction. There were some indications that Soviet economic help had not been as abundant as anticipated and that P'yŏngyang wanted to build a military and economic base more independent of Moscow.

NORTH KOREA'S FRIENDLY RELATIONS
WITH PEKING

A major factor contributing to the revival of P'yŏngyang-Peking friendship was their shared hostility toward Japan and their increased fear of Japan's growing strength. During 1969 and 1970, three significant developments seemed to forerun a larger future role for the Japanese in Asian security arrangements, reinforcing North Korean fears. First was the Nixon Doctrine announced in November 1969, which implicitly urged a more positive Japanese role in the maintenance of Asian security.[1] Second was the Nixon-Sato joint communiqué in which Premier Eisaku Sato stated that "the maintenance of peace and security in the Taiwan area was . . . a most important factor for the security of Japan" and that "the security of the Republic of Korea was essential to Japan's own security."[2] Speaking at the

National Press Club in Washington, the premier reemphasized the importance of Korea to Japan's security:

> Specially, if an armed attack should occur against the Republic of Korea, this would gravely affect the security of our country. Accordingly, if the situation arose where the United States, in meeting the armed attack against the Republic of Korea, should find it necessary to use the facilities located in Japan as forward bases from which to stage combat operations, the Government of Japan, based on such recognition, would enter prior consultation [with the United States] and determine its attitude positively and promptly.[3]

The third event was the automatic extension of the U.S.-Japan Security Treaty in June 1970.

Following the Nixon-Sato communiqué, North Korea and China accelerated their campaign against the U.S.-Japanese "collusion" and expressed their concern over the possibility of South Korea and Taiwan falling into the grasp of a presumably resurgent Japan. In an August 1971 interview with James Reston of *The New York Times,* Chou En-lai warned of the revival of Japanese militarism: "The United States is promoting Japanese economic and military power, and if Washington does not handle the Taiwan-Korean questions carefully Japan will move in as the United States pulls back."[4] During his visit to North Korea in April 1970, Chou said the November Nixon-Sato communiqué was "a naked confession of intensified military collusion between the United States and Japanese reactionaries." "The revival of Japanese militarism is," he continued, "beyond all doubt, a matter of reality." Under such circumstances, Chou urged the further strengthening of the militant solidarity between the peoples of the two countries. Echoing Chou's statement, Kim Il-sŏng pledged that ". . . the Korean people will again, as in the past, together with the Chinese people, fight against the enemy [the U.S. and Japan] to the end."[5]

During this period, Peking constantly reminded P'yŏngyang of the U.S.-Japanese threat and of Moscow's warming relations with Tokyo. By early 1969, P'yŏngyang was wary of Moscow's friendly gestures toward Japan. In his report to the Fifth Congress of the KWP held November 2–13, 1970, Kim Il-sŏng denounced Moscow obliquely for increasing the danger of war in Asia by promoting friendship with Japan.[6]

The Chinese policy of playing upon North Korea's fear of a Washington-Tokyo-Seoul collusion worked. For the first time since 1965, North Korea sent a special delegation, which was headed by Ch'oe Yong-gŏn, to China's twentieth anniversary celebrations in October 1969. Chou En-lai met the P'yŏngyang delegation at the airport, and North Korea was placed first on all official lists of visiting delegations. Reportedly, Ch'oe was given a place beside Mao Tse-tung on the reviewing stand at T'ien-an men Square.[7]

The main turning point in Sino-North Korean relations probably was Premier Chou En-lai's visit to North Korea during April 5–7, 1970. His visit was the first by a top-level Chinese official since President Liu Shao-ch'i visited North Korea in 1963. Chou's speech, delivered upon his arrival at the P'yŏngyang airport, clearly conveyed Peking's desire to restore friendly relations with North Korea. Recalling their "blood-cemented militant friendship," Chou said: "China and Korea are neighbors as closely related as lips and teeth, and our two peoples are intimate brothers."[8] During his visit, Chou loudly denounced U.S.-Japanese collusion and, probably out of consideration for his hosts, avoided public attacks on the Soviet Union.

Sino-North Korean contacts, which had withered since 1965, resumed after late 1969. In February 1970, a new North Korean ambassador was sent to Peking, and a new Chinese ambassador took up his North Korean post on March 23, 1970. In January 1970, China and North Korea concluded the Yalu and Tuman Rivers Navigation Agreement.[9] In November 1970, Peking reportedly dropped its long-standing claim for cession of a hundred-square-mile strip of North Korean territory around Mt. Paektu.[10] As noted earlier, Peking initially made the demand in 1965 when North Korea drifted to the Soviet camp.

The twentieth anniversary of the outbreak of the Korean Conflict was celebrated in both countries with more enthusiasm and fanfare than at any other time during the 1960s. Gen.

Huang Yung-sheng, chief of general staff of the Chinese armed forces, headed the Chinese delegation to North Korea. Addressing a mass rally in P'yŏngyang, Huang restated old rhetoric used when the two countries were close: "China and Korea are neighbors linked by mountains and rivers and share weal and woe. The peoples of our two countries are brothers as closely related as flesh and blood."[11] Pak Sŏng-ch'ŏl, Politburo member of the KWP Central Committee and vice-premier, attended the Peking rally for the war anniversary.[12] The anniversary of the entrance of the Chinese troops into the Korean Conflict was also marked with large-scale celebrations.[13]

P'YŎNGYANG-MOSCOW RELATIONS: COOL BUT CORRECT?

As Sino-North Korean relations improved considerably after late 1969, North Korea's relations with Moscow cooled somewhat. However, it should be emphasized that North Korea did not intend to break away from Moscow as she had done in 1962.

P'yŏngyang's relations with Moscow slipped in the wake of the downing of an EC-121 American intelligence aircraft on April 15, 1969. While China promptly praised North Korea, the Soviet Union waited three days to endorse the North Korean attack, and Soviet ships joined the U.S. Navy in the search for possible survivors.[14] President Nikolai Podgorny's visit to North Korea the following month probably was designed to restrain P'yŏngyang's excessively bellicose posture. The Soviet reaction to the EC-121 incident did not please North Korea.

While in P'yŏngyang, Podgorny attempted to gain North Korean support for Moscow's position concerning the Sino-Soviet border dispute of 1969 and to win P'yŏngyang's participation in the Moscow Conference of world Communist parties the following month. But North Korea took a neutral position on the border dispute issue, and the KWP refused to attend the Moscow Conference, joining China on the list of absent parties.[15]

Peking and P'yŏngyang stood together on two important issues: support for Cambodia's ousted chief of state, Prince Norodom Sihanouk, and opposition to the revival of "Japanese militarism and aggression." When Sihanouk formed a government-in-exile in Peking early in 1970, China and North Korea immediately recognized the exile government, while the Soviet Union continued to recognize Lon Nol's government in Phnom Penh. Despite North Korea's veiled criticism of Moscow's "insensitivity" to growing Japanese militarism, Moscow continued its friendly gestures toward Tokyo.[16]

The first indication of disagreement between North Korea and the Soviet Union surfaced publicly when North Korea announced its decision to withdraw from a joint Soviet-North Korean oceanographic study of the Sea of Japan. The reason was Moscow's unilateral decision to include Japanese scientists in the research project, which was originally undertaken on the basis of scientific and technological cooperation between Moscow and P'yŏngyang.[17]

North Korea's deteriorating relations with Moscow were confirmed at the Fifth Congress of the KWP held in November 1969. In his report to the congress, Kim criticized the Soviet Union, asserting that "revisionism appeared in the international Communist movement and obstructed its unity and cohesion, causing ideological confusion." But Kim did not attack dogmatism as before.[18]

However, P'yŏngyang continued to maintain substantial contacts with the Soviet Union. Following Chou En-lai's visit to North Korea, a Soviet military delegation led by Marshal Matvei Zakharov, chief of staff of the Soviet armed forces, made an official call on North Korea. According to *The Christian Science Monitor,* Zakharov may have offered additional deliveries of sophisticated military equipment on easy terms, perhaps as a reminder that North Korea needed Moscow's military assistance and to offset Chinese encroachments.[19]

In March 1970, M. N. Suloyev, deputy chairman of the USSR State Commission for Foreign Economic Relations, arrived in North Korea. Deputy Foreign Minister Yakov Malik came to P'yŏngyang in late 1970. His visit resulted in the signing of an economic cooperation agreement in September, in which the Soviet Union extended its assistance in the construction and expansion of industrial plants in North Korea. In January 1971, a Soviet delegation headed by Vice-Premier I. T. Novikov journeyed to P'yŏngyang to attend the sixth session of the economic, scientific, and technical consultation committee of the two countries.[20] Perhaps these Soviet delegations visited P'yŏngyang to remind the North Korean Communists that Moscow had more resources to offer than China.

President Ch'oe Yong-gŏn traveled to Moscow to attend Lenin's hundredth birthday celebration. While in Moscow, Ch'oe reportedly discussed Moscow-P'yŏngyang relations with Leonid Brezhnev.[21] In March 1971, North Korea sent Vice-Premier Kim Il to Moscow to represent P'yŏngyang at the Twenty-fourth Congress of the CPSU.

PRESIDENT NIXON'S VISIT TO PEKING AND SINO-NORTH KOREAN RELATIONS

On July 16, 1971, President Richard M. Nixon announced that he would make an official trip to Peking in 1972, and less than three months later, on October 12, Washington and Moscow announced that Nixon would also visit the Soviet Union that year. Nixon's scheduled visits to both Peking and Moscow in 1972 undoubtedly caused serious apprehension in P'yŏngyang, but North Korea was much more concerned with the consequences of Nixon's journey to Peking than with his trip to Moscow. This was perhaps because the Moscow visit was the less dramatic and unusual by far.

North Korea referred to Nixon's forthcoming Peking visit as "not the march of a victor but a trip of the defeated." Although North Korea offered reassurance that Nixon's visit would not affect P'yŏngyang's relations with Peking, the KWP organ expressed some misgivings and subtly demanded an acceptable explanation of the trip.[22] North Korea's concern about Washington-Peking rapprochement had some impact on P'yŏngyang's relationship with Peking. For example, the October 25, 1971, commemoration of China's entry into the Korean Conflict passed almost unmarked in each country, in sharp contrast to 1970.[23]

Realizing North Korea's apprehension over Nixon's Peking visit, Chinese leaders made a considerable effort to reassure North Korea. Even before the announcement, Peking proclaimed July 9–15 as "Chinese-Korean Friendship Week."[24] A few days before the Nixon announcement, a Chinese delegation left for P'yŏngyang. The delegation, led by Li Hsien-nien, vice-premier of the State Council, and Li Te-sheng, director of the General Political Department of the Chinese People's Liberation Army (PLA), came to North Korea to explain China's reason for inviting President Nixon.[25] On July 9, 1971, a senior Chinese delegate returned to the P'anmunjŏm armistice talks after an absence of nearly five years.[26] *Jen-min Jih-pao,* on July 11, editorially promised unlimited aid for North Korea to fight against "expanding Japanese militarism."[27] According to *The New York Times,* reports (unconfirmed) from Peking indicated that Premier Chou had secretly traveled to Hanoi and P'yŏngyang between July 12 and 14 to inform both countries of the imminent announcement of the Nixon visit.[28]

At the invitation of Peking, a North Korean economic delegation, led by Vice-Premier Chŏng Chun-t'aek, visited China during August 8–16, 1971. During this visit, the two countries signed an economic agreement for mutual aid and economic cooperation, in which Peking apparently promised economic assistance to North Korea.[29] Furthermore, a high-level North Korean military delegation, led by O Chin-u, chief of general staff of the North Korean armed forces, visited Peking from August 18 to September 9, 1971. During the visit, O Chin-u and Huang Yung-sheng signed an agreement for Chinese military aid to North Korea, the first such agreement to be concluded in more than fifteen years.[30] It is interesting to note that North Korea had reportedly received a considerable amount of economic aid from the Soviet Union immediately after Khrushchev's visit to the United States in 1959.

Upon receiving additional economic and military assistance and assurances from China, Kim Il-sŏng then announced that Nixon's China trip would "temporarily ease international tension." In his statement, Kim again stressed that Sino-American rapprochement had no direct bearing on North Korea. Chou En-lai had apparently succeeded in persuading Kim Il-sŏng to accept the new Sino-American relationship.[31]

SINO-AMERICAN RAPPROCHEMENT AND P'YŎNGYANG-MOSCOW RELATIONS

North Korea's concern over Nixon's journey to Peking was shared fully by Moscow. Apparently to counter the Sino-American rapprochement, for instance, Soviet Foreign Minister Andrei Gromyko suddenly visited Japan just before President Nixon's visit to Peking and agreed with Japanese leaders to open negotiations within 1972 for a Japanese-Soviet peace treaty. The Soviet Union seemed to use the situation to strengthen her position in North Korea by providing additional economic and military assistance and exchanging high-level delegations. Meanwhile, North Korea made an effort to utilize the Nixon visit to Peking to strengthen its relations with Moscow. There is no doubt that P'yŏngyang became more intimate with Moscow.

As Nixon's visit to Peking neared, there were unusually frequent exchanges of high-ranking delegations between Moscow and P'yŏngyang. In December 1971, Vice-Premier Chŏng Chunt'aek visited Moscow, as a result of which the Soviet Union reportedly agreed to provide additional economic and military assistance for the 1971–1975 period. A few days later, a high-level Soviet delegation, led by Sharaf R. Rashodov, first secretary of the Uzbekistan Communist Party, came to P'yŏngyang, probably to inform and assure the North Korean Communists about Nixon's forthcoming Moscow visit. While in North Korea, Rashodov made an unusually strong statement in support of "Korean unification under Communist leadership."[32] From February 22 to 26, 1972, while Peking was hosting Nixon, Foreign Minister Hŏ Tam went to the Soviet Union, and *Pravda* gave the Brezhnev-Hŏ meeting front page coverage.[33]

During the week prior to Nixon's Peking visit, the Soviet press accused Peking of breaking the solidarity of the Communist camp by receiving President Nixon. Although North Korea bit-

terly criticized the United States, without mentioning Nixon's
arrival in Peking, the North Koreans shied away from siding
with Moscow's criticism of Peking.[34]

Immediately after Nixon's Moscow visit, the Soviet Union dis-
patched two separate delegations to North Korea. The first delegation, composed of Foreign Ministry officials, came to P'yŏngyang apparently to inform the North Koreans of the Nixon-
Brezhnev talks and agreements. Vice-Premier Yevgnity Novikov,
who led the second delegation, visited North Korea presumably
to give details of Nixon's Moscow visit and to officially attend the
eighth session of the Intergovernmental Economic Commission.[35] During the conference, the Soviet Union reportedly
agreed to increase its deliveries of certain industrial equipment
and raw materials, to expand scientific and technical cooperation, and to help develop oil and gas production in the continen-
tal shelf of North Korea and the Soviet Union.[36] A Soviet delegation led by Konstantin Katushev, secretary of the CPSU Central
Committee, made a week-long visit to North Korea on the occasion of the twenty-fourth national-day celebrations. During the
national celebrations, the North Koreans gave more praise for
Soviet aid, both past and present, than for Peking's assistance.[37]

The display of friendship between Moscow and P'yŏngyang
during these periods served the common interests of both countries. For North Korea, the display of friendship toward the
Soviets might have been a well planned act of political maneuvering both to reassure Soviet assistance and to warn Peking not
to go too far in its relations with Washington. For the Soviet
Union, it was a good opportunity to bring North Korea closer to
its side by capitalizing on P'yŏngyang's apprehension over the
new Sino-American relationship. Despite the warm display of
North Korean-Soviet cooperation and the obvious campaign
that the Russians waged to promote their influence in North
Korea at China's expense, the Soviet Union apparently had only
limited success. The North Koreans continued to refrain from
siding with Moscow against Peking. In general, North Korea
appeared to be still closer to Peking than to Moscow.

CHAPTER 8
NORTH KOREA BETWEEN
PEKING AND MOSCOW,
1973-1975

Throughout 1973-1975 North Korea maintained a policy of neutrality in the Sino-Soviet schism and close contacts with both Peking and Moscow. Because of mounting economic problems, the North Korean regime exerted a concerted effort to obtain as much economic assistance and other support as possible from both Communist neighbors, to which Peking responded more favorably than Moscow did. Emerging Asian power alignments also have affected P'yŏngyang's leverage in dealing with the PRC and the Soviet Union. Although North Korea tried to preserve equidistance from both Peking and Moscow during this period, the P'yŏngyang regime continued to have a slight tilt toward Peking, as had been the case during the 1969-1972 period.

P'YŎNGYANG'S FRIENDLY RELATIONS
WITH PEKING

During the 1973-1975 period, North Korea maintained warm and close relationships with the PRC, and there were frequent exchanges of military and economic delegations between the two countries. On February 10, 1973, Foreign Minister Hŏ Tam visited Peking, where he conferred with Chou En-lai and high-ranking military officers.[1] On May 28, 1974, a Chinese military delegation, led by the vice-chief of general staff of the PLA, traveled to North Korea for military conferences.[2] In June 1974, a friendship-inspection delegation of the Chinese People's Liberation Army toured various places in North Korea. Peking warmly supported the South-North Korean dialogue[3] and P'yŏngyang's reunification policies, including the recent five-point program proposed by Kim Il-sŏng.[4] In July 1975, a North Korean military delegation led by Cho Myŏng-sŏn, vice-chief of the North Korean armed forces, visited Peking, where he met Chinese Defense Minister Yeh Chien-ying. In a speech made by the vice-chief of the PLA at a banquet held for the visiting P'yŏngyang delegation, the Chinese military leader said that, in any case, Chinese and North Korean troops would fight to the end, with tightened cooperation, for the execution of their common revolutionary struggle.[5] During September 21–27, 1975, Chang Chun-chiao, member of the Standing Committee of the Politburo of the CCP, visited North Korea and conferred with Kim Il-sŏng.[6] On the occasion of the twenty-sixth anniversary of the founding of the DPRK, *Jen-min Jih-pao* carried an editorial employing rhetoric which symbolized the close relationship between P'yŏngyang and Peking:

> China and Korea are close neighbours linked by the same mountains and rivers. The great friendship between the peoples of the two countries is cemented with blood.[7]

Jen-min Jih-pao also carried an identical editorial on the twenty-seventh anniversary of the founding of the DPRK.[8]

The increased number of Sino-North Korean economic delegations was indicative of P'yŏngyang's effort to obtain Chinese economic assistance for its financial difficulties.[9] A North Korean economic delegation, headed by Vice-Premier Ch'oe Chae-u, came to Peking on June 15, 1973, and talked with Vice-Premier Li Hsien-nien, who is known as the Chinese economic expert. Three days later, the two vice-premiers signed an agreement and a protocol for economic and technical cooperation between the two countries.[10] In January 1974, North Korea and China signed a 1974 commodity exchange protocol. On February 8, 1974, a North Korean agriculture-technology delegation visited China. On November 6, 1974, an agreement for continued cooperation between the two countries was signed in Peking at the fifteenth meeting of the Scientific and Technological Cooperation Commission.[11] A North Korean trade delegation headed by Yi T'ae-paek, vice-minister of foreign trade, arrived in Peking on December 18, 1974, and, three days later, an agreement for 1975 mutual delivery of commodities was signed.[12]

The PRC appears to have increased its assistance to North Korea in the wake of the latter's financial problems. Peking apparently sent one million tons of oil to North Korea in 1974, when the Soviet Union, from whom P'yŏngyang buys most of its oil, demanded a sharp price increase for Soviet oil.[13] A new oil pipeline linking China and North Korea was completed in January 1976, but the scale or site of the new pipeline has not been disclosed.[14] Either in late 1975 or in early 1976, the North Koreans reportedly signed a new economic agreement with China. No details of the agreement have been announced.[15] Moreover, it is reported that the Chinese, since 1973, have delivered more military assistance to North Korea than the Soviets have done. According to a South Korean source, in mid-1975, Peking completed a plan to provide P'yŏngyang with Chinese-made fighter planes, T54 and T55 tanks, warships such as R-class submarines, destroyers and torpedoes, and industrial facilities necessary for the production of airplane parts.[16]

The most significant event during this period in regard to North Korea's relation to China was Kim Il-sŏng's visit to Peking from April 18 through 26, 1975. The Chinese apparently gave an elaborate welcome for Kim Il-sŏng, and he immediately met Mao Tse-tung.[17] The North Korean leader's hurried trip to China, the first since 1961, came just after the fall of Phnom Penh and on the verge of the South Vietnam debacle and, thus, provoked intense speculation on the purposes of his visit. Kim Il-sŏng's ten-member delegation included: Kim Tong-gyu, member of the Political Committee of the KWP Central Committee and vice-president; Pak Sŏng-ch'ŏl, member of the Political Committee of the KWP and then vice-premier (now premier); Hŏ Tam, vice-premier and minister of foreign affairs; Kye Ŭng-t'ae, minister of foreign trade; Chŏng Song-nam, minister of external economic affiars; O Chin-u, member of the Political Committee and army chief of staff; Chŏn Mun-sŏp, army colonel general; and O Guk-yŏl, air force commander.[18]

The composition of the P'yŏngyang delegation certainly indicates the three priority items on Kim's agenda. Kim Il-sŏng's visit to Peking aimed to gather Chinese support for the crucial forthcoming session of the U.N. General Assembly debate on the Korean issue. North Korea waged an all-out effort to pass the pro-North Korean Resolution,[19] which called for the dissolution of the U.N. Command in Korea and the withdrawal of American forces from Korea. The main purposes of Kim Il-sŏng's extended visit to East European and African countries during May 22 to June 9, 1975, also were aimed at obtaining the support of nonaligned nations for the General Assembly discussion on the Korean peninsula and at consolidating support from the Balkan Communist states for his goal of unifying Korea after the collapse of South Vietnam and Cambodia.[20]

The North Korean leader apparently had gone to China to look for financial aid for P'yŏngyang's ailing economy. The Chinese probably promised to increase economic aid to North Korea, but there is no substantiated evidence on this except that North Korean economic experts accompanying Kim Il-sŏng had taken part in the talks with their Chinese counterparts.[21] It was reported that Kim also asked Peking leaders to extend military assistance and that high-ranking Chinese and North Korean military leaders held unannounced meetings for several days.[22]

A more compelling reason for Kim's official visit to Peking may have been to solicit Chinese backing for his hope to achieve reunification of Korea by military means, capitalizing on the defeats of Cambodia and South Vietnam and a weakening of the American credibility in Asia. The timing of Kim's trip and his aggressive statements in Peking support this view. In a speech delivered at a banquet on April 18, 1975, Kim Il-sŏng pledged to launch an intervention if a revolution were to break out in South Korea. He went on further:

> If the enemy ignites war recklessly, we shall resolutely answer it with war and completely destroy the aggressors. In this war we will only lose the military demarcation line and will gain the country's reunification.[23]

On the same occasion, Teng Hsiao-p'ing emphasized the close friendship between the two countries, employing such rhetoric as "fraternal neighbors as close as the lips to the teeth." He also stressed that "The Chinese people will forever stand together with the Korean people and together with you fight to the end for our common revolutionary cause."[24] Both Kim and Teng denounced in bitter language the ROK government and U.S. military presence in South Korea.

It has been reported that the Chinese are believed to have discouraged Kim Il-sŏng from any effort to take advantage of the Indochina debacle with a thrust at South Korea.[25] Of course, how much or whether Peking exerted a moderating influence over the impetuous Kim Il-sŏng is a subject for speculation. But neither all the reports of Chinese statements nor the Sino-North Korean joint communiqué of April 26 could be taken as a strong commitment by the Chinese side to support Kim's military venture in Korea.[26] At least for the time being, the Chinese might fear that renewed hostilities on the Korean peninsula: (1) would destroy its fragile rapprochement with the United States; (2) could lead Japan to rearming and going nuclear; and (3) would result in greater Soviet influence in North Korea because the P'yŏngyang regime would have to depend on Soviet arms supplies for the war. Finally, it is noteworthy that, while Kim was in China, he refused to join Peking in denouncing the dangers of Soviet "hegemony" in Asia. Apparently by the request of the North Korean visitor, the joint communiqué also did not include anti-Soviet statements.

P'YŎNGYANG'S RELATIONS WITH MOSCOW

Despite its warm relations with Peking, P'yŏngyang kept up many personnel and economic exchanges with Moscow. Ch'oe Yong-gŏn visited Moscow on December 22, 1972, to attend the fiftieth anniversary of the formation of the USSR.[27] On February 28, 1973, a KWP delegation, headed by Kim Tong-gyu, member of the Political Committee and secretary of the KWP Central Committee, went to Moscow at the invitation of the CPSU Central Committee. Leonid Brezhnev and the KWP delegation met and reportedly exchanged opinions "in a comradely fashion on the question of the further development and strengthening of fraternal friendship and cooperation" between the CPSU and the KWP.[28] A delegation from the North Korean Supreme People's Assembly, led by Sŏ Ch'ŏl, was in Moscow May 5–7 en route home following a visit to Bulgaria.[29] It was reported that the Soviet Union gave crucial support to North Korea's admission to the World Health Organization on May 17, 1973. The Kremlin supported Kim Il-sŏng's reunification policies, but the Russians reportedly were more guarded than the Chinese in their support of the South-North Korean talks, perhaps because of European implications for reuniting divided states. In November 1973, a Soviet governmental delegation led by Vice-Premier I. T. Novikov visited North Korea to attend the joint economic and scientific-technological consultative conference.

A similar pattern in the contacts between P'yŏngyang and Moscow continued throughout 1974–1975. In January 1974, a North Korean fisheries delegation headed by Kim Yun-sang, minister of fisheries, visited the Soviet Union, where an agreement on cooperation in fishing was signed.[30] The North Korean ambassador to Bulgaria attended the twenty-eighth regular session of CEMA held June 18–21, 1974, in Sofia as an observer.[31] On September 1, 1974, the Soviet Union and North Korea agreed to open round-trip airline service between P'yŏngyang and Khabarovsk.[32] In September 1974, a Soviet party delegation led by I. I. Bodyul, member of the CPSU Central Committee, made a seven-day visit in North Korea.[33] On October 8, 1974, a Soviet Union delegation headed by M. A. Orlov, vice-minister of Soviet fisheries, came to P'yŏngyang to attend the fifth meeting of the North Korean-Soviet Fisheries Committee.[34] In May 1975, a North Korean delegation led by Sŏ Ch'ŏl, member of the Political Committee of the KWP Central Committee, visited the Soviet Union. The Soviet Union and North Korea agreed to extend, for another five years, the agreement on mutual cooperation and defense which expired in July 1976.[35]

North Korean-Soviet relations were not so cordial as the intimate relationships that existed between P'yŏngyang and Peking during the same period. Kim Il-sŏng's China trip was not followed by a similar visit to the Soviet Union in 1975. Kim reportedly wanted to visit Moscow before he went to Peking, but the Soviets showed little enthusiasm for a visit by Kim Il-sŏng prior to his Peking trip. The reason may have been Soviet concern about American sensitivities following the defeat of U.S. supported Cambodia and South Vietnam. The Soviet Union perhaps did not intend to identify closely with the militant stance of Kim Il-sŏng at a time when the Americans were in a very tense mood and also when the tension on the Korean peninsula reached its peak after the American setbacks in Indochina. Other sources report that Kim Il-sŏng planned to visit Moscow subsequent to his trip to China, but the Soviet Union rebuffed Kim's intended visit to Moscow probably because he had gone to Peking first.[36] During his extended tour of East Europe and Africa from May 22 to June 9, 1975, Kim Il-sŏng easily could have included Moscow in his visiting list. The North Korean leader reportedly "avoided" even traveling to East Europe through the Soviet Union and returned to P'yŏngyang via Peking.[37] Kim Il-sŏng has not visited Moscow since 1961.

Moscow's response to North Korean economic problems has been less than enthusiastic. There has been no indication that the Soviet Union provided North Korea with any substantial economic assistance. From January 27 to February 10, 1976, a North Korean economic delegation led by Vice-Premier Kong Chin-t'ae visited the Soviet Union and met Premier Kosygin. But no announcement of any trade or other economic agreement was made. Moreover, the Soviet Union reportedly refused to commit further loans to P'yŏngyang because of North Korea's unpaid debt of $700 million to the Soviet Union.[38]

NORTH KOREA'S DILEMMA AHEAD

There are a number of important issues and developments that could have a significant bearing on North Korea's balanced relations with both Peking and Moscow and that could create a delicate situation for the P'yŏngyang regime in attempting to pursue a neutral posture in the Sino-Soviet dispute.

The pattern of power structure in East Asia has undergone a fundamental change from a bipolar confrontation to a new Asian power balance among the United States, the Soviet Union, China, and Japan. The new four-power arrangement is a complex one, characterized by overlapping patterns of quadrilateral, as well as bilateral and triangular, relationships among the powers involved in the region. These relationships by no means have been structured in final form, and continuing changes are inevitable. But the distribution of power among the four states will increasingly become more even in the future, especially in political influence, as the American influence is definitely decreasing and the Chinese, as well as Soviet, political and military strength will be substantially increased. Japan has been rapidly establishing a position of economic preeminence throughout much of Asia. Since 1968, Japan has been the world's third industrial power and may become the second within a decade's time. Further, as the result of the shifting tides of international politics in East Asia, the drift of American foreign policy and the deeper involvement of Japan in regional nonmilitary affairs, the possibility of Japan's decision to develop its own defense capability, even including nuclear weapons, is greater than ever before, despite Japan's previous unwillingness to do so, and the turbulent implications surrounding such a possibility. For the four major powers, East Asia must be considered, therefore, in the context of a quadrilateral relationship, which increasingly will be based on more balanced conditions of influence and power among them in the region. Accordingly, North Korea will have to adjust and adapt to the new Asian power alignments in its relations with the Soviet Union and China.

As the four major powers begin to establish a new power balance in Asia, North Korea's interests will likely diverge from those of Moscow and Peking on such issues as Korean reunification and the desire of Moscow and Peking to improve their relations with the United States and Japan. Since the Korean peninsula is being tied to the major power bilateral alliance systems, the security of the four powers in Asia converges on the peninsula. The United States is committed to the security of the ROK, which is closely linked to that of Japan. North Korea is allied with the Soviet Union and China. Thus, there is little doubt that each of the four would be likely to regard armed conflict or any drastic political change in the peninsula as a threat to their security and other interests. Such a development would affect the Sino-American rapprochement and the U.S.-Soviet détente and destroy any possibility of achieving long-term stability in East Asia through solidification of a new Asian balance of power system. Therefore, neither the Russians nor the Chinese would place as high a priority on Korean reunification as does Kim Il-sŏng, who has been obsessed with the aim of unifying Korea by any means. The Republic of Korea expressed interest in establishing relations with "nonhostile" Communist states, including the Soviet Union. In his Independence Day message to the Korean people, President Park Chung Hee himself declared:

> I will encourage relations of cooperation and reciprocal benefit in as many fields as possible between our Republic and any nation that respects our national integrity and does not engage in acts of hostility against us, irrespective of political system and ideology.[39]

South Korea's motivations appear to be to counterbalance North Korea's diplomatic expansion into non-Communist countries, to enhance South Korea's diplomatic flexibility vis-à-vis "nonhostile" Communist states, to help ensure against possible Chinese domination in the aftermath of American military withdrawal from Asia, and to adjust to the new multipolar power balance.

Responding favorably to South Korea's expressed interest in relations with "nonhostile" Communist states, the Soviet Union reportedly signalled an interest in establishing cultural relations with South Korea. For the first time since Korea was divided, a Soviet citizen, Igor A. Neto, entered South Korea on September 8, 1971. North Korea protested against the Soviet action and issued a warning to Moscow not to engage in contacts of any kind with the ROK government.[40] But following the visit of Korean dramatist Yu Dŏk-hyŏng, the first South Korean to enter the Soviet Union with a Korean passport, several South Korean businessmen, a few scientists, and other South Koreans also visited the Soviet Union. P'yŏngyang was obviously annoyed and expressed its displeasure by boycotting the Universaid (World University Games) in Moscow in August 1973 because a South Korean team was invited and participated in the Games.[41] In September 1975, the Soviet Union also granted entry visas to South Korean sportsmen.[42]

At the United Nations, the ROK correspondents reportedly revealed that there had been increased "amicability on the part of Russian correspondents toward South Koreans."[43] On August 28, 1974, Soviet diplomats at the U.N. hinted that diplomatic relations could be established between Seoul and Moscow if U.N. forces in Korea were dissolved. The Soviet diplomats also indicated that Moscow would not be concerned about the American military presence in Korea because the matter should be settled by an agreement between the United States and the ROK. A Soviet diplomatic source, however, subsequently denied in part the earlier report.[44] When P'yŏngyang opposed India's plan to establish friendly relations with both Koreas, according to unconfirmed diplomatic sources, General Secretary Leonid Brezhnev served as the "middleman" in ironing out the differences involving the three parties.[45] Responding to a South Korean initiative, the Lenin National Library expressed its desire to establish a regular exchange of materials with the Library of the ROK National Assembly.[46] In October 1974, the Lenin Library sent five books to the ROK National Assembly Library.[47] Since March 1974, for the first time, the ROK has been importing a limited amount of Soviet raw materials through a third party—Japan.[48] According to a pro-Peking newspaper in Hong Kong, the Soviet Union wants to obtain naval passages through the Korean Straits.[49]

Any sign of Moscow's interest in establishing informal contacts with South Korea has created an air of apprehension in P'yŏngyang, and Peking also promptly seized on the issue in criticizing Moscow. This strong reaction from North Korea evidently discouraged the Soviet Union, for *Pravda* denied the existence of a "political rapprochement between Seoul and Moscow" and "Soviet-South Korean contacts and rapprochement in trade and other areas," which was previously reported by a West German correspondent.[50] According to Professor Robert Scalapino, the Soviet Union has given some indications of "being satisfied with the status quo" in the Korean peninsula and "privately a number of Russians admit that 'in due time' the logic of events may well dictate an acceptance of two Koreas, de jure as well as de facto."[51] However, no sudden mellowing of relations between the ROK and the Soviet Union is expected in the near future.

Since the recent changes in Asian power politics, there have been increasing contacts between the Soviet Union and Japan. As noted, Foreign Minister Andrei Gromyko made a sudden visit to Japan shortly before President Richard Nixon's trip to Peking and agreed with Japanese leaders to reopen negotiations for a Japanese-Soviet peace treaty. Japan signed an agreement in Tokyo on April 22, 1974, to provide a long-term bank credit of $1,050 million to the Soviet Union for the exploitation of Yakutsk coal, natural gas, and forestry resources. This was the largest bank credit in the history of Soviet trade. It is to be repaid to Japan with deliveries of coal, gas, and timber. The Japanese and Russians are also negotiating two other Siberian projects.[52] Recently, a group of Soviet and Japanese social scientists held informal discussions regarding the future of Asia and their mutual relations. The growth of these ties is more likely to be steady than to be dramatic, and the Soviet-Japanese relation will be that of mutual convenience and benefits. Japan has an obvious interest in Soviet Asian natural resources, and improved relations with Moscow also would increase Japan's political leverage against Peking and even Washington in the future. On the other hand, good relations with Japan serve Moscow's political interest not only in counterbalancing the Sino-American rapprochement but also in containing Peking's influence in Asia. The Soviet Union also needs Japanese technical capabilities and capital for the development of natural resources in Siberia and the Far East. Implications of Soviet-Japanese ties on future Soviet-North Korean relations remain unclear. As indicated earlier, P'yŏngyang previously expressed its displeasure over Moscow's warming relations with Japan. It is also noteworthy that the Soviets have not objected to the U.S.-Japan Security Treaty at this point in time, mainly because they view the pact as a guarantee against "Japanese Gaullism."[53]

One of the characteristics of the post-Indochina era has been an increase in Sino-Soviet competition for influence in Asia. China has emerged as a more active and influential political and military power in Asia, an increase precipitated by the decline in American presence and aided by the Communist victories in Indochina. The Soviet Union also has adjusted to the changes in the region by strengthening its military position in Asia and by stepping up its political and economic activities on a broad front to try to compete against the Chinese. Intensifying Sino-Soviet competition to enhance their influence in Asia will affect their policies toward the Korean peninsula and, in particular, will put pressure on the North Korean regime to side one way or the other.

The Soviet Union appears to have launched a campaign against the Communist states that have remained neutral in the Sino-Soviet conflict. According to *The Washington Post,* the P'yŏngyang regime's decision to turn to the non-Communist world for technology and industrial equipment beginning in the early 1970s aimed to decrease its reliance on the Soviet Union because Moscow attempted to use trade as a political weapon to gain North Korean support in the Sino-Soviet quarrel.[54] An editorial in *Kommunist,* a journal published by the Central Committee of the CPSU, criticized the Communists who remained neutral in the Sino-Soviet struggle, saying that they served the anti-Marxist interest of Peking and called on them to adopt a policy of "smashing Maoism."[55] Even though the article did not single out North Korea as its target, it was an obvious warning directed against the North Korean Communists as well as other Communist parties that have sought to pursue a neutral policy in the dispute.

The North Korean regime reportedly has undertaken a major effort to modernize its military forces with the same kind of equipment that the Soviet Union supplied the Arab countries during the 1973 Yom Kippur War.[56] For such a military modernization program, North Korea will have to rely heavily on a Soviet supply of sophisticated weapons. The North Korean armed forces are already equipped primarily with Soviet-supplied weapons, including 150 MIG-21, 40 MIG-19, and 300 MIG-17/-15 jet fighters, 12 FROG-5/-7 surface-to-surface missiles, 180 SA-2 surface-to-air missiles, 28 Su-7 fighter-bombers, 60 Il-28 bombers, 8 submarines (4 ex-Soviet W-class, 4 ex-Chinese R-class), 10 Komar and 8 Osa-class missile equipped warships, 15 submarine chasers (ex-Soviet SOI-class), and 90 torpedo boats (45 P-4, 30 P-6 class, ex-Soviet).[57]

Because of heavy pressure from Moscow, North Korea reportedly cancelled its participation in the Asian table tennis tournament held in Yokohama in April 1974. It is noteworthy that North Korea was one of the countries, along with China and Japan, which sponsored the tournament and that the next year's tournament was scheduled to be held in P'yŏngyang. According to Japanese sources, Soviet pressure on North Korea to follow pro-Soviet policy and North Korea's desire to obtain more modern military weapons, in particular, MIG-23's, were the major reasons for North Korea's sudden decision not to attend the tournament.[58]

Since the early 1970s, North Korea has been undergoing serious economic stagnation, and its Six-Year Economic Plan (1971–1976) has been behind schedule.[59] North Korea's continuing inability to pay its foreign debts appears to have slowed industrial growth. By mid-1975, sources estimated North Korea's outstanding external debts at $1.7 billion. The figure included $1 billion owed mainly to Japan, West Germany, France, England, Austria, Sweden, Finland, Italy, Switzerland, and Denmark, and $700 million to the Soviet Union.[60] P'yŏngyang's trade with the Western European nations and Japan has shown a tremendous growth since the early 1970s and reportedly accounted for about half of its total trade by early 1975. But North Korea's trade position with these countries deteriorated from a surplus of $18 million in 1970 to a deficit of $430 million in 1974.[61]

Major West European creditors have been demanding repayment of overdue debts and "either cutting off or threatening to cut-off governmental guarantees for trade credits." A Bank of Japan source estimated that North Korea's outstanding trade loans from Japanese businessmen amounted to over $200 million, of which $67 million already was overdue for payment in 1975.[62] France had extended about $150 million in credits to North Korea; and delinquent debts to England were estimated at $28 million.[63] Hermes Export Credit Insurance of West Germany announced that it would no longer insure trade with North Korea, because "the country's unpaid bills were piling up, while servicing of its foreign debt was in arrears."[64]

West European nations and Japan are becoming increasingly

reluctant to deal with the North Koreans, and Western observers believe that financial problems will continue to plague P'yŏngyang for a considerable period. It appears that North Korea will have to look once again to the Soviet Union and China for friendship and economic support, thus making the economic arena a particularly intense focus of Sino-Soviet rivalry over North Korea. Information concerning both Chinese and Soviet economic assistance to North Korea in recent years is scanty. But as indicated earlier, China apparently has responded more positively than the Soviet Union has done in the wake of North Korea's economic difficulties. But the Chinese themselves reportedly are short of foreign exchange, and it is doubtful that Peking's aid alone would meet North Korean needs for financial recovery. Under a similar previous situation, P'yŏngyang tended to lean toward Moscow for additional economic and military assistance.

Not only has the Soviet Union been North Korea's primary source of foreign credit and capital goods, but Moscow has been P'yŏngyang's largest single trade partner throughout the existence of the North Korean regime (see Table 8).[65] According to Soviet sources, Moscow has been aiding North Korea's thirty industrial projects under construction and has increased export of various forms of industrial equipment as well as raw materials. Also, the Soviet Union reportedly has provided North Korea with technical assistance for constructing major projects of the current Six-Year Economic Plan including a thermal electric power plant at Pukchŏng, oil refinery at Unggi, and the reconstruction of the Kim Ch'aek Steel Mill at Chŏngjin.[66] Moscow claimed that, in 1972–1973 alone, more than 3,000 North Korean specialists underwent practical training at major Soviet factories.[67] North Korea's continuing and renewed interest in close economic ties with Moscow clearly indicates P'yŏngyang's need for such Soviet economic aid.

Peking seems anxious to prevent Soviet advances in the Pacific-Asian area. Indeed, the Chinese appear more apprehensive about a Soviet military build-up in Asia than about the U.S. troops in both Japan and South Korea because they view the American presence as a deterrent to Soviet designs on China. Fearing possible Japanese remilitarization and development of

TABLE 8

NORTH KOREAN TRADE WITH THE U.S.S.R., 1965–1974
(Unit: Million Dollars)

Year	Exports to U.S.S.R.	Imports from U.S.S.R.	Total Trade with U.S.S.R.	As % of Total North Korean Trade Volume
1965	88.3	89.8	178.1	40.4
1966	92.3	85.6	177.9	38.4
1967	108.0	110.3	218.3	43.7
1968	120.9	172.2	293.1	n.a.
1969	126.6	201.6	328.2	47.1
1970	143.2	230.0	373.2	n.a.
1971	135.7	366.7	502.4	n.a.
1972	154.8	303.5	458.3	n.a.
1973	181.0	304.2	485.2	n.a.
1974	196.9	256.3	453.2	n.a.

Note: n.a. refers to figures that are not available. During 1970–1974, North Korean trade with the Soviet Union very likely exceeded 30% of total North Korean trade volume annually.

Sources: Joseph Sang-hoon Chung, *The North Korean Economy: Structure and Development* (Stanford: Hoover Institution Press, 1974), p. 112; United Nations, *Yearbook of International Trade Statistics 1974,* p. 296.

nuclear weapons, the Chinese have supported the maintenance of the U.S.-Japan Mutual Security Treaty at least temporarily. The Peking regime reportedly believes that any wavering of the American stance in Korea not only would push Japan into rearming[68] but would encourage the unpredictable Kim Il-sŏng to engage in military adventurism in Korea. It should be noted, too, as Professor Scalapino has pointed out, that Peking was interested in the Americans because the Chinese assumed that the United States would continue to be a major power in the region.[69]

Thus, Peking prefers as an alternative the retention of an American military presence in Japan as well as in South Korea, for the time being at least. According to reports that emerged

from private conversations with the Chinese leaders, the maintenance of U.S. military forces in Korea is acceptable to Peking.[70] When Dr. Henry Kissinger visited Peking to confer with
the Chinese, Peking reportedly did not demand the withdrawal
of American troops from South Korea.[71] But China, publicly,
has always supported North Korea's demand for the withdrawal
of American forces from the ROK and the dissolution of the
U.N. Command in Korea,[72] perhaps because of Peking's delicate
position on this sensitive issue vis-à-vis P'yŏngyang. Nonetheless, it is generally believed that Peking has taken a passive attitude toward the withdrawal, hoping that the American military
presence would impede Soviet advancement in Asia and the
pace of Japanese rearmament.[73]

The future course of Chinese domestic and external politics
will have a very important bearing on North Korea's precarious
relations with its two Communist neighbors. For example, China's relations with North Korea came under a cloud during Peking's savage "anti-Lin Piao, anti-Confucius" campaign. During
the Chinese Cultural Revolution of 1966–1969, as noted earlier,
Sino-North Korean relations reached their lowest point. As for
Peking's external politics, the PRC will play an increasingly large
role in international relations in Asia and in the global arena as
well. Chinese leadership is currently experiencing an uncertain,
transitional period. Should a pragmatic policy line prevail in
Peking, the Chinese may be willing to accept friendly relations
between P'yŏngyang and Moscow. However, the manner in
which a future Chinese leadership will deal with North Korea's
neutral attitude in the Sino-Soviet dispute remains to be seen.

North Korea cannot afford to alienate either Peking or
Moscow. The P'yŏngyang regime needs continuous economic
and military assistance as well as political support from both the
PRC and the Soviet Union. So far, North Korea, with a considerable degree of success, has maneuvered the Sino-Soviet rift by
obtaining economic, military, and political support from the two
Communist powers, while maintaining a neutrality in the conflict. However, the various issues and developments that have
been discussed will likely create a dilemma for the North Korean
regime in its continuing attempt to steer a neutral course in the
dispute between Peking and Moscow.

SUMMARY AND CONCLUSION

The Sino-Soviet dispute has had major implications for North Korea in formulating policy toward Peking and Moscow. The dispute presented a serious dilemma to the North Korean leaders because various political, economic, and military factors made it difficult for them to avoid alienating either of the neighboring Communist powers. However, the dispute presented an opportunity to deal with the two powers in such a way as to augment North Korea's national interest.

Until 1950, North Korea was a veritable satellite of the Soviet Union. The Democratic People's Republic of Korea and the Korean Workers' Party were created and totally dominated by the Soviet Union. During the same period, the Chinese Communists participated very little, if at all, in North Korean politics. By 1958, however, a state of equilibrium between the Soviet and Chinese influence was reached.

In the 1950s, a number of factors contributed to the reduction of Soviet, and the increase of Chinese, influence in North Korea. Contributing factors to this change were: (1) Mao Tse-tung's successful seizure of power in 1949; (2) the massive intervention of Chinese troops for the North Korean Communists during the Korean War; (3) the continued presence of Chinese armed forces in North Korea following the 1953 armistice; (4) reduction of Soviet aid and increase of Chinese assistance to North Korea; (5) the death of Stalin and the subsequent internal struggle within Soviet leadership; and (6) Khrushchev's insistence on de-Stalinization and peaceful coexistence with the West.

North Korea began to emulate Chinese economic policies in 1958 and showed a strong affinity for Peking's militant policy of unremitting struggle against the West, particularly the United States. During 1958-1961, however, the North Korean leaders tried to steer a neutral course in the face of worsening Sino-Soviet relations. After 1960, as the conflict became further embittered, the P'yŏngyang regime frequently showed that it was incapable of total detachment. The North Korean leaders also attempted to balance Soviet and Chinese influence and sought to minimize the extent of either direct Chinese or Soviet involvement in the internal affairs of the P'yŏngyang regime.

By the autumn of 1962 the North Korean regime had begun gradually to lean toward the Chinese line in the course of the Communist camps' dispute over such matters as Soviet-Yugoslav rapprochement, the Sino-Indian border dispute, and the Cuban missile crisis. From the beginning of 1963 until Khrushchev's downfall in October 1964, North Korea became Peking's strongest ally in Asia in the Sino-Soviet rift. In addition to their geographic propinquity and cultural closeness, the major reasons for North Korea's shift to the Chinese orbit were economic and ideological. Soviet economic and political interference in North Korea's internal affairs seemed to be another important factor. In short, P'yŏngyang's alignment with Peking was primarily based upon a coincidence of the two regimes' immediate practical interests and needs at that time.

But Khrushchev's ouster in 1964 changed the situation. While North Korea's relations with the Soviet Union began to improve, its relations with China deteriorated slowly. This change reflected an altered view of North Korea's national interest: namely, P'yŏngyang's desire to modernize its armed forces with new weapons as well as to seek economic assistance from the Soviet Union to complete the Seven-Year Economic Plan which had already been extended for three years. However, this change did not mean the conversion of the North Korean regime to the Soviet line, nor did it mean a return to the pre-1950 Soviet-North Korean relationship. Rather, North Korea returned to a neutralist posture in the Sino-Soviet dispute.

At the end of the Chinese Cultural Revolution in 1969, North Korea and China restored their friendly relations. The major factors contributing to the revival of P'yŏngyang-Peking friendship were their mutual interest in improving the deteriorated relationship that had existed during the 1966–1969 period and their common fear of Japan's growing strength, which was becoming increasingly evident. But despite its warm relations with China, North Korea continued to maintain substantial ties with the Soviet Union.

President Nixon's visits to Peking and Moscow in 1972 undoubtedly caused serious apprehension within the North Korean regime. North Korea was more concerned with the outcome of Nixon's trip to Peking than with his journey to Moscow. P'yŏngyang and Moscow fully shared their apprehension over Nixon's visit to Peking, and the Soviet Union apparently used the situation to promote its influence in North Korea at China's expense by exchanging high-ranking delegations and by providing additional economic and military assistance. But the Soviet Union achieved only partial success. As a result of the Soviet efforts and North Korea's concern over the Sino-American rapprochement, the P'yŏngyang regime returned to a more balanced relationship with both Peking and Moscow, but still with a tilt toward the former.

North Korea, like any other Asian country, faces a serious challenge from the dynamic changes occurring in Asian and world politics. There are many uncertain issues and developments that could have a significant bearing on North Korea's attitude in the Sino-Soviet dispute. The major issues are: the U.S.-Chinese relations; Japan's relations with Moscow and Peking; a possibility of Japanese rearmament; China's domestic politics; P'yŏngyang's economic and political situations; Peking's and/or Moscow's policies toward South Korea; and, of course, the Sino-Soviet conflict itself.

Most Asian Communist regimes and parties seem to be trying to preserve relations with both Moscow and Peking without being excessively dependent upon, or subordinate to, either. Kim Il-sŏng's domestic and foreign policies claimed to be, and to a large extent were, based on the principle of *chuch'e*. For economic, military, and political reasons, however, North Korea most likely will continue to live in the shadow of the two Communist powers: the Soviet Union, to which North Korea owes its creation immediately after World War II, and China, to which North Korea owes its survival during the Korean War.

As long as the Sino-Soviet dispute continues, North Korea indeed is and increasingly will be in a delicate position in its relations with the two neighboring powers, both very sensitive about their prestige and power position. Should the North Korean leaders decide to take a positive stance in the Sino-Soviet rift, they will have to pay a high price, regardless of the side they favor. Therefore, the P'yŏngyang regime will probably continue to be cautious and circumspect on issues and events that divide Moscow and Peking, while attempting to maintain correct and balanced relations with both Peking and Moscow.

NOTES

Chapter 1

1. Dae-Sook Suh, *The Korean Communist Movement, 1918–1948* (Princeton: Princeton University Press, 1967), pp. 69–70.

2. Ibid., pp. 53–84; Glenn D. Paige, "Korea and the Comintern, 1919–1935," *Bulletin of the Korean Research Center,* no. 13 (December 1960), pp. 1–25; Robert A. Scalapino and Chong-Sik Lee, "The Origins of the Korean Communist Movement (II)," *The Journal of Asian Studies,* vol. XX, no. 2 (February 1961), p. 161.

3. Soon Sung Cho, *Korea in World Politics, 1940–1950* (Berkeley: University of California Press, 1967), pp. 47–58.

4. Suh, *Korean Communist Movement,* pp. 295–99.

5. Robert A. Scalapino and Chong-Sik Lee, *Communism in Korea,* Part I (Berkeley: University of California Press, 1972), pp. 314–24; Chong-Sik Lee, "Politics in North Korea: Pre-Korean War State," in Robert A. Scalapino, ed., *North Korea Today* (New York: Praeger, 1963), p. 4; Kim Ch'ang-sun, *Pukhan siponyŏn sa* (Fifteen Year History of North Korea) (Seoul: Chimungak, 1961), pp. 90–94.

6. Lee, "Politics in North Korea," pp. 4–5; Philip Rudolph, *North Korea's Political and Economic Structure* (New York: Institute of Pacific Relations, 1959), p. 11; Scalapino and Lee, *Communism in Korea,* Part I, pp. 338–40.

7. Suh, *Korean Communist Movement,* pp. 301–302; Kim, *Pukhan siponyŏn sa,* p. 93; Koon Woo Nam, *The North Korean Communist Leadership, 1945–1965: A Study of Factionalism and Political Consolidation* (University, Alabama: The University of Alabama Press, 1974), pp. 71–76.

8. Scalapino and Lee, *Communism in Korea,* Part I, pp. 322–23; Nam, *North Korean Communist Leadership,* pp. 21–23; Kim, *Pukhan siponyŏn sa,* pp. 65–68 and 90–92.

9. Kim, *Pukhan siponyŏn sa,* pp. 92–96. For a detailed discussion on this subject, see Chong-Sik Lee, "Korean Communists and Yenan," *The China Quarterly,* no. 9 (January–March 1962), pp. 182–92.

10. Rudolph, *Political and Economic Structure,* p. 26; Scalapino and Lee, *Communism in Korea,* Part I, pp. 383–84.

11. U.S., Department of State, *North Korea: A Case Study in the Techniques of Takeover,* Department of State Publication 7119, Far Eastern Series no. 103 (Washington, D.C.: U.S. Government Printing Office, 1961), pp. 12–16. Hereinafter referred to as *North Korea.*

12. Ibid., p. 101; Nam, *North Korean Communist Leadership,* pp. 1 and 16–17.

13. For further discussion, see Chong-Sik Lee and Ki-Wan Oh, "The Russian Faction in North Korea," *Asian Survey,* vol. VIII (April 1968), pp. 207–88.

14. Scalapino and Lee, *Communism in Korea,* pp. 227–28 and 477.

15. For further discussion on the background and early life of Kim Il-sŏng, see ibid., pp. 200–226; Kim, *Pukhan siponyŏn sa,* pp. 56–58.

16. Suh, *Korean Communist Movement,* pp. 267 and 281–93.

17. Department of State, *North Korea,* p. 13; Kim, *Pukhan siponyŏn sa,* pp 54–61; Scalapino and Lee, *Communism in Korea,* Part I, p. 324.

18. Democratic People's Republic of Korea, Academy of Science Center for Historical Studies, *Chosŏn t'ongsa* (Outline History of Korea) (Tokyo: Hak-u Sŏbang, 1959), vol. III, pp. 16–17.

19. Department of State, *North Korea,* p. 103.

20. Ibid., pp. 12–16; Rudolph, *Political and Economic Structure,* p. 12. For detailed study of the transformations of governmental structure in North Korea, see Tong-un Pak, *Pukhan t'ongch'i kiguron* (On the Government Structure in North Korea) (Seoul: Center for Asian Studies, Korea University Press, 1964), pp. 7–16. Hereinafter referred to as Pak, *Pukhan.*

21. Kim, *Pukhan siponyŏn sa,* pp. 99–101.

22. Ibid. According to Kim Ch'ang-sun, who was one of the delegates at the conference of the NPP and Communist Party, the Communist Party was planning to make Kim Il-sŏng chairman. But the election of Kim Tu-bong was the result of tactical mistakes of Kim Il-sŏng's supporters at the conference.

23. Ibid., p. 105; Lee, "Politics in North Korea," pp. 11–13.

24. *New Korea* (Monthly magazine, published by the Foreign Languages Publishing House, P'yŏngyang), no. 11 (1957), p. 25.

25. Kim, *Pukhan siponyŏn sa,* p. 219.

26. Ibid., p. 232; Glenn D. Paige, "North Korea and the Emulation of Russian and Chinese Behavior," in A. Doak Barnett, ed., *Communist Strategies in Asia* (New York: Praeger, 1963), pp. 225–37.

27. For an analysis of governmental structure under the new constitution, see Chin O. Chung, "The Government and Power Structure in North Korea," in Se-Jin Kim and Chang-hyun Cho, eds., *Korea: A Divided Nation* (Silver Spring, Md.: Research Institute on Korean Affairs, 1976), pp. 153–62.

28. Department of State, *North Korea,* pp. 100–03.

29. Kim, *Pukhan siponyŏn sa,* pp. 115–20.

30. Glenn D. Paige, *The Korean People's Democratic Republic* (Stanford: The Hoover Institution, Stanford University, 1964), p. 30; Lee, "Politics in North Korea," p. 14; Scalapino and Lee, *Communism in Korea,* pp. 335–63.

31. Suh, *Korean Communist Movement,* pp. 313–25.

32. Soon Sung Cho, "North Korea and the Sino-Soviet Rift," (paper presented at the Association for Asian Studies 1968 Conference at Philadelphia), p. 7.

33. Lee, "Politics in North Korea," p. 16.

34. George M. McCune and Arthur L. Grey, Jr., *Korea Today* (Cambridge: Harvard University Press, 1950), p. 180; Department of State, *North Korea,* pp. 100–03.

35. Department of State, *North Korea,* p. 120.

36. Ibid., p. 103.

37. Ibid., pp. 109–13.

38. Ibid., p. 104.

39. Vsevolod Holubnychy, "Soviet Economic Aid to North Korea," *Bulletin* (Institute for the Study of the U.S.S.R., Munich), vol. IV (January 1957), p. 15; Paige, *People's Democratic Republic,* p. 31.

40. *Pravda,* March 21, 1949, trans. in the *Current Digest of the Soviet Press,* vol. I, no. 11 (April 12, 1949), pp. 47–49. Hereinafter referred to as *CDSP.*

41. Department of State, *North Korea,* p. 108; Holubnychy, "Soviet Economic Aid," p. 15.

42. Holubnychy, "Soviet Economic Aid," pp. 15–17.

43. Department of State, *North Korea,* p. 109.

44. Ibid., p. 105.

45. Ibid., p. 180.

46. Holubnychy, "Soviet Economic Aid," p. 20.

47. Department of State, *North Korea,* p. 109.

48. Ibid., pp. 108–09. See also *Nodong Shinmun* (The Workers' Daily; the organ of the KWP Central Committee), September 7, 1964.

49. Department of State, *North Korea,* p. 109.

50. Ibid., pp. 114–18.

51. Ibid., p. 115.

52. Paige, *People's Democratic Republic,* p. 34.

53. Department of State, *North Korea,* pp. 115–16.

54. Rudolph, *Political and Economic Structure,* p. 19.

55. Paige, *People's Democratic Republic,* p. 37.

56. Kim, *Pukhan siponyŏn sa,* pp. 130–31.

57. Cho, "Sino-Soviet Rift," p. 7.

58. *History of the Just Fatherland War* (P'yŏngyang: Foreign Languages Publishing House, 1961), pp. 227–29; Kim, *Pukhan siponyŏn sa,* pp. 121–30.

59. Kim Il-sŏng, *Kim Il-sŏng Sŏnjip* (Selected Works of Kim Il-sŏng) (6 vols.; P'yŏngyang: Chosŏn Nodong-dang Ch'ulp'ansa, 1960–66), vol. IV, p. 192. Hereinafter referred to as *Selected Works.*

60. *The New York Times,* December 19, 1955, p. 6.

61. Bertram D. Wolfe, *Khrushchev and Stalin's Ghost* (New York: Praeger, 1957), p. 172.

62. Kim, *Pukhan siponyŏn sa,* pp. 155–56.

63. Lee Tong-jun, *Hwansang kwa hyŏnsil* (Illusions and Reality) (Seoul: Dongbang T'ongshinsa, 1961), p. 187.

64. Lee and Oh, "The Russian Faction," p. 287.

65. Kim, *Pukhan siponyŏn sa,* pp. 57–58.

66. Chong-Sik Lee, "Kim Il-sŏng of North Korea," *Asian Survey,* vol. VII (June 1967), pp. 374–82.

67. Lee and Oh, "The Russian Faction," pp. 286–87; *New Korea* (November 1957), p. 25; Glenn D. Paige and Dong Jun Lee, "The Post-War Politics of Communist Korea," in Scalapino, *North Korea Today,* p. 22.

68. Chung, "Government and Power Structure in North Korea," pp. 167–70.

69. There was, for example, some evidence of professional jealousy among North Korean army officers who had to take orders from Chinese commanders. Paige, *People's Democratic Republic,* pp. 36–37.

70. Editorial, *Jen-min Jih-pao,* October 25, 1953.

71. Paige and Lee, "Post-War Politics," pp. 18–19.

72. Kim, *Selected Works,* vol. V, pp. 416–21; *New China News Agency* (Hereinafter referred to as *NCNA*), October 25, 1958; *Peking Review* (A weekly magazine of Chinese news and views), vol. I, no. 17 (June 24, 1958), p. 19.

73. *Peking Review,* vol. I, no. 4 (March 25, 1958), p. 19.

74. "North Korean Recovery," *Eastern World,* vol. XII, no. 9 (1958), p. 14.

75. Scalapino, *North Korea Today,* p. 45.

76. Kim, *Selected Works,* vol. IV, p. 444, cited in Paige and Lee, "Post-War Politics," p. 19; *NCNA,* October 30, 1958; *Current Background* (published by American Consulate General of Hong Kong), no. 535 (November 11, 1958), p. 15.

77. Alexander Eckstein, *Communist China's Economic Growth and Foreign Trade* (New York: McGraw-Hill Book Co., 1966), pp. 324–25.

78. For the full text of the agreement, see *NCNA*, November 23, 1953.

79. *The New York Times*, November 24, 1953, pp. 1 and 12; S. B. Thomas, "Chinese Communists' Economic and Cultural Agreement with North Korea," *Pacific Affairs*, vol. XXVII, no. 1 (March 1954), pp. 62–63.

80. *The New York Times*, November 24, 1953.

81. U.S. Department of Commerce, Joint Publications Research Service, *Economic Information on North Korea*, JPRS no. 9834 (August 17, 1961), p. 27. Hereinafter referred to as JPRS.

82. Yoon T. Kuark, "A Comparative Study of Economic Development Between North and South Korea During the Post-War Period," (unpublished M.A. thesis, University of Minnesota, 1961), p. 27.

83. Harold C. Hinton, *Communist China in World Politics* (Boston: Houghton Mifflin Co., 1966), pp. 386–87.

84. Editorial, *Jen-min Jih-pao*, November 24, 1953, cited in Thomas, "Chinese Communists' Economic and Cultural Agreement with North Korea," p. 63.

85. Paige, "Emulation," pp. 235–36.

86. David J. Dallin, *Soviet Foreign Policy After Stalin* (New York: J.B. Lippincott Co., 1961), p. 461.

87. Holubnychy, "Soviet Economic Aid," p. 19.

88. Paige and Lee, "Post-War Politics," p. 25.

89. Rudolph, *Political and Economic Structure*, p. 63.

90. *The Korean People's Righteous Fatherland Liberation War for Freedom and Independence* (P'yŏngyang: Chosŏn Nodong-dang Ch'ulp'ansa, 1955), p. 300.

91. Kim, *Selected Works*, vol. V, p. 209.

92. Paige, "Emulation," p. 242.

93. Ibid. See also pp. 31–37.

94. *The New York Times*, November 24, 1953, p. 1.

95. Eckstein, *Economic Growth and Foreign Trade*, p. 163.

96. V. Wolpert, "Turns in North Korea Trade," *Far Eastern Economic Review* (Hong Kong), no. 143 (February 13, 1964), p. 386; Ernst Kux, "East Europe's Relations With Asian Communist Countries," in Kurt London, ed., *Eastern Europe in Transition* (Baltimore: Johns Hopkins University Press, 1966), pp. 291–95.

97. The word, *chuch'e*, has been variously translated as "autonomy," "independence," "self-identity," and "subjectivity." See Paige and Lee, "Post-War Politics," p. 25; Paige, "Emulation," p. 260; Cho, "Sino-Soviet Rift," p. 8; Chong-Sik Lee, "Stalinism in the East," in Robert A.

Scalapino, ed., *The Communist Revolution in Asia* (Berkeley: University of California Press, 1965), p. 124.

98. Soon Sung Cho, "The Politics of North Korea's Unification Policies, 1950–1965," *World Politics,* vol. XIX, No. 2 (January 1967), p. 22.

99. Paige, *People's Democratic Republic,* p. 39.

100. Kuark, "Industrial Development," p. 52; *Facts About Korea* (P'yŏngyang: Foreign Languages Publishing House, 1961), pp. 92–93.

101. *Facts About Korea,* pp. 95–96; *Pravda,* August 17, 1956, cited in Holubnychy, "Soviet Economic Aid," p. 18.

102. "North Korean Recovery," *Eastern World,* p. 14.

103. Rudolph, *Political and Economic Structure,* p. 42; North Korean radio broadcast, February 18, 1958.

104. Kim, *Selected Works,* vol IV, pp. 230–31.

105. Kim Il-sŏng, *On Eliminating Dogmatism and Formalism and Establishing Jooche [chuch'e] in Ideological Work* (P'yŏngyang: Foreign Languages Publishing House, 1964), pp. 1–3 and 12; *The New York Times,* January 29, 1968, p. 30.

106. For detailed discussion on this subject, see Klaus Mehnert, *Peking and Moscow,* translated by Leila Vennewitz (New York: Mentor Book, 1964); Robert C. North, *Moscow and Chinese Communists,* 2nd ed. (Stanford: Stanford University Press, 1963); Benjamin Schwartz, *Chinese Communism and the Rise of Mao* (Cambridge: Harvard University Press, 1959).

107. For the full text of Khrushchev's speech at the 20th CPSU Congress, see *Pravda,* February 15, 1956, trans. in *CDSP,* vol. VIII, no. 4 (March 7, 1956), pp. 8–12; G.F. Hudson, et al., *The Sino-Soviet Dispute* (New York: Praeger, 1961), pp. 42–46; David Floyd, *Mao Against Khrushchev* (New York: Praeger, 1963), pp. 228–31.

108. "On Historical Experience Concerning the Dictatorship of the Proletariat," *Jen-min Jih-pao,* April 5, 1956, trans. in *Current Background,* no. 403 (July 25, 1956), pp. 1–5.

109. Donald S. Zagoria, *The Sino-Soviet Conflict, 1956–1961* (New York: Atheneum, 1966), pp. 42–46; Richard L. Walker, "Bases of the Sino-Soviet Dispute," *The Journal of Asian Studies* (Seoul), vol. IX, no. 3 (September 1960), p. 4; William E. Griffith, *The Sino-Soviet Rift* (Cambridge: The M.I.T. Press, 1964), p. 16.

110. Ho Il Hun, "Various Problems in the Correct Fulfillment of the Principle of Collective Leadership," *Kŭlloja* (The Workers; the theoretical journal of the KWP Central Committee) (December 1956), pp. 92–102.

111. Kim, *Pukhan siponyŏn sa*, pp. 151–52.
112. Rudolph, *Political and Economic Structure*, p. 33.
113. Lee, "Stalinism," p. 130.
114. Edward Crankshaw, *The Cold War: Moscow V. Pekin[g]* (Harmondsworth, Eng.: Penguin Books, 1963), pp. 64–65. The major issue at the Moscow Conference was the basis of intrabloc relationships. The conference, at which sixty-four world Communist leaders were present, was convened to celebrate the fortieth anniversary of the October Revolution.
115. See *Nodong Shinmun*, November and December 1957 issues.

Chapter 2

1. See the editorials of *Nodong Shinmun*, January 3, June 27, September 30, 1958, and September 27, 1959; editorial, *Peking Review*, vol. I, no. 39 (November 25, 1958), p. 3.
2. In 1959 alone, eight major North Korean delegations visited Communist China, and an equal number of Chinese delegations came to North Korea. See *Chosŏn Chungang Nyŏngam 1960* (Korean Central Yearbook 1960, published by Chosŏn Chungang T'ongshinsa in P'yŏngyang), pp. 39 and 301.
3. *Minju Chosŏn* (Democratic Korea, published by the DPRK), February 15, 1958.
4. *Peking Review*, vol. I, no. 1 (March 4, 1958), p. 21; *New Korea*, no. 3, supplement (1958), pp. 2–5.
5. North Korean radio broadcast, home service, November 21, 1958.
6. *Peking Review*, vol. I, no. 39 (November 25, 1958), p. 18.
7. Ibid., vol. I, no. 42 (December 16, 1958), p. 20.
8. Peter S. H. Tang, "The Soviet and Chinese Communists in Korea," *Free World Forum*, vol. I, no. 5 (September–October 1959), p. 73; *Korean Central News Agency* (Official news agency of North Korea; hereinafter referred to as *KCNA*), September 30, 1958.
9. *Peking Review*, vol. I, no. 35 (October 28, 1958), pp. 6–7; *Nodong Shinmun*, October 4, 1958.
10. *Peking Review*, vol. II, no. 26 (June 30, 1959), p. 8.
11. Alexander Eckstein, *Communist China's Economic Growth and Foreign Trade* (New York: McGraw-Hill, 1966), p. 163.
12. *Peking Review*, vol I, no. 39 (November 25, 1958), p. 19.
13. *NCNA*, October 21, 1958; *Peking Review*, vol. II, no. 46 (November 17, 1959), p. 26.
14. *Nodong Shinmun*, January 1, 1958.
15. Tang, "Communists in Korea," p. 73.

16. *Peking Review,* vol. I, no. 39 (November 25, 1958), p. 19.

17. *Chosŏn Chungang Nyŏngam 1959,* p. 39; *Peking Review,* vol. I, no. 1 (March 4, 1958), p. 17.

18. *Peking Review,* vol. II, no. 35 (September 1, 1959), p. 24.

19. Tang, "Communists in Korea," p. 73.

20. *Peking Review,* vol. I, no. 39 (November 25, 1958), p. 19; U.S. Department of Commerce, Joint Publications Research Service, *Political and Social Information on North Korea,* JPRS no. 9834 (August 17, 1961), p. 27.

21. *New Korea,* no. 3 (1958), p. 50; *KCNA,* November 19, 1958.

22. *Chosŏn Chungang Nyŏgam 1959,* p. 39; ibid., *1960,* p. 301; *Peking Review,* vol. I, no. 1 (March 4, 1958), p. 17.

23. *KCNA,* February 13, 1959; *Peking Review,* vol. II, no. 9 (March 3, 1959), p. 20.

24. North Korean radio broadcast, January 15, 1959.

25. For detailed discussion of the new Chinese policies, see Chu-yuan Ch'eng, *Communist China's Economy, 1949–1962: Structural Changes and Crisis* (South Orange, New Jersey: Seton-Hall, 1963); *People's Communes in China* (Peking: Foreign Languages Press, 1958); Richard Hughes, *The Chinese Communes* (London: The Badley Head, 1960); Ch'eng-chih Shih, *Urban Commune Experiments in Communist China* (Hong Kong: Union Research Institute, 1962); Henry J. Lethbridge, *The Peasant and the Communes* (Hong Kong: Dragonfly Books, 1963).

26. *Hsueh Hsi* (Study, published in Peking), May 31, 1958; Donald S. Zagoria, *The Sino-Soviet Conflict, 1956–1961* (New York: Atheneum, 1966), p. 85; Donald S. Zagoria, "Strains in the Sino-Soviet Alliance," *Problems of Communism,* vol. IX, no. 3 (May–June 1960), pp. 4–5.

27. *Hung Ch'i* (Theoretical organ of the Central Committee of the CCP), July 16, 1958.

28. *Nodong Shinmun,* August 29, 1958.

29. Kim, *Selected Works,* vol. VI (1960), p. 9, cited in Glenn D. Paige, "North Korea and the Emulation of Russian and Chinese Behavior," in A. Doak Barnett, ed., *Communist Strategies in Asia* (New York: Praeger, 1963), p. 244.

30. John Bradbury, "Sino-Soviet Competition in North Korea," *The China Quarterly,* no. 6 (April–June 1961), p. 17.

31. Ibid.

32. Some indication of the demands being placed upon the population for increased production can be seen in the following table of annual industrial production to be attained in the next four years and grain output to be reached in the near future.

PRODUCTION GOALS

	1957	Goal	
Electric power (KWH)	6.9 billion	20	billion
Coal (tons)	5.0 million	25	million
Pig iron and granulated iron (tons)	330,000	4	million
Steel (tons)	277,000	3.0–3.5	million
Chemical fertilizer (tons)	323,000	1.5–2.0	million
Cement (tons)	895,000	5	million
Grain (tons)	3.2 million	over 7	million

Source: *New Korea,* no. 30 (1958), pp. 7–8.

33. North Korean radio broadcast, home service, September 18, 1958; *New Korea,* no. 29 (1958), p. 7. The North Korean Communists claimed that the First Five-Year program was accomplished in two and one-half years in terms of the total industrial output value. North Korean radio broadcast, home service, January 16, 1960.

34. Paige, "Emulation," pp. 244–45.

35. Philip Rudolph, "North Korea and the Path to Socialism," *Pacific Affairs,* vol. XXXII, no. 2 (June 1959), p. 137.

36. *Nodong Shinmun,* December 12, 1963.

37. *Iron kwa silchŏn* (Theory and Practice) (P'yŏngyang: Chosŏn Nodong-dang Ch'ulp'ansa, 1962), pp. 234–35.

38. At the sixth plenum of the KWP Central Committee in August 1953, Kim Il-sŏng called for the collectivization of agriculture. By the end of 1953, however, only 0.6 percent of the arable land and 1.2 percent of the peasants were in collectives. At the KWP Central Committee's plenum in early November 1954 the P'yŏngyang regime decided to launch a full-scale collectivization movement. By December 1955, about 49 percent of the farmers were organized into cooperatives, and another 30 percent were forced into them during the following year. By the end of 1957, over 95.6 percent of the peasants were embraced in 16,032 cooperatives averaging sixty-four households each. By August 1958, all of the North Korean farmers were in 13,309 cooperatives with an average of about seventy-nine households each; the drop in number was caused by the amalgamation of some of the

early cooperatives during 1956–1957. Collectivized farms in North Korea were known officially as "agricultural cooperatives" and not collective farms. But these cooperatives were actually somewhat like the Soviet collectives (the artel type *kolkhoz*), in that the collective farmers were permitted to retain small private plots, fruit trees, and some cattle for their own use. Philip Rudolph, *North Korea's Political and Economic Structure* (New York: Institute of Pacific Relations, 1959), pp. 50–53; Chong-Sik Lee, "Land Reform, Collectivization and the Peasants in North Korea," in Robert A. Scalapino, ed., *North Korea Today* (New York: Praeger, 1963), pp. 76–81; Chong-Sik Lee, " 'The Socialist Revolution' in the North Korean Countryside," *Asian Survey,* vol. II, no. 8 (October 1962), pp. 9–22.

39. North Korean radio broadcast, October 14 and November 4, 1958; *New Korea,* no. 3 (1958), p. 49.

40. For further discussion, see pp. 35–36.

41. The new rules for agricultural cooperatives stipulated that the cooperative "shall construct socialist cultural, rural villages" by building various kinds of production establishments and educational, cultural, health, and welfare facilities. The cooperatives were to operate such things as schools, day nurseries, rest houses, clinics, and community restaurants. Paige, "Emulation," p. 245; Rudolph, *Political and Economic Structure,* p. 54.

42. *New Korea,* no. 3 (1958), p. 49.

43. *Nodong Shinmun,* November 28, 1958; *Jen-min Jih-pao,* November 27, 1958.

44. *Nodong Shinmun,* December 11, 1958; *KCNA,* December 10, 1958; *NCNA,* December 11, 1958.

45. North Korean radio broadcast, home service, December 20, 1958.

46. *Pravda,* January 14 and 28, 1959; David Floyd, *Mao Against Khrushchev* (New York: Praeger, 1963), pp. 64–65; Zagoria, "Strains," p. 4.

47. Bradbury, "Sino-Soviet Competition," p. 20. See also *Jen-min Jih-pao,* November 7, 1958.

48. *Life,* vol. XLVI, no. 2 (January 12, 1959), p. 86.

49. *KCNA,* January 30, 1959.

50. *Pravda,* March 17, 1959.

51. Kim, *Selected Works,* vol. VI, pp. 441–50; *KCNA,* September 28, 1959; *Jen-min Jih-pao,* September 26, 1959; *Current Background,* no. 594 (October 2, 1959), pp. 12–13.

52. *NCNA,* April 16, 1959; *Minju Chosŏn,* April 16, 1959.

53. North Korean radio broadcast, home service, December 6, 1959.

54. *Korea Today* (Monthly magazine, published by the Foreign Languages Publishing House, P'yŏngyang), no. 51 (August 1960), pp. 4–8; North Korean radio broadcast, August 8, 1960.

55. Cited in Floyd, *Mao Against Khrushchev*, p. 65.

56. *Pravda*, December 2, 1959, cited in Bradbury, "Sino-Soviet Competition," p. 22.

57. Paige, "Emulation," pp. 244–45.

58. Chong-Sik Lee, "Stalinism in the East," in Robert A. Scalapino, ed., *The Communist Revolution in Asia* (Berkeley: University of California Press, 1965), p. 131.

59. Paige, "Emulation," p. 247.

60. Bradbury, "Sino-Soviet Competition," p. 22; *Nodong Shinmun*, December 6, 1959.

61. For the full text of the P'yŏngyang proposal, see *Nodong Shinmun*, February 5, 1958. The proposal was apparently made with advance understanding with Moscow. The Soviet-North Korean joint communiqué, issued in July 1956, indicated that P'yŏngyang and Moscow had discussed the withdrawal of the CPV from North Korea. *Nodong Shinmun*, July 14, 1956; *Pravda*, July 13, 1956.

62. For the full text of the Chinese statement, see *Chosŏn Chungang Nyŏngam 1959*, pp. 5–6.

63. For the full text of the Moscow statement, see ibid., pp. 6–7.

64. *New Korea*, no. 3, supplement (1958), p. 4.

65. *Pravda*, February 21, 1958.

66. *NCNA*, October 30, 1958, in *Current Background*, no. 535 (November 1, 1958), p. 10.

67. Paige, "Emulation," p. 243.

68. Rudolph, "Path to Socialism," p. 142; *Nodong Shinmun*, September 29, 1959; *Jen-min Jih-pao*, September 27, 1959.

69. *Nodong Shinmun*, July 18, 1958; *KCNA*, July 18, 1958.

70. *Korea Today*, no. 34 (1959), p. 4.

71. Kim, *Selected Works*, vol. VI, pp. 225–50; *Nodong Shinmun*, July 30, 1958.

72. *Nodong Shinmun*, July 18, 1958; *Kŭlloja*, vol. CXIV, no. 10 (November 15, 1957), pp. 5–15.

73. Kim, *Selected Works*, vol. VI, pp. 249–50; *Chosŏn Chungang Nyŏngam 1960*, p. 34.

74. *Korea Today*, August 9, 1960; *Pravda*, March 18, 1960; Paige, *People's Democratic Republic*, p. 41; *KCNA*, August 30, 1958.

75. *KCNA*, March 17, 1959; *Chosŏn Chungang Nyŏngam 1960*, p. 173;

V. N. Azov, et al., "Foreign Trade of the U.S.S.R. in 1958," in *CDSP*, vol. XI, no. 34 (September 23, 1959), pp. 3–5.

76. *Nodong Shinmun*, September 8, 1959; *Chosŏn Chungang Nyŏngam 1960*, p. 173; *Pravda*, September 8, 1959.

77. *The New York Times*, September 14, 1963, pp. 1 and 6–9.

78. *Nodong Shinmun*, September 8, 1959.

79. *New Korea*, no. 3 (1958), p. 50.

80. *CDSP*, vol. XI, no. 34 (September 23, 1959), pp. 4–5.

81. *Pravda*, December 31, 1958, trans. in *CDSP*, vol. X, no. 52 (February 1, 1959), p. 35.

82. Ibid., December 30, 1958, trans. in *CDSP*, vol. X, no. 59 (February 4, 1959), p. 35.

83. *KCNA*, February 17, 1959; *Chosŏn Chungang Nyŏngam 1960*, p. 173; *Korea Today*, no. 35 (1959), p. 61.

84. *Korea Today*, no. 34 (1959), p. 38.

85. For the full text of Khrushchev's Twentieth Congress speech, see *Pravda*, February 15, 1956; G. F. Hudson, et al., *The Sino-Soviet Dispute* (New York: Praeger, 1961), pp. 42–46; Floyd, *Mao Against Khrushchev*, pp. 228–31.

86. Nikita S. Khrushchev, "On Peaceful Coexistence," *Foreign Affairs*, vol. XXXVIII, no. 1 (October 1959), p. 4.

87. Ibid., p. 7.

88. Zagoria, *Sino-Soviet Conflict*, pp. 42 and 236–44.

89. People's Republic of China, *The Polemics of the General Line of the International Communist Movement* (Peking: Foreign Languages Press, 1965), p. 59.

90. Zagoria, *Sino-Soviet Conflict*, p. 241.

91. *Hung Ch'i*, April 15, 1960.

92. *CDSP*, vol. VIII, no. 29 (August 29, 1956), p. 3.

93. Crankshaw, *Cold War*, pp. 64–65.

94. *Nodong Shinmun*, November 9, 1957.

95. *Korea Today*, no. 34 (1959), p. 37; *KCNA*, January 30, 1959.

96. *Nodong Shinmun*, October 27, 1959.

97. *KCNA*, August 29, 1958; North Korean radio broadcast, home service, September 3, 1958.

98. The Peking statement offered to resume the interrupted talks between the Chinese and American ambassadors at Warsaw to bring about a lessening of tension. *The New York Times*, September 9, 1958, pp. 1 and 12.

99. Ibid.

100. For the full text of the P'yŏngyang statement, see *Nodong Shin-*

mun, September 13, 1958; *New Korea,* no. 29, supplement (1958), pp. 9–10.

101. *The New York Times,* September 28, 1959, p. 1.

102. *Pravda,* September 29, 1959.

103. *Peking Review,* vol. III, no. 33 (August 18, 1959), pp. 6–9.

104. For the entire editorial of *Jen-min Jih-pao,* see Floyd, *Mao Against Khrushchev,* pp. 374–85.

105. *Minju Chosŏn* and *KCNA,* August 7, 1959. See also *Nodong Shinmun,* August 4 and 5, 1959.

106. *Nodong Shinmun,* September 16, 1959.

107. Ibid., September 29, 1959.

108. Ibid.

109. Ibid., September 30, 1959.

110. Ibid., October 27, 1959.

111. Ibid., August 8 and 18, 1958.

112. Ibid., January 29, 1958; *KCNA,* June 8, 1960.

113. Kim, *Selected Works,* vol. IV, pp. 189 and 343; Cho, "Political Development," p. 158.

114. Bradbury, "Sino-Soviet Competition," p. 24.

115. *Pravda,* November 1, 1959, cited in Zagoria, *Sino-Soviet Conflict,* p. 283.

116. *Nodong Shinmun,* January 18, 1960; *KCNA,* January 19, 1960; *Current Background,* no. 613 (February 26, 1960), p. 44; *NCNA,* P'yŏng-yang, February 15, 1960.

117. *Nodong Shinmun,* January 11, 1958.

118. *KCNA,* September 12, 1959.

119. For the full text of the Soviet statement, see Floyd, *Mao Against Khrushchev,* pp. 261–62.

Chapter 3

1. This was not a formal conference, such as those held in Moscow in November 1957 and again in November–December 1960, but rather an impromptu gathering. Communist leaders were assembled in Bucharest for the Third Congress of the Rumanian Communist Party held on June 20–25, 1960.

2. Donald S. Zagoria, *The Sino-Soviet Conflict, 1956–1961* (New York: Atheneum, 1966), pp. 325–27.

3. The Russians evidently came to the Bucharest Conference with the intention of forcing a Chinese retreat, and decided at the very last moment of the conference to use the occasion to attack for the first

time Chinese policies and attitudes in front of delegates from other Communist parties. Edward Crankshaw, "The Moscow-Peking Clash Exposed," *Observer* (London), February 12 and 19, 1961; Edward Crankshaw, "Khrushchev and China," *The Atlantic,* vol. CCVII (May 1961), pp. 43–47.

4. For the full text of Khrushchev's Bucharest speech, see G. F. Hudson, et al., *The Sino-Soviet Dispute* (New York: Praeger, 1961), pp. 132–38.

5. Ibid., pp. 139–40.

6. *Nodong Shinmun,* June 25, 1960; William E. Griffith, *Albania and the Sino-Soviet Rift* (Cambridge: The M.I.T. Press, 1963), pp. 43–45.

7. See *Nodong Shinmun,* June and July 1960 issues. Especially see *Nodong Shinmun,* July 5, 1960.

8. *KCNA,* August 12, 1960.

9. Tong-un Pak, "Communist China's Impact on North Korea," *The Journal of Asian Studies* (Seoul), vol. IX, no. 3 (September 1966), p. 93; Zagoria, *Sino-Soviet Conflict,* pp. 326–31.

10. *Nodong Shinmun,* August 9, 1960.

11. Ibid., August 15, 1960; *KCNA,* August 14, 1960. Kim's speech was carried in full by *Pravda* under the title, "Our Banner is the Banner of Friendship, Brotherhood, and Peace," August 15, 1960, trans. in the *CDSP,* vol. XII, no. 33 (September 14, 1960), p. 16.

12. *Chosŏn Chungang Nyŏngam 1961,* p. 133; *Korea Today,* no. 53 (October 1960), p. 20; Soon Sung Cho, "Politics of North Korea's Unification Policies, 1950–1965," *World Politics,* vol. XIX, no. 2 (January 1967), pp. 218–41.

13. *Chosŏn Chungang Nyŏngam 1961,* p. 134. For the full text of Khrushchev's speech at the United Nations General Assembly, see *The New York Times,* September 24, 1960, pp. 6–9.

14. *KCNA,* October 1, 1960; *Korea Today,* no. 53 (October 1960), p. 20.

15. *Jen-min Jih-pao,* December 10, 1960.

16. *Peking Review,* vol. VI, no. 33 (August 16, 1960), pp. 6–8.

17. P. J. Honey, "North Vietnamese Party Congress," *China Quarterly,* no. 4 (October–December, 1960), pp. 66–75; P. J. Honey, "The Position of the DRV Leadership and the Succession of Ho Chi Minh," *China Quarterly,* no. 9 (January–March 1962), pp. 24–36.

18. *NCNA,* October 13, 1960; *Peking Review,* vol. III, no. 42 (October 18, 1960), p. 8.

19. According to the Chinese source, the members of the Chinese military mission included: Senior Gen. Lo Jui-ching; Ho Lung; Air

Force Gen. Liu Yu-lau, vice-minister of national defense and commander of the People's Liberation Army (PLA) Air Force; Gen. Yang Yung; Lt. Gen. Chen Hsi-lien, commander of PLA units in Shenyang; Gen. Wang Ping, former political commissar of the CPV; Vice Adm. Hsiao Hsiang-jung, director of the general office of the Ministry of National Defense. *NCNA,* October 23, 1960.

20. *Nodong Shinmun,* October 23, 1960; *NCNA,* October 23, 1960.

21. *NCNA,* P'yŏngyang, October 24, 1960; *Peking Review,* vol. III, no. 44 (November 1, 1960), pp. 7–8.

22. *KCNA,* October 24, 1960; *Jen-min Jih-pao,* October 24, 1960. See also Lo Jui-ching's speech in *NCNA,* October 31, 1960.

23. *Nodong Shinmun,* August 12, 1960; North Korean radio broadcast, home service, August 11, 1960.

24. *The New York Times,* October 13, 1960, p. 14; North Korean radio broadcast, home service, October 11, 1960.

25. *Nodong Shinmun,* October 12, 1960; *Chosŏn Chungang Nyŏngam 1961,* pp. 135–45; *Time,* vol. LXXVI, no. 20 (November 14, 1960), p. 35.

26. Zagoria, *Sino-Soviet Conflict,* pp. 343–69.

27. Griffith, *Albania,* pp. 51–52.

28. Zagoria, *Sino-Soviet Conflict,* p. 365.

29. Ibid., pp. 367–68.

30. North Korean radio broadcast, home service, December 11, 1960; *Kŭlloja,* no. 6 (May 6, 1962), pp. 11–12.

31. *Chosŏn Chungang Nyŏngam 1961,* pp. 5–6.

32. Ibid. According to Edward Crankshaw, the North Korean delegates, along with the Albanians, Indonesians, Thais, North Vietnamese, Burmese, Malaysians, and Japanese, took a pro-Chinese position at the conference. See *Observer,* May 6, 1962.

33. *Nodong Shinmun,* December 7, 1960.

34. For the text of the resolution, see *Nodong Shinmun,* December 24, 1960; *KCNA,* December 25, 1960.

35. *KCNA,* December 25, 1960.

36. *Nodong Shinmun,* December 7, 1960.

37. *KCNA,* June 22, 1960. The treaty came into force on March 3, 1961. See *KCNA,* March 3, 1961.

38. *Nodong Shinmun,* August 10 and 15, 1960.

39. *KCNA,* December 6, 1960.

40. *Kyong Hyang Shinmun* (A Korean daily newspaper, published in Seoul), August 29, 1963. See also note 25, above.

41. *Chosŏn Chungang Nyŏngam 1961,* pp. 65–66 and 135–36; *Nodong*

Shinmun, December 27, 1960; *Pravda,* December 28, 1960; *KCNA,* December 26, 1960.

42. *KCNA,* December 26, 1960.

43. *Chosŏn Chungang Nyŏngam 1961,* p. 135.

44. *Current Background,* no. 651 (April 19, 1961), p. 5.

45. *KCNA,* August 24, 1960.

46. See note 18, above. China also provided similar sizable loans to Outer Mongolia and North Vietnam.

47. *Chosŏn Chungang Nyŏngam 1961,* p. 136; *Nodong Shinmun,* October 14, 1960; *Peking Review,* vol. III, no. 42 (October 18, 1960), p. 8.

48. *NCNA,* March 28, 1961.

49. North Korea also reportedly agreed to provide China with designs and documents for an annual capacity of 10,000 tons of vinylon synthetic fiber and other technical data and agricultural seeds. *Current Background,* no. 679 (March 7, 1962), p. 21.

50. During early 1960, China was facing acute setbacks in industrial and agricultural developments mainly due to the withdrawal of the Soviet technicians, the national calamities, and the disastrous failures of the commune system and the Great Leap Forward movement.

51. Moscow was apparently rallying support from the Asian Communist parties for the forthcoming Twenty-second CPSU Congress in November 1961. Kim's Moscow trip probably had been prepared for during Kosygin's visit (May 30–June 6) to North Korea. During his stay in North Korea, Kosygin stressed that "in the Soviet Union the Korean people have a true and reliable friend ready to come to their aid at any minute if an aggressive force attempts to infringe on the peaceful labor of the Korean people." *KCNA,* June 5, 6, and 7, 1961.

52. For the full text of the treaty, see *Chosŏn Chungang Nyŏngam 1962,* pp. 157–58; *Pravda* and *Izvestia,* July 7, 1961, trans. in the *CDSP,* vol. XIII, no. 27 (August 21, 1961), pp. 23–24.

53. The unexpected military coup of May 16, 1961, and the subsequent development of its leaders' strong anti-Communist program in South Korea apparently led the P'yŏngyang leaders to seek an explicit guarantee for their national safety from the Soviet Union and Communist China. "Atlantic Report: North Korea," *The Atlantic,* vol. CCVIII, no. 3 (September 1961), pp. 14–15.

54. Zbigniew K. Brzezinski, *The Soviet Bloc: Unity and Conflict,* 1st rev. ed. (Cambridge: Harvard University Press, 1967), p. 467.

55. *Chosŏn Chungang Nyŏngam 1962,* pp. 159–60; *Tass* in English to Europe, July 10, 1961.

56. Kim Il-sŏng had also visited the Soviet Union and Eastern Europe during June–July 1956 seeking support for the First Five-Year Plan (1957–1961).

57. See *Jen-min Jih-pao,* July 10, 12, and 16, 1961.

58. For the full text of the treaty, see *Jen-min Jih-pao,* July 12, 1961; *Peking Review,* vol. IV, no. 28 (July 14, 1961), pp. 5–6; *Chosŏn Chungang Nyŏngam 1962,* pp. 157–58.

59. *NCNA,* September 10, 1961; *Current Background,* no. 679 (March 7, 1962), p. 9.

60. *Peking Review,* vol. IV, no. 29 (July 21, 1961), pp. 7–8.

61. *Tass* in English to Europe, July 10, 1961.

62. During his five-day visit in Communist China, Kim Il-sŏng met only once with Mao Tse-tung, who was in Hankow.

63. *KCNA,* July 15, 1961.

64. For further discussion on the congress, see Il-pyong Kim, "North Korea's Fourth Party Congress," *Pacific Affairs,* vol. XXXV, no. 1 (Spring 1962), pp. 37–50; Ho Sen Kim, "Fourth Congress of the Korean Party of Labour," *World Marxist Review* (Moscow), vol. V (January 1962), pp. 61–63.

65. There was a strong indication that North Korea's announcement of a new Seven-Year Plan was not well received by the Soviet Union, because the latter insisted on united economic planning within the entire Communist bloc. It was also reported that the Soviet Union cut off economic assistance to North Korea when Moscow was not able to dissuade the North Koreans from putting the plan into effect in 1961. Joungwon A. Kim, "The Long March of North Korea's Kim," *The New York Times Magazine,* February 25, 1968, p. 188.

66. By the completion of the Seven-Year Plan, the North Korean Communists claimed that the annual output would reach 17 billion kilowatts in electricity, 23 million tons in coal, 2.5 million tons in steel, 4.4 million tons in cement, and 1.5 million tons in chemical fertilizer. Kim Il-sŏng, "The Central Committee Reports," *Nodong Shinmun,* September 12, 1961; *Documents of the Fourth Congress of the Workers' Party of Korea* (P'yŏngyang: Foreign Languages Publishing House, 1961), pp. 102–04.

67. Eckstein, *Economic Growth and Foreign Trade,* p. 182. Moscow also waged extensive economic and propaganda sanctions against Albania in 1960–1961. The Russians and other East European bloc countries pulled out their technicians from Albania in 1960. According to Hoxha, Moscow cut all credits to Albania, demanded repayment of old credits,

and withdrew its technicians. *The New York Times,* October 22, 1961, p. 3; Griffith, *Albania,* pp. 63–64; Crankshaw, "Khrushchev and China," p. 46. See also note 50, above.

68. *Korea Today,* no. 12 (1961), p. 11; *Nodong Shinmun,* September 12, 1961.

69. *Nodong Shinmun,* September 12, 1961.

70. Ibid.

71. Ibid.

72. For detailed discussion on the Albanian relations with the Soviet Union and Communist China, see Griffith, *Albania,* pp. 1–176.

73. Ibid., pp. 111–21. The open Albanian-Soviet polemics resulted in the final diplomatic break between Moscow and Tirana in December 1961. Early in 1962 Albania was expelled from the Warsaw Treaty Organization. Alexander Dallin, et al., eds., *Diversity in International Communism* (New York: Columbia University Press, 1963), pp. 99–111.

74. Dallin, *Diversity,* p. 3; Griffith, *Albania,* pp. 80–99; Robert A. Scalapino, "Moscow and the Communist Parties of Asia," *Foreign Affairs,* vol. XL, no. 2 (January 1963), p. 323.

75. The twenty-two bloc countries were: North Korea, North Vietnam, Indonesia, India, United Kingdom, Canada, Algeria, Japan, Burma, Malaya, Dominican Republic, Guadeloupe, Sweden, Martinique, Australia, New Zealand, Norway, Denmark, Iceland, Belgium, and Switzerland. Dallin, *Diversity,* p. 83.

76. For further discussion on North Korea's relationship with Albania, see pp. 65–66.

77. Dallin, *Diversity,* p. 83; Zagoria, *Sino-Soviet Conflict,* p. 381.

78. For the full text of Kim Il-sŏng's speech at the congress, see *KCNA,* October 21, 1961. See also Scalapino, *North Korea Today,* pp. 38–39; Dallin, *Diversity,* p. 387; *The New York Times,* October 22, 1961, pp. 1 and 3.

79. For the full text of Kim's speech, see *Nodong Shinmun,* November 28, 1961; *Jen-min Jih-pao,* December 1, 1961; Dallin, *Diversity,* pp. 388–94.

80. Dallin, *Diversity,* pp. 388–89 and 391.

81. Quoted in Dallin, *Diversity,* pp. 389–90.

82. Ibid. This passage was omitted by *Pravda* when the Soviet organ reprinted Kim Il-sŏng's speech on December 4, 1961. The omitted passages obviously hurt the feelings of the Soviet leaders. But *Jen-min Jih-pao* carried the full text of Kim's speech.

83. Robert A. Scalapino, "Korea: The Politics of Change," *Asian Survey,* vol. III (January 1963), p. 37.

84. *Nodong Shinmun*, November 28, 1961; Dallin, *Diversity*, p. 390.

85. Dallin, *Diversity*, pp. 392–93.

86. The closing month of 1961 saw two major international Communist meetings: the Fifth World Federation of Trade Unions (WFTU) Congress at Moscow, December 4–15, and a meeting of the World Peace Council (WPC) in Stockholm, December 16–19. Both meetings were dominated by the Sino-Soviet dispute. In the WFTU debate, three issues were of significance for the Sino-Soviet conflict: the relative priority of the struggle for peace and of that for national liberation, joint action with non-Communist trade unions, and the degree of autonomy of national trade-union federations. The North Korean delegation to the WFTU Congress reportedly sided with the Chinese Communists. At the Stockholm meeting of the WPC, the Soviet Union, supported by a vast majority of the delegates, insisted that the overriding priority of the world peace movement must be the struggle against atomic war and for the Soviet plan of "general and complete disarmament." The Chinese and North Korean delegates, along with the North Vietnamese, Albanian, and some African and Latin American delegates, declared, on the contrary, that the first priority must be given to the struggle against imperialism and colonialism and for national liberation. See Griffith, *Albania*, pp. 122–23 and 125–26; Floyd, *Mao Against Khrushchev*, pp. 151–52.

87. Dallin, *Diversity*, p. 395.

88. *Minju Chosŏn*, November 29, 1960.

89. *Nodong Shinmun*, February 20, 1961; Griffith, *Albania*, p. 73.

90. *KCNA*, April 30 and May 2, 1961.

91. *Nodong Shinmun*, November 8, 1961; *KCNA*, November 7, 1961.

92. *Nodong Shinmun*, November 29, 1961; Dallin, *Diversity*, pp. 394–95.

93. *Chosŏn Chungang Nyŏngam 1963*, p. 353.

94. Ibid., p. 355.

Chapter 4

1. Thus, it was reported that Kim Il-sŏng, along with Ho Chi Minh, applied maximum pressure upon Moscow and Peking to reconcile their differences in the interest of Communist unity and strength, and to avoid splitting every Communist party in the world. See Robert A. Scalapino, ed., *North Korea Today* (New York: Praeger, 1963), pp. 40–41.

2. *Nodong Shinmun*, February 13, 1962.

3. *KCNA*, April 18, 19, and 20, 1962.

4. Ibid., July 5, 1962.

5. *Nodong Shinmun,* August 15, 1962.

6. *KCNA,* July 5, 1962.

7. V. Wolpert, "Turns in North Korea Trade," *Far Eastern Economic Review,* no. 143 (February 13, 1964), p. 386.

8. *Chosŏn Chungang Nyŏngam 1963,* p. 196.

9. Ibid., pp. 196 and 426.

10. Ibid., p. 426; *KCNA,* May 8, 1962.

11. A. M. Halperin, "The Emergence of an Asian Communist Coalition," *The Annals of American Academy of Political and Social Sciences,* vol. CCCII (September 1963), p. 121.

12. *KCNA,* March 16, 1962.

13. Ibid., July 5, 1962.

14. *Chosŏn Chungang Nyŏngam 1963,* p. 381.

15. *Peking Review,* vol. V, no. 17 (April 27, 1962), pp. 7–8.

16. Ibid., vol. V, no. 25 (June 22, 1962), pp. 5–6; *Chosŏn Chungang Nyŏngam 1963,* pp. 190–93.

17. *Chosŏn Chungang Nyŏngam 1963,* pp. 191–92.

18. *Peking Review,* vol. V, no. 16 (April 20, 1962), p. 25.

19. *NCNA,* July 10, 1962.

20. On the occasion of the thirteenth anniversary of the founding of the Chinese People's Republic, Ch'oe Yong-gŏn said that "the invincible vitality of the militant friendship between the Korean and Chinese peoples sealed with blood ... has already been tested in the trials of history ... and will be everlasting, and no force in earth will break them." *KCNA,* October 1, 1962.

21. *Chosŏn Chungang Nyŏngam 1963,* pp. 195–96.

22. Ibid.; *Current Background,* no. 684 (June 20, 1962), p. 35.

23. *Current Background,* no. 705 (February 20, 1963), p. 17.

24. *NCNA,* November 5, 1962; *Peking Review,* vol. V, no. 45 (November 9, 1962), p. 24.

25. When India became independent in 1947, its leaders were determined to prevent resurgent Communist China from reoccupying Tibet. The Indian government then protested at the loss of its rights there and later granted asylum to the Dalai Lama when the Chinese crushed the Tibetan "rebellion" in 1959. This infuriated but did not check the Chinese. The P'yŏngyang regime categorically supported the measure taken by the Chinese Communists against Tibet. The Chinese had built a strategic military post in East Ladakh during 1956–1957. At the same period, the Indians decided secretly to infiltrate and outflank the Chinese border posts in Ladakh. *Nodong Shinmun,* March 31, 1959.

For further background, see Margaret W. Fisher, et al., *Himalayan Background: Sino-Indian Rivalry in Ladakh* (New York: Praeger, 1963); John W. Lewis, "Communist China's Invasion of the Indian Frontier: The Framework of Motivation," *Current Scene*, vol. II, no. 7 (January 2, 1963); George Patterson, *Peking Versus Delhi* (London: Oxford University Press, 1964). For the official views, see People's Republic of China, *The Sino-Indian Boundary Question* (Peking: Foreign Languages Press, 1962); Government of India, *The Chinese Threat* (New Delhi: Ministry of Information and Broadcasting, 1963).

26. For the full statement of the Soviet Union, see *Tass,* September 9, 1959. See also David Floyd, *Mao Against Khrushchev* (New York: Praeger, 1963), pp. 261–62.

27. William E. Griffith, *The Sino-Soviet Rift* (Cambridge: The M.I.T. Press, 1964), pp. 5–7.

28. *Peking Review,* vol V, no. 44 (November 2, 1962), pp. 10–12; ibid., vol. V, no. 46 (November 16, 1962), pp. 5–7.

29. "In the Interests of the Peoples, in the Name of Universal Peace," *Pravda,* October 25, 1962.

30. Griffith, *Sino-Soviet Rift,* p. 59.

31. *Jen-min Jih-pao,* October 26, 1962.

32. *Pravda,* November 5, 1962.

33. Alexander Dallin, et al., *Diversity in International Communism: A Documentary Record, 1961–1963* (New York: Columbia University Press, 1963), p. 660; *The New York Times,* November 3, 1962, p. 2; *Christian Science Monitor,* January 2, 1963.

34. *KCNA,* September 12, 1959.

35. Ibid., December 17, 1961; *Nodong Shinmun,* December 16, 1961; *Minju Chosŏn,* December 17, 1961.

36. *Nodong Shinmun* and *KCNA,* September 26, 1962.

37. *KCNA,* November 18, 1962; *Nodong Shinmun,* November 5, 1962; North Korean radio broadcast, November 9, 1962; *Chosŏn Chungang Nyŏngam 1963,* pp. 193–94.

38. *Korea Today,* no. 81 (February 1963), pp. 45–46; *The New York Times,* November 4, 1962, p. 2.

39. *Nodong Shinmun,* October 26, 1962; *Minju Chosŏn,* November 23, 1962.

40. *Peking Review,* vol. V, no. 45 (November 9, 1962), p. 24.

41. *Nodong Shinmun,* November 22, 1962.

42. *Minju Chosŏn,* November 23, 1962.

43. *Nodong Shinmun,* November 24, 1962; *Chosŏn Chungang Nyŏngam 1963,* pp. 103–04.

44. *Chosŏn Chungang Nyŏngam 1963,* pp. 193–94.

45. "The Sino-Indian Border Question Should Be Settled Peacefully," *Korea Today,* no. 81 (February 1963), pp. 45–46.

46. U.S. Department of Commerce, Joint Publications Research Service, *Political and Social Information on North Korea,* JPRS no. 2691 (May 21, 1960), p. 186.

47. *Tass* in English to Europe and Moscow Radio, July 5, 1961.

48. *Chosŏn Chungang Nyŏngam 1963,* p. 354.

49. Kim's message to Nehru reads: "On the occasion of the thirteenth anniversary of the founding of the Republic of India, I extend my congratulations to the Indian people...." Nehru's reply to Kim went: "On behalf of the government and people of India and on my own behalf, I thank your Excellency for your kind message of greetings...." *KCNA,* February 1, 1963.

50. For further studies on the Cuban crisis, see *The New York Times,* November 3, 1962, pp. 1–4 and 7–9; David L. Larson, *The Cuban Crisis of 1962* (Boston: Houghton Mifflin, 1963); Harry M. Pachter, *Collision Course: The Cuban Missile Crisis and Coexistence* (New York: Praeger, 1963).

51. The Cuban crisis was so serious, because it was a potentially thermonuclear Soviet-American confrontation, that for Khrushchev its negative effect on Sino-Soviet relations was probably a secondary element in Soviet considerations. According to Dr. Doolin, the overt controversy over the Sino-Soviet border in early 1963 was actually an unforeseen byproduct of the Cuban missile crisis. Dennis J. Doolin, *Territorial Claims in the Sino-Soviet Conflict: Documents and Analysis* (Stanford: The Hoover Institute, Stanford University Press, 1965), p. 19.

52. Dallin, *Diversity,* p. 658; Griffith, *Sino-Soviet Rift,* pp. 60–61.

53. *Jen-min Jih-pao,* October 31, 1962.

54. Ibid., October 31, 1962; *Peking Review,* vol. V, no 44 (November 2, 1962), p. 5.

55. *Jen-min Jih-pao,* November 5, 1962; *Peking Review,* vol. V, no. 45 (November 7, 1962), pp. 12–13.

56. *Chosŏn Chungang Nyŏngam 1963,* p. 195; *Nodong Shinmun,* October 29, 1962; *Korea Today,* no. 80 (1963), pp. 42–45.

57. *Nodong Shinmun,* November 17, 1962.

58. Ibid., November 30, 1962.

59. Leopold Labedz, ed., *International Communism After Khrushchev* (Cambridge: The M.I.T. Press, 1965), pp. 154–67.

60. *Chosŏn Chungang Nyŏngam 1963,* pp. 361 and 426.

61. Kim Il-sŏng, in his report to the Fourth Congress of the KWP,

emphasized the self-sufficient economy as the major goal of the Seven-Year Plan. *KCNA,* September 16, 1961.

62. See note 2, above.

63. *Nodong Shinmun,* October 24, 1962.

64. Ibid., June 12, 1963.

65. *Chosŏn Nodong-dang yŏksa kyojae* (The Textbook of History of the Korean Workers' Party) P'yŏngyang: Chosŏn Nodong-dang Ch'ulp'-ansa, 1964), p. 489.

66. The 1962 meeting of the CEMA was mapping the new course in the intrabloc economic cooperation and adding new dimensions to the program of integration. Khrushchev's report indicated that the CEMA would include the entire socialist commonwealth of nations: "The works of the Council on Mutual Economic Aid in organizing collective economic cooperation does not yet extend to all the socialist countries. The differences in the times when various countries entered upon the road to socialism prevented them from embarking upon collective economic cooperation simultaneously. However, the success of the member states of the Council . . . in drawing together economically, will make it easier for all the countries of socialism to turn to the path of collective economic cooperation. Extensive economic ties . . . are developing between the Council members and socialist states that do not belong to the Council." Cited in Kazimierz Grzybowski, *The Socialist Commonwealth of Nations* (New Haven: Yale University Press, 1964), pp. 212–13.

67. *Pravda,* June 9, 1962; *Izvestia,* June 10, 1962.

68. Griffith, *Sino-Soviet Rift,* pp. 38–39.

69. There was a period in 1958–1959 when it looked as if China were going to associate itself more closely with the CEMA. The fact that China did not actually belong to this body was attributed to the Council being essentially a European organization. This was hardly tenable after June 1962 when Mongolia was admitted to membership. Audrey Donnithorne, *China's Economic System* (New York: Praeger, 1967), pp. 331–32.

70. At the meeting of the CEMA in May 1956, the observer status was accorded to Communist China, North Korea, Mongolia, and North Vietnam. Grzybowski, *Socialist Commonwealth,* p. 71.

71. Griffith, *Albania,* pp. 147–48; Floyd, *Mao Against Khrushchev,* p. 156.

72. Paul F. Langer, "Outer Mongolia, North Korea, [and] North Viet-Nam," in Adam Bromke, ed., *The Communist States at the Crossroads: Between Moscow and Peking* (New York: Praeger, 1965), p. 153.

73. *Chosŏn Nodong-dang yŏksa kyojae,* pp. 487–89.

74. *Korea Today,* no. 88 (September 1963), p. 15.

75. "Socialist Revolution and Building of a New Life Through Self-Reliance," *Kŭlloja,* no. 19 (December 1962), cited in Halperin, "Asian Communist Coalition," p. 122. The entire article was quoted by *NCNA* on December 22, 1962.

76. *Nodong Shinmun,* December 16, 1962.

77. Five congresses of pro-Soviet European Communist parties were held from November 5, 1962 to January 21, 1963. They were: Bulgaria, November 5–14, 1962; Hungary, November 20–24; Italy, December 2–8; Czechoslovakia, December 4–8; and East Germany, January 15–21, 1963. This chapter deals with only the Czechoslovakian and East German congresses. For further discussion on the congresses, see Griffith, *Sino-Soviet Rift,* pp. 67–84 and 97–103.

78. Cited in Ryu Hun, *Study of North Korea* (Seoul: Research Institute of Internal and External Affairs, 1966), pp. 129–30.

79. Lee, "Stalinism," p. 133. See also *Jen-min Jih-pao,* December 15, 1962.

80. Dallin, *Diversity,* p. 661.

81. *Nodong Shinmun,* January 30, 1963.

82. Griffith, *Sino-Soviet Rift,* pp. 102–03.

83. *Nodong Shinmun,* January 22, 1963. This speech was published in *Jen-min Jih-pao* on the same day.

84. *Nodong Shinmun,* January 30, 1963.

85. Ibid.

Chapter 5

1. *Nodong Shinmun,* June 12, 1963; *Korea Today,* no. 85, supplement (June 1963), p. 8; ibid., no. 89 (October 1963), pp. 4–6; ibid., no. 101 (October 1964), pp. 2–4.

2. *Chosŏn Chungang Nyŏngam 1964,* p. 364. There were also unusually frequent exchanges of nonofficial delegations between Peking and P'yŏngyang. For example, in April 1963, the North Korean lawyers' delegation and a five-member delegation from *Nodong Shinmun* visited Communist China. *Peking Review,* vol. VI, no. 19 (May 10, 1963), p. 5; ibid., vol. VI, no. 16 (April 19, 1963), p. 6.

3. Ch'oe Yong-gŏn was accompanied on the visit by Yi Hyo-sun, member of the SPA Presidium of the DPRK and vice-chairman of the KWP Central Committee, Pak Sŏng-ch'ŏl, member of the KWP Central Committee and minister of foreign affairs, Kang Hi-won, deputy to the

SPA and member of the KWP Central Committee, and Hwang Chang-yŏp, deputy to the SPA and vice-director of a department of the KWP Central Committee. *KCNA*, June 5, 1963.

4. *Nodong Shinmun*, June 5, 1963. Emphasis supplied.

5. *Korea Today*, no. 88 (September 1963), pp. 8–9.

6. *Peking Review*, vol. VI, no. 24 (June 14, 1963), pp. 2–12; *The Economist*, vol. CCVII, no. 6252 (June 22, 1963), p. 1,247.

7. For the full text of the joint communiqué, see *Chosŏn Chungang Nyŏngam 1964*, pp. 16–21; *Korea Today*, no. 87 (August 1963), pp. 3–9; *Peking Review*, vol. VI, no. 26 (June 28, 1963), pp. 8–12; *Nodong Shinmun*, June 24, 1963.

8. *Peking Review*, vol. VI, no. 26 (June 28, 1963), p. 10; *Nodong Shinmun*, June 24, 1963.

9. *Nodong Shinmun*, June 24, 1963.

10. Ibid.

11. Ibid.

12. Ibid.

13. Ibid.

14. For the full text of Ch'oe's report on his visit to Peking, see *NCNA*, P'yŏngyang, July 25, 1963; *Korea Today*, no. 88 (September 1963), pp. 1–12.

15. Liu Shao-ch'i's visit to North Korea will be discussed later in detail.

16. William E. Griffith, *The Sino-Soviet Rift* (Cambridge: The M.I.T. Press, 1964), pp. 154–55.

17. Ryu Hun, *Study of North Korea* (Seoul: Research Institute of Internal and External Affairs, 1966), pp. 132–34.

18. *KCNA*, September 15 and 22, 1963.

19. *Nodong Shinmun*, September 15, 1963.

20. See pp. 86–87.

21. For the full text of Liu Shao-ch'i's speech, see *Nodong Shinmun*, September 19, 1963; *Peking Review*, vol. VI, no. 39 (September 27, 1963), pp. 8–14.

22. *Peking Review*, vol. VI, no. 39 (September 27, 1963), p. 13.

23. *KCNA*, September 15 and 24, 1963.

24. *Korea Today*, no. 90 (November 1963), pp. 1–2.

25. *Nodong Shinmun*, September 28, 1963; *KCNA*, September 26, 1963.

26. For further discussion on the subject, see pp. 86–87.

27. Griffith, *Sino-Soviet Rift*, p. 192.

28. North Korean radio broadcast, international service, December

25, 1963, cited in Paul F. Langer, "Outer Mongolia, North Korea, [and] North Vietnam," in Adam Broke, ed., *The Communist States at the Cross-roads: Between Moscow and Peking* (New York: Praeger, 1965), pp. 151–53. By this time Peking and P'yŏngyang had reportedly solved the long pending border issue between China and North Korea. The 1965 edition of *Chosŏn Chungang Nyŏngam* clearly indicated that "Mts. Paektu and Changpaek are within the boundary of Korea." For further discussion on the subject, see U.S. Department of State, *China-Korean Boundary*, International Boundary Study no. 17 (Washington, D.C.: U.S. Government Printing Office, 1962); *Chosŏn Chungang Nyŏngam 1965*, pp. 101–02.

29. Griffith, *Sino-Soviet Rift*, p. 192.

30. *Peking Review*, vol. VI, no. 33 (August 16, 1963), p. 15.

31. Morton H. Halperin and Dwight H. Perkins, *Communist China and Arms Control* (Cambridge: East Asian Research Center, Harvard University Press, 1965), pp. 114–19.

32. The Chinese proposals for total nuclear disarmament were as follows: (a) dismantle all military bases, including nuclear bases, on foreign soil, and withdraw from abroad all nuclear weapons and their means of delivery; (b) establish a nuclear weapon-free zone of the Asian and Pacific region, including the United States, the Soviet Union, China and Japan; a nuclear weapon-free zone of Latin America; and a nuclear-free zone of Africa; (c) refrain from exporting and importing in any form nuclear weapons and technical data for their manufacture; and (d) cease all nuclear tests, including underground nuclear tests. *Peking Review*, vol. VI, no. 34 (August 9, 1963), p. 7.

33. *Nodong Shinmun*, August 4, 1963; *Peking Review*, vol. VI, no. 32 (August 9, 1963), pp. 17–18.

34. *Nodong Shinmun*, August 4, 1963.

35. Ibid., October 11, 1963.

36. *Minju Chosŏn* and *KCNA*, October 22, 1963.

37. *Nodong Shinmun*, December 6, 1963.

38. Ibid., May 27, 1963; *Kŭlloja*, vol. XIV, no. 228 (July 1963), pp. 16–18.

39. "Yugoslav Revisionists Serve Imperialism," editorial, *Nodong Shinmun*, August 22, 1963.

40. Langer, "North Korea," p. 153.

41. *Nodong Shinmun*, September 20, 1963.

42. Kim Suk Hyung, Kim Heui Il, and Son Yung Jong, *On the Grave Errors in the Description on Korea of the 'World History' Edited by the U.S.S.R. Academy of Sciences* (P'yŏngyang: Foreign Languages Publishing House, 1963), p. 2.

43. *Nodong Shinmun* and *KCNA*, October 28, 1963; *Korea Today*, no. 92 (January 1964), pp. 13–16; *Chosŏn Chungang Nyŏngam 1964*, pp. 115–31. See also *Kŭlloja*, vol. XXI, no. 235 (November 5, 1963); *Nodong Shinmun*, December 6, 1963.

44. *Nodong Shinmun*, October 28, 1963.

45. Ibid.

46. Ibid.

47. Ibid. For further discussion of the so-called August 1956 incident, see pp. 15–16.

48. Ibid., October, 28, 1963.

49. "North Korea Bites Moscow's Hand," *Atlas*, vol. IX (April 1965), p. 227; "Freudian Slip," *The Economist*, p. 1,247. For further discussion on the Sino-North Korean and Soviet-North Korean economic relations, see pp. 91–93, 115–16, 124–25, and 155–57.

50. Donald S. Zagoria, *Sino-Soviet Conflict 1956–61* (New York: Atheneum, 1966), p. xvi.

51. See note 49, above.

52. *NCNA*, June 10, 1963; *Chosŏn Chungang Nyŏngam 1964*, p. 163.

53. *NCNA*, June 22, 1963; *Chosŏn Chungang Nyŏngam 1964*, p. 163.

54. *Chosŏn Chungang Nyŏngam 1965*, p. 163; *KCNA*, October 14, 1963.

55. *NCNA*, November 12, 1963.

56. Douglas M. Johnston and Hungdah Chiu, eds., *Agreements of the People's Republic of China 1949–1967: A Calendar* (Cambridge: Harvard University Press, 1968), p. 254.

57. The major agreements between Moscow and P'yŏngyang during 1963–1964 were: (1) a protocol on commodity exchange for 1963 signed on January 26, 1963; (2) a 1963 plan for a cultural cooperation agreement signed on April 17, 1963; (3) an agreement on cultural and scientific cooperation for 1963 signed on May 13, 1963; and (4) a protocol on commodity delivery and payments for 1964 signed on February 27, 1964. *Chosŏn Chungang Nyŏngam 1964*, pp. 193–451; *Nodong Shinmun* and *KCNA*, February 28, 1964.

58. It is noteworthy, however, that Soviet economic and technical aid to North Korea was never completely interrupted. Unlike the en masse withdrawal from Communist China, a small number of Soviet experts remained in North Korea even after party relations came to a breaking point. According to *Pravda* of September 9, 1964, the Soviet Union, in fulfilling an agreement concluded in 1959, was helping in the construction of an atomic power hydroelectric plant. *Pravda*, September 9, 1964; *The New York Times*, September 9, 1964.

59. *Nodong Shinmun*, October 28, 1963.

60. Only eight official delegations were exchanged between Moscow and P'yŏngyang in 1963, while there were twenty-two delegations exchanged during the same period between P'yŏngyang and Peking. *Chosŏn Chungang Nyŏngam 1964*, pp. 364 and 451.

61. Alexander Eckstein, *Communist China's Economic Growth and Foreign Trade* (New York: McGraw-Hill, 1966), pp. 293–94; Ernst Kux, "East Europe's Relations with Asian Communist Countries," in Kurt London, ed., *Eastern Europe in Transition* (Baltimore: The Johns Hopkins University Press, 1966), pp. 291–92. The ruble-dollar exchange rate since 1961 is 0.90 rubles to the dollar. From 1950 to 1959, the official exchange rate was 4.00 rubles to the dollar, and the special rate for noncommercial payments was 10.00 rubles to the dollar.

62. Kux, "East Europe's Relations," p. 291.

63. North Korea did not have diplomatic relations with any of these countries. In their economic relations, the North Koreans usually deal directly with private firms in these countries with no government-to-government negotiation involved.

64. Kux, "East Europe's Relations," p. 294.

65. Soon Sung Cho, "Japan's Two Koreas Policy and the Problems of Korean Unification," *Asian Survey*, vol. VII (October 1967), pp. 712–16; *JPRS* no. 27,724 (December 8, 1964), pp. 1–8.

66. *Nitcho Boeki* (Japan-Korea Trade) (Tokyo, Japan), vols. I–II (February 15, 1963), pp. 1–27, trans. in *JPRS* no. 19,572 (June 5, 1963), pp. 1–3.

67. J. K. Lee and Donald Wellington, "North Korea's Trade with the West: 1956–1968," *Journal of Korean Affairs*, vol. I, no. 1 (April 1971), p. 27.

68. By early 1964, the percentage of Japan's share in North Korea's total trade with the non-Communist countries drastically decreased, although Japan's actual trade volume with P'yŏngyang was increased as shown in Table 4. Wolpert, "North Korea Trade," p. 387.

69. M. T. Haggard, "North Korea's International Position," *Asian Survey*, vol. V, no. 8 (August 1965), p. 377.

70. Wolpert, "North Korea Trade," p. 387.

71. *Far Eastern Economic Review: 1965 Yearbook*, p. 233.

72. During the first half of 1963, French imports from North Korea amounted to 171,000 francs, consisting mainly of plastic materials. Ibid.; Haggard, "International Position," p. 377.

73. *Nodong Shinmun*, January 27, 1964.

74. Cited in Young Hoon Kang, "North Korea's Mysterious Kim Il Sung," *Communist Affairs*, vol. II, no. 2 (March–April 1964), p. 26.

75. Kyosuke Hirotsu, "Japan," in Leopold Labedz, ed., *International Communism After Khrushchev* (Cambridge: The M.I.T. Press, 1965), pp. 123–30; "Subversive Machinations Against Japanese Communist Party Can Never Be Tolerated," editorial, *Nodong Shinmun*, July 27, 1964.

76. "We Must Prevent the World Communist Parties Conference That Would Split the Socialist Camp," editorial, *Nodong Shinmun*, August 31, 1964.

77. Ibid.

78. *Second Asian Economic Seminar: P'yŏngyang* (Colombo, Ceylon: The Asian Economic Bureau, 1964), vol. I, p. 1. The first seminar was held in Colombo in 1962. The eight members of the Asian Economic Conference were Japan, North Korea, Ceylon, Communist China, North Vietnam, Viet Cong, Indonesia, and Pakistan. Pakistan was absent but sent a message of greetings to the seminar.

79. Ibid., pp. 6–11. The twenty-eight countries which participated in the seminar were Algeria, Angola, Australia, Basutoland, Bolivia, Bechuanaland, Cameroon, the Congo (Brazzaville), the Congo (Leopoldville), Gambia, Ghana, Iraq, Kenya, Mali, Mozambique, Nepal, New Zealand, Niger, North Kalimantan, Palestine, Rwanda, Somalia, Sudan, Southwest Africa, Syria, Thailand, Uganda, and Zanzibar.

80. Ibid., p. 23.

81. Ibid., p. 21.

82. Ibid., p. 30.

83. Ibid., vol. II, p. 136.

84. Ibid., vol. II, p. 137.

85. Ibid., vol. II, pp. 232–36; *Korea Today*, no. 100 (September 19, 1964), pp. 14–15.

86. "In Whose Interest?" *Pravda*, August 18, 1964, trans. in *CDSP*, vol. XVI, no. 33 (September 9, 1964), pp. 16–17.

87. Ibid., p. 16.

88. Ibid., p. 17.

89. "Why Do They [the Russians] Condemn the Success of the P'yŏngyang Economic Seminar? Response to the Attacks made by *Pravda* on the Second Asian Economic Seminar," *Nodong Shinmun*, September 7, 1964.

90. Ibid.

91. Ibid.

92. Soviet officials appear to have closely supervised North Korea's gold production, with 6.5 tons exported in 1949 and 9 tons of refined gold in 1950. Small exports of monazite, a mineral of possible uranium content, were also reported but such exports do not appear in available

documents. The editorial was apparently referring to these "exports." Department of State, *North Korea*, p. 103.

93. *Chosŏn Chungang Nyŏngam 1964*, pp. 162–63 and 333–41; *Korea Today*, no. 84 (May 1963), p. 46; ibid., no. 90 (November 1963), p. 26. North Korea had also established relations with the following countries: the Soviet Union (1948), Mongolia (1948), Poland (1948), Czechoslovakia (1948), Yugoslavia (1949), Albania (1949), Communist China (1949), East Germany (1949), North Vietnam (1950), Guinea (1960), Cuba (1960), and Mali (1960).

94. Haggard, "International Position," p. 376; *Far Eastern Economic Review: 1965 Yearbook*, p. 231.

95. Haggard, "International Position," p. 377; Chong-Sik Lee, "Korea: Troubles in a Divided State," *Asian Survey*, vol. V (January 1965), p. 29; *Far Eastern Economic Review: 1965 Yearbook*, p. 231.

96. North Korea praised the success of the first Chinese nuclear test. See the editorial entitled "The Great Success of the Chinese People in the Struggle for Peace," *Nodong Shinmun*, October 19, 1964.

97. For further analysis on the subject, see Chong-Sik Lee, "Stalinism in the East," in Robert A. Scalapino, ed., *The Communist Revolution in Asia: Tactics, Goals, and Achievements* (Englewood Cliffs, N.J.: Prentice-Hall, 1965), pp. 135–36; Griffith, *Sino-Soviet Rift*, pp. 191–92; Langer, "North Korea," pp 154–55; Ryu, *North Korea*, pp. 130–31; Zagoria, "Asia," in Labedz, *International Communism*, pp. 101–03.

98. For detailed discussion on the subject, see Reinhard Bendix, "Reflections on Charismatic Leadership," *Asian Survey*, vol. VII (June 1967), pp. 348–49; Chong-Sik Lee, "Kim Il-sŏng of North Korea," *Asian Survey*, vol. VII (June 1967), pp. 374–82; Richard Walker, "Chairman Mao and the Cult of Personality," *Encounter*, June 1960, pp. 32–38; James T. Myers, "De-Stalinization and the Hero Cult of Mao Tse-tung," *Orbis*, vol. IX, no. 2 (Summer 1965), pp. 472–93; Stuart R. Schram, "Mao Tse-tung as a Charismatic Leader," *Asian Survey*, vol. VII (June 1967), pp. 383–88; Stuart R. Schram, *The Political Thought of Mao Tse-tung* (New York: Praeger, 1963), pp. 315–18. For the Chinese official response to the problem of the cult of personality, see the *Jen-min Jih-pao* articles entitled "On the Historical Experience of the Dictatorship of the Proletariat." They were published on April 5 and December 29, 1956. Some excerpts of the Chinese official statement are: "Marxist-Leninists hold that leaders play a big role in history. . . . But when any leader of the Party or the state places himself over and above the Party and the masses instead of in their midst . . . he ceases to have an all-round, penetrating insight into the affairs of the state. . . ." "The cult of

personality is a foul carry-over from the long history of mankind [and] . . . even after a socialist society has been founded, certain rotten, poisonous ideological survivals may still remain in people's minds for a very long time. . . . We must therefore give unremitting attention to opposing elevation of oneself, individual heroism, and the cult of the individual." See Edgar Snow, *The Other Side of the River: Red China Today* (New York: Random House, 1962), pp. 334–39.

99. Yoon T. Kuark, "North Korea's Industrial Development During the Post-War Period," *The China Quarterly*, no. 14 (April–June, 1963), pp. 61–62; Lee, "Stalinism," p. 136.

100. *Nodong Shinmun*, October 28, 1963, and September 7, 1964.

101. Robert A. Scalapino, ed., *North Korea Today* (New York: Praeger, 1963), pp. 44–45.

Chapter 6

1. See Chong-Sik Lee, "North Korea Between Dogmatism and Revisionism," *Journal of Korean Affairs*, vol. 1 (April 1971), pp. 14–24.

2. William E. Griffith, *Sino-Soviet Relations, 1964–1965* (Cambridge: The M.I.T. Press, 1967), pp. 61–62.

3. *Pravda*, October 17, 1964, trans. in *Current Digest of the Soviet Press (CDSP)*, vol. XVI, no. 40 (October 28, 1964), pp. 3 and 6.

4. The CPSU Central Committee resolution that announced Khrushchev's "resignation" also reaffirmed the validity of the Twentieth Congress of the CPSU. Griffith, *Sino-Soviet Relations*, pp. 59–60.

5. *Pravda*, November 7, 1964, trans. in *CDSP*, vol. XVI, no. 43 (November 18, 1964), pp. 3–9.

6. Other Chinese delegates included Ho Lung, Kang Sheng, and Wu Hsiu-ch'uan.

7. "Why Krushchev Fell?" *Hung Ch'i*, November 21–22, 1964; *Peking Review*, vol. VII, no. 48 (November 27, 1964), pp. 6–9.

8. Although invitations were extended to them, the Communist parties of China, North Korea, North Vietnam, Rumania, Algeria, Indonesia, and Japan did not attend the meeting.

9. *Pravda*, March 27, 1965.

10. *Far Eastern Economic Review: 1967 Yearbook*, p. 282.

11. *Hung Ch'i* and *Jen-min Jih-pao*, November 11, 1965; *Peking Review*, vol. VII, no. 46 (November 12, 1965), pp. 1–5. On February 11, 1966, a *Hung Ch'i* article waged an identical attack against the new Soviet leaders. *Hung Ch'i*, February 11, 1966; *Peking Review*, vol. IX, no. 8 (February 18, 1966), pp. 6–12.

12. *NCNA,* April 9, 1965; *Jen-min Jih-pao,* November 11, 1965; Kevin Devlin, "Which Side Are You On?" *Problems of Communism,* vol. XVI, no. 1 (January–February 1967), p. 56.

13. North Korean radio broadcast, October 16, 1964.

14. *KCNA,* October 17, 1964.

15. *Far Eastern Economic Review: 1966 Yearbook,* p. 249.

16. "Strengthen the Unity of the International Communist Movement and Intensify the Revolutionary Struggle Against Imperialism," *Nodong Shinmun,* December 3, 1964; *Global Digest* (Hong Kong), vol. II, no. 5 (February 1965), pp. 68–70.

17. *Nodong Shinmun,* December 3, 1964.

18. Joseph C. Kun, "North Korea: Between Moscow and Peking," *The China Quarterly,* no. 31 (July–September 1967), pp. 49–50.

19. *Nodong Shinmun,* February 11, 1965.

20. *Pravda,* February 13, 1965, trans. in *CDSP,* vol. XVII, no. 7 (March 10, 1965), p. 6.

21. *Nodong Shinmun,* February 14, 1965.

22. Ibid., February 15, 1965; *Minju Chosŏn,* February 16, 1965; *Pravda,* February 15, 1965, trans. in *CDSP,* vol. XVII, no. 7 (March 10, 1965), pp. 7–8.

23. *Pravda,* February 15, 1965.

24. North Korean radio broadcast, February 14, 1965.

25. *KCNA,* February 14, 1965, cited in Kun, "North Korea," p. 52.

26. *Pravda,* February 27, 1965, trans. in *CDSP,* vol. XVII, no. 9 (March 24, 1965), p. 5.

27. Ibid.

28. *Nodong Shinmun,* February 15, July 6, and September 30, 1965.

29. *The Economist,* November 6, 1965, p. 600.

30. See pp. 99–100.

31. M. T. Haggard, "North Korea's International Position," *Asian Survey,* vol. V (August 1965), pp. 377–78.

32. *Chosen Shiryo,* vol. V, no. 9 (September 1965), pp. 5–10.

33. *Pravda,* August 14, 1965, trans. in *CDSP,* vol. XVII, no. 33 (September 8, 1965), p. 7.

34. *Nodong Shinmun,* August 10 and 13, 1965; *Pravda* and *Izvestia,* trans. in *CDSP,* vol. XVII, no. 32 (September 1, 1965), p. 17.

35. *KCNA,* August 13, 1965.

36. *Nodong Shinmun,* August 18, 1965; *Pravda,* August 18, 1965, trans. in *CDSP,* vol. XVII, no. 33 (September 8, 1965), pp. 7–8.

37. *Izvestia,* February 5, 1965, trans. in *CDSP,* vol. XVII, no. 5 (February 24, 1965), p. 17; *Pravda,* March 17, 1965, trans. in *CDSP,* vol.

XVII, no. 11 (April 9, 1965), pp. 21–22; ibid., June 25, 1965, trans. in *CDSP*, vol. XVII, no. 25 (July 14, 1965), pp. 19–20; *Izvestia*, July 6, 1965, trans. in *CDSP*, vol. XVII, no. 27 (July 28, 1965), pp. 22–23; *Pravda*, October 10, 1965, trans. in *CDSP*, vol. XVII, no. 41 (November 3, 1965), p. 23.

38. *Pravda*, September 30, 1965. As early as May 1965, a Soviet spokesman, Demichev, stated that "... the positions of our party and the positions of ... the Korean Workers' Party coincide or have come closer together." *Tass*, May 31, 1965, cited in Devlin, "Which Side Are You On?" p. 56.

39. *Nodong Shinmun*, December 31, 1964; "Premier Kim Il Sung's New Year's Message," *Korea News* (P'yŏngyang), January 1965, p. 4.

40. The complete cessation of Soviet military aid and growing tension in Asia probably forced the North Korean regime to concentrate on building up its own armament industry, thereby causing shortages of manpower and raw materials in other branches of industry. *Nodong Shinmun*, October 11, 1966; *Far Eastern Economic Review: 1967 Yearbook*, p. 283.

41. See pp. 97–98.

42. Concerned over possible repercussions in South Korea, Japan did nothing to promote trade with the North Korean regime, and in 1966 refused to let North Korean engineers enter Japan to negotiate purchase of machinery, at a time when North Korea was said to be showing increasing interest in purchases of sophisticated machinery and plants. *Far Eastern Economic Review: 1968 Yearbook*, p. 257.

43. Griffith, *Sino-Soviet Relations*, p. 78.

44. *Nodong Shinmun*, March 4, 1965.

45. Soon Sung Cho, "North Korea and the Sino-Soviet Rift" (paper presented at the Association for Asian Studies 1968 Conference at Philadelphia), p. 7.

46. Ernst Kux, "East Europe's Relations With Asian Communist Countries," in Kurt London, ed., *Eastern Europe in Transition* (Baltimore: Johns Hopkins University Press), p. 297.

47. *Pravda*, September 9, 1964; Glenn D. Paige, *The Korean People's Democratic Republic* (Stanford: The Hoover Institution, Stanford University, 1966), p. 41.

48. *International Affairs* (Moscow), August 1966, p. 77; *Izvestia*, February 24, 1965, trans. in *CDSP*, vol. XVII, no. 5 (February 24, 1965), p. 17; ibid., March 14, 1965, trans. in *CDSP*, vol. XVII, no. 11 (April 7, 1965), pp. 21–22.

49. Thomas An, "New Winds in P'yŏngyang?" *Problems of Com-*

munism, vol. XV, no. 4 (July–August 1966), p. 70; Carl Berger, *The Korean Knot: A Military-Political History*, rev. ed. (Philadelphia: University of Pennsylvania Press, 1964), p. 228.

50. Ryu Hun, *Study of North Korea* (Seoul: Research Institute of Internal and External Affairs, 1966), p. 147.

51. *Tass*, February 8, 1965.

52. The instruments of ratification were exchanged in Seoul on December 18, 1965. Kwan Bong Kim, *The Korea-Japan Treaty Crisis and the Instability of the Korean Political System* (New York: Praeger, 1971), pp. 40–41.

53. "Korean-Japanese Treaty and Plot of Organizing NEATO," *Nodong Shinmun*, October 2, 1965.

54. North Korean radio broadcast, June 24, 1965; *Nodong Shinmun*, June 23, 1964.

55. "Nobody's Little Brother," *The Economist*, vol. CCXVII, no. 6,376 (November 6, 1965), p. 600; *Tass*, May 31, 1965; *Nodong Shinmun*, June 2, 1965. A North Korean military delegation which had visited Moscow for V. E. Day anniversary celebrations (May 8, 1965) spent nearly a month in the Soviet Union. The delegation was led by Gen. Ch'oe Kwang, the chief of the North Korean general staff and deputy minister of defense, and included Col.-Gen. Kim Tae-hyŏn, the commander of the North Korean air force and antiaircraft defense and deputy minister of defense, and two other general officers. Kun, "North Korea," p. 51.

56. *Nodong Shinmun*, June 2, 1965; An, "New Winds in P'yŏngyang?" p. 70.

57. *New York Herald Tribune*, January 29, 1966.

58. Kun, "North Korea," p. 51.

59. *Nodong Shinmun*, December 3, 1964. See also *Nodong Shinmun*, September 30, 1965; Kim Il-sŏng, *Report on the Occasion of the 20th Anniversary of the Establishment of the Korean Workers' Party* (P'yŏngyang: Chosŏn Nodong-dang Ch'ulp'ansa, 1965), pp. 1–46.

60. *Nodong Shinmun*, December 3, 1964.

61. Cited in An, "New Winds in P'yŏngyang?" p. 68.

62. Wu Hsin-yu was deputy secretary-general of the Chinese National People's Congress Standing Committee. *Nodong Shinmun*, August 13, 1965; *KCNA*, August 14, 1965.

63. Griffith, *Sino-Soviet Relations*, p. 79.

64. *Nodong Shinmun*, August 15, 1965.

65. *Far Eastern Economic Review: 1966 Yearbook*, p. 249.

66. An, "New Winds in P'yŏngyang?" p. 68.

67. Douglas M. Johnston and Hungdah Chiu, eds., *Agreements of the*

People's Republic of China 1949–1967: A Calendar (Cambridge: Harvard University Press, 1968), p. 254.

68. Ibid.; *NCNA*, February 15, 1966. For a comparison with P'yŏng-yang's economic and military relations with Moscow particularly during 1966, see pp. 124–26.

69. *KNCA*, July 9, 1965; *Peking Review*, vol. IX, no. 29 (July 15, 1966), p. 30.

70. Joseph C. Kun, "Vietnamese, Korean Delegates Demonstrate Neutral Attitudes," *Radio Free Europe*, Munich, July 23, 1965, cited in Griffith, *Sino-Soviet Relations*, pp. 78–79.

71. *Nodong Shinmun* and *KCNA*, September 17, 1965; *KCNA*, September 28, 1965.

72. *KCNA*, April 19 and 22, 1965; *Nodong Shinmun*, April 22, 1965.

73. See p. 110.

74. *Nodong Shinmun*, December 6, 1965; Ryu, *North Korea*, p. 146.

75. Cited in Kux, "East Europe's Relations," pp. 300–01.

76. The congress was opened on March 29 and closed on April 8, 1966. Other members of the P'yŏngyang delegation were foreign minister and candidate member of the Politburo, Pak Sŏng-ch'ŏl, the director and deputy director of the KWP Central Committee's international affairs department, Hŏ Sŏk-sŏn and Kim U-ch'ang, and the North Korean ambassador to Moscow, Kim Pyŏng-jik, Kun, "North Korea," p. 54.

77. Hanoi sent a high-ranking delegation to the congress, but the Communist parties of Japan, Albania, and New Zealand, along with the Chinese-dominated parties of Burma, Malaya and Thailand, followed Peking's lead in boycottting the congress. *The New York Times*, March 26, 1966, pp. 1 and 8.

78. *Nodong Shinmun*, April 2, 1966; North Korean radio broadcast, April 1, 1966; *Tass*, international service in English, April 1, 1966.

79. *Pravda* and *Izvestia*, March 30, 1966, trans. in *CDSP*, vol. XVIII, no. 12, Part I (April 30, 1966), pp. 6–7.

80. *CDSP*, vol. XVIII, no. 45 (November 30, 1966), pp. 3–8.

81. *Izvestia*, March 17, 1966, trans. in *CDSP*, vol. XVIII, no. 11 (April 6, 1966), p. 19; *Pravda*, July 6, 1966, trans. in *CDSP*, vol. XVIII, no. 27 (July 27, 1966), p. 19.

82. *KCNA*, March 22, 1966.

83. The North Korean delegations attended the following party congresses during 1966: Thirteenth Congress of the Czechoslovakian Communist Party, May 31–June 4; Fifteenth Congress of the Mongolian People's Revolutionary Party, June 7–11; Fifth Congress of the Albanian Workers' Party, November 1–8; Ninth Congress of the Bulgarian

Communist Party, November 14–19; and Ninth Congress of the Hungarian Socialist Workers' Party, November 28–December 3. Kun, "North Korea," p. 53.

84. The Soviet consumer goods fair was held from March 13 to April 6, 1966. At the end of the fair, the main exhibits and amounts were presented to North Korea. *KCNA,* March 16, 1966.

85. *KCNA,* June 22, 1966; *Far Eastern Economic Review: 1967 Yearbook,* p. 283; *Nodong Shinmun,* November 8, 1966.

86. *Far Eastern Economic Review: 1967 Yearbook,* p. 283; D. Usatov, "In the Interests of Peace and Socialism," *International Affairs* (Moscow), August 1966, pp. 76–77.

87. *Nodong Shinmun,* December 13, 1966; Byung Chul Koh, *The Foreign Policy of North Korea* (New York: Praeger, 1969), p. 99. Hereinafter referred to as *Foreign Policy.*

88. Cho, "Sino-Soviet Rift," p. 36.

89. *Izvestia,* February 16, 1967, trans. in *CDSP,* vol. XIX, no. 7 (March 8, 1967), p. 21; ibid., March 4, 1967, trans. in *CDSP,* vol. XIX, no. 9 (March 22, 1967), pp. 15–16; *Pravda,* March 6, 1967; *Nodong Shinmun,* March 4 and 6, 1967.

90. *Minju Chosŏn* (Democratic Korea), May 23, 1967, cited in Koh, *Foreign Policy,* p. 99.

91. *KCNA,* October 17, 1967.

92. *Pravda,* October 23, 1967 and *Izvestia,* October 24, 1967, trans. in *CDSP,* vol. XIX, no. 43 (November 15, 1967), p. 27.

93. Ibid., p. 28.

94. Ibid., p. 27.

95. *The New York Times,* October 29, 1967; Koh, *Foreign Policy,* p. 101.

96. Koh, *Foreign Policy,* p. 101; *Dong-A Ilbo,* October 3 and November 4, 1967.

97. *The New York Times,* February 1, 1968, p. 15.

98. Robert R. Simmons, "China's Cautious Relations with North Korea and Indochina," *Asian Survey,* vol. XI (July 1971), p. 633; *The New York Times,* January 26, 27, and 30, 1968; Jan Sejna, "Russia Plotted the Pueblo Affair," *Reader's Digest* (July 1969), pp. 73–76.

99. *Nodong Shinmun,* August 22 and 23, 1968; *Peking Review,* no. 37 (September 13, 1968), p. 31; ibid., no. 44 (November 1, 1968), pp. 17–18; B. C. Koh, "North Korea and the Sino-Soviet Schism," *The Western Political Quarterly,* vol. XXII, no. 4 (December 1969) p. 960.

100. *NCNA,* April 1, 1966; Kevin Devlin, "Ten Years that Shook the

World," *Problems of Communism*, vol. XV, no. 5 (September–October 1966), p. 55.

101. *The New York Times*, January 24, 1968, p. 15.

102. Ibid., August 13, 1966, p. 2; *Nodong Shinmun*, August 12, 1966.

103. *Nodong Shinmun*, August 12, 1966. This *Nodong Shinmun* editorial also criticized revisionism.

104. Ibid.

105. Ibid.

106. The fourteenth plenum following the party conference abolished the rank of chairmanship of the party. Instead, it established a Presidium within the Politburo, and set up an all-member secretariat. Kim Il-sŏng became secretary general. At the same time, a number of ministerial changes were made, which apparently aimed at strengthening Kim Il-sŏng's position and eliminating pro-Chinese men from the party and the government. On October 18, it was announced that Kim Ch'ang-bong, minister of defense, and Pak Sŏng-ch'ŏl, minister of foreign affairs, had been named vice-premiers and appointed to the party's Politburo. *Far Eastern Economic Review: 1967 Yearbook*, p. 282; Kun, "North Korea," p. 57.

107. Kim Ch'ang-man was one of the Korean Communists who spent some time in Yenan, China, during the early 1940s and returned to Korea at the end of 1945 under the leadership of Kim Tu-bong who had been purged in 1958 by Kim Il-sŏng. See Chong-Sik Lee and Ki-Wan Oh, "The Russian Faction in North Korea," *Asian Survey*, vol. VIII (April 1968), p. 278.

108. *Pravda*, September 17, 1966, trans. in *CDSP*, vol. XVIII, no. 38 (October 13, 1966), p. 25.

109. *Nodong Shinmun*, September 15, 1966.

110. Ibid. As early as October 1959, Khrushchev, though not explicitly naming the Chinese leadership, made a highly unusual reference to Trotsky's "adventuristic policy" expressed in the "notorious slogan of 'neither peace nor war.'" *Pravda*, November 1, 1959, cited in Donald S. Zagoria, "Strains in the Sino-Soviet Alliance," *Problems of Communism*, vol. IX, no. 3 (May–June 1960,) p. 1.

111. *Nodong Shinmun*, September 15, 1966.

112. Ibid., October 6, 1966; *KCNA*, October 5, 1966. The condensed text of Kim's speech was carried by *Pravda* under the title of "Kim Il-sŏng asserts Independence," October 8, 1966, trans. in *CDSP*, vol. XVIII, no. 40 (October 26, 1966), p. 16.

113. *KCNA,* October 5, 1966.

114. Ibid., April 9, 1966.

115. Republic of Korea, Ministry of Public Information, *Intensified Aggression in Korea: A Report on Armed Infiltrators Sent by Communists in the North, 1968* (Seoul), p. 33.

116. *Dong-A Ilbo,* February 21, 23, and 27, 1967; *Far Eastern Economic Review: 1968 Yearbook,* p. 255.

117. *KCNA,* October 27, 1967.

118. Simmons, "China's Cautious Relations," pp. 633–34; *Dong-A Ilbo,* May 29, 1969.

119. For an excellent discussion on the subject, see Chong-Sik Lee, "North Korea Between Dogmatism and Revisionism," *Journal of Korean Affairs,* vol. 1 (April 1971), pp. 14–24.

120. *The New York Times,* February 23 and 27, 1968.

121. *Nodong Shinmun,* December 3, 1964. See also note 118, above.

122. *KCNA,* April 19, 1965.

123. *Nodong Shinmun,* October 11, 1965; *Far Eastern Economic Review: 1966 Yearbook,* p. 249.

124. *Nodong Shinmun,* August 12, 1966.

125. Ibid.

126. Ibid.

127. Ibid., October 6, 1966.

128. Cho, "Sino-Soviet Rift," p. 38; Lee and Oh, "Russian Faction," p. 278.

129. *Nodong Shinmun,* December 17, 1967; *The People's Korea* (Tokyo, published in English), January 17, 1968, p. 2.

130. *The New York Times,* January 25, 1968, p. 14.

131. Koh, *Foreign Policy,* p. 102.

Chapter 7

1. Ralph N. Clough, *East Asia and U.S. Security* (Washington: The Brookings Institution, 1975), pp. 2–5; Richard Nixon, *U.S. Foreign Policy for the 1970's: A New Strategy for Peace* (Washington: U.S. Government Printing Office, 1970), pp. 53–61.

2. *The New York Times,* November 22, 1969, pp. 1 and 14; *United States Foreign Policy, 1969–1970* (Washington, D.C.: U.S. Government Printing Office, 1971), pp. 503–05.

3. Cited in Kwan Ha Yim, "Korea in Japanese Foreign Policy," (Paper presented at the 1973 Annual Meeting of the American Political Science Association at New Orleans), pp. 10–11.

4. *The New York Times,* August 10, 1971.

5. Cited in Chong-Sik Lee, "North Korea Between Dogmatism and Revisionism," *Journal of Korean Affairs,* vol. 1 (April 1971), p. 23; Robert R. Simmons, "China's Cautious Relations with North Korea and Indochina," *Asian Survey,* vol. XI (July 1971), p. 630.

6. *Nodong Shinmun,* November 3, 1970; *The New York Times,* November 8, 1970, p. 5.

7. "North Korean Leader Visits Peking," *Radio Free Europe Research,* October 2, 1969, pp. 1–2; *The New York Times,* April 5, 1970.

8. *Dong-A Ilbo,* April 8 and 9, 1970; *The New York Times,* April 7 and 8, 1970; *Far Eastern Economic Review,* April 11, 1970, pp. 33–34.

9. *NCNA,* January 30, 1970; *Dong-A Ilbo,* March 15, 1970.

10. *The New York Times,* November 23, 1970.

11. *Peking Review,* vol. 13, no. 27 (July 3, 1970), p. 60. The entire July 3rd issue of *Peking Review* was devoted to the coverage of the twentieth anniversary of the outbreak of the Korean Conflict.

12. *The New York Times,* June 26, 1970, p. 9; *Peking Review,* vol. 13, no. 27 (July 3, 1970), p. 9.

13. *Peking Review,* vol. 13, no. 30 (September 30, 1970), p. 27; ibid., vol. 13, no. 50 (December 18, 1970), p. 23; *Dong-A Ilbo,* October 19, 1970.

14. *The New York Times,* April 16 and May 15, 1969; *Pravda,* April 18, p. 5, trans. in *CDSP,* vol. XXI, no. 16 (May 7, 1969), p. 8. See also B. C. Koh, "Dilemmas of Korean Reunification," *Asian Survey,* vol. XI (May 1971), p. 486.

15. *The New York Times,* May 11, 1969, p. 8; ibid., May 20, 1969, p. 18; *Dong-A Ilbo,* May 20, 1969; *Pravda,* May 17, 1969, trans. in *CDSP,* vol. XXI, no. 20 (June 4, 1969), pp. 7–9.

16. *The New York Times,* May 8, 1970, p. 2; ibid., June 30, 1970, p. 22.

17. *KCNA,* P'yŏngyang, March 7, 1970; "North Korea Leaves Joint Soviet-Korean Oceanographic Project," *Radio Free Europe Research,* March 14, 1970, pp. 1–3.

18. *The New York Times,* November 8, 1970; Lee, "Dogmatism and Revisionism," p. 23.

19. *The Christian Science Monitor,* May 7, 1970, pp. 1 and 4; *Dong-A Ilbo,* May 8, 1970.

20. Koh, "Korean Reunification," p. 487.

21. *Dong-A Ilbo,* April 24, 1970.

22. *The New York Times,* August 11, 1971, p. 5.

23. Robert Simmons, "North Korea: Year of the Thaw," *Asian Survey,* vol. XII (January 1972), p. 31.

24. Ibid., pp. 30–31; *Dong-A Ilbo,* July 12, 1971.

25. *Dong-A Ilbo,* July 12, 1971.

26. Ibid., July 8, 1971; *The New York Times,* July 10, 1971; Harold Hinton, "Chinese Policy Toward Korea," in Young C. Kim, ed., *Major Powers and Korea* (Silver Spring, Md.: Research Institute on Korean Affairs, 1973), p. 25.

27. *Jen-min Jih-pao,* July 11, 1971.

28. *The New York Times,* September 2, 1971, p. 2.

29. *Dong-A Ilbo,* October 11, 1971; Roy U. T. Kim, "North Korea's Relations with the Soviet Union and the PRC," in Young C. Kim, ed., *Foreign Policies of Korea* (Washington: Institute for Asian Studies, 1973), p. 106.

30. *Dong-A Ilbo,* September 9 and October 11, 1971; *The New York Times,* March 5, 1972.

31. *The Washington Post,* October 6, 1971; *The New York Times,* September 27, 1971; *Dong-A Ilbo,* October 11, 1971.

32. *The Christian Science Monitor,* December 16, 1971; *Dong-A Ilbo,* December 17, 1971.

33. *The New York Times,* February 27, 1972, p. 31; *Dong-A Ilbo,* February 22, 1972.

34. Ibid.

35. Kim, "North Korea's Relations," p. 109.

36. D. Matvevev, "Soviet-Korean Consultative Commission," *International Affairs* (Moscow), December, 1972, p. 117.

37. *Radio Free Europe Research,* September 11, 1972, pp. 1–2.

Chapter 8

1. *Dong-A Ilbo,* February 12, 1973.

2. Ibid., May 29, 1974.

3. Beginning in May 1972, high officials of South and North Korea exchanged unprecedented visits between P'yŏngyang and Seoul, and issued the joint communiqué of July 4, 1972. The communiqué announced basic agreements on a number of important principles concerning Korean reunification. Despite the earlier expectations, the South-North dialogue soon resulted in complete stalemate. For further discussion, see Chong-Sik Lee, "The Impact of the Sino-American Détente on Korea," in Gene T. Hsiao, ed., *Sino-American Détente* (New York: Praeger, 1974), pp. 189–206.

4. *Peking Review,* vol. 16, no. 26 (June 29, 1973), p. 16; ibid., vol. 17, no. 4 (April 5, 1974), p. 25; *Jen-min Jih-pao,* September 9, 1975. The five-point program includes: (1) stopping arms reinforcement and the arms race; (2) reducing the military strength of the North and South to 100,000 men or less; (3) stopping the introduction of all weapons and war materials from foreign countries; (4) withdrawing the U.S. and other foreign troops from Korea; and (5) concluding a peace agreement guaranteeing that the above proposals would be fulfilled and that the North and South would not use military forces against each other. For an excellent analysis on the subject, see B. C. Koh, "North Korea: Old Goals and New Realities," *Asian Survey,* vol. XIV (January 1974), pp. 36–39.

5. *The Korea Herald,* July 11, 1975.

6. *The Pyongyang Times,* October 4, 1975.

7. For the English text, see *Peking Review,* vol. 37, no. 31 (September 13, 1974), p. 7.

8. *Jen-min Jih-pao,* September 9, 1975.

9. For a detailed discussion on North Korea's economic problems, see pp. 115–16 and 155–56.

10. *Peking Review,* vol. 16, no. 25 (June 22, 1973), p. 3.

11. *Journal of Korean Affairs,* vol. IV, no. 4 (January 1975), p. 51.

12. Ibid., p. 54.

13. David Rees, "North Korea: Undermining the Truce," *Conflict Studies,* no. 69 (March 1976), p. 12; *The Washington Post,* December 21, 1975, p. 2; *Barron's,* vol. LVI, no. 9 (March 1, 1976), p. 4.

14. *The People's Korea,* January 21, 1976; *The Korea Herald,* January 9, 1976.

15. North Korea also signed new agreements with North Vietnam, Mongolia, Poland, Czechoslovakia, and Hungary. *The New York Times,* February 26, 1976, p. 43 and 47; Rees, "North Korea: Undermining the Truce," p. 12.

16. *The Korea Herald,* June 20, 1975.

17. *The Washington Post,* April 19, 1975, p. 16.

18. *Peking Review,* vol. 18, no. 17 (April 25, 1975), pp. 6–17; *Dong-A Ilbo,* April 18, 1975; *The Pyongyang Times,* April 26 and May 3, 1975.

19. On November 18, 1975, the U.N. General Assembly adopted two contradictory resolutions on Korea, one supported by South Korea and the other by North Korea. See *The New York Times,* November 19, 1975, p. 7.

20. For a detailed discussion on Kim Il-sŏng's tour to East Europe and Africa which included stops in Rumania, Algeria, Mauritania, Bulgaria,

and Yugoslavia, see Robert R. King, "Kim Il Song Visit Highlights Differences Among Balkan Communist States," *Radio Free Europe Research*, June 12, 1975, pp. 1–7; "Kim Il Song in Rumania," ibid., June 6, 1975, pp. 1–14; *The Pyongyang Times*, May 31, June 7, and June 14, 1975.

21. *Dong-A Ilbo*, April 17, 1975; *The New York Times*, April 29, 1975, p. 5; *Barron's*, vol. LV, no. 20 (May 19, 1975), p. 27.

22. *The Korea Herald*, June 20, 1975.

23. For the text of Kim Il-sŏng's speech, see *The Pyongyang Times*, April 26, 1975.

24. *Peking Review*, vol. 18, no. 17 (April 25, 1975), pp. 11–14.

25. "Not now, Mr. Kim," *The Economist*, vol. 255, no. 6874 (May 24, 1975), pp. 12–13; *The Korea Herald*, December 19, 1975; Young C. Kim, "The Democratic People's Republic of Korea in 1975," *Asian Survey*, vol. XVI (January 1976), p. 84.

26. Peking's statement on the Korean unification in the joint communiqué reads: "The Chinese side reaffirms its resolute support to the Korean people in their just struggle for the independent and peaceful reunification of their fatherland." For the text of the communiqué, see *The Pyongyang Times*, May 3, 1975.

27. *Pravda*, December 23, 1972, trans. in *CDSP*, vol. XXIV, no. 51 (January 17, 1973), p. 2.

28. Ibid., March 1, 1973, trans. in *CDSP*, vol. XXV, no. 9 (March 28, 1973), p. 23.

29. *Tass*, February 5, 1975, in *Daily Report*, Foreign Broadcast Information Service, May 16, 1973.

30. V. Tikhomirov, "People's Korea: 30 Years," *International Affairs* (Moscow), September, 1975, p. 53.

31. *Pravda*, June 22, 1974, trans. in *CDSP*, vol. XXVI, no. 25, (July 17, 1974), p. 10.

32. *Journal of Korean Affairs*, vol. IV, no. 3 (October 1974) p. 43.

33. Ibid., p. 44.

34. Ibid., vol. IV, no. 4 (January 1975), p. 49.

35. *The Korea Herald*, July 13, 1975.

36. For other possible reasons for the Soviet refusal to receive Kim Il-sŏng, see Kim, "Democratic People's Republic of Korea in 1975," pp. 85–86; *The Korea Herald*, June 24, 1975.

37. King, "Kim Il Song Visit," pp. 2–3.

38. *The New York Times*, February 26, 1976, pp. 43 and 47; *The Korea Herald*, February 21 and 27, 1976.

39. For the full text, see *Dong-A Ilbo*, August 15, 1971.

40. *Radio Free Europe Research*, September 15, 1971.

41. *Peking Review,* Vol. 16, No. 34 (August 24, 1973), p. 20; *Dong-A Ilbo,* August 16, 1973.

42. Donald S. Zagoria and Young Kun Kim, "North Korea and the Major Powers," *Asian Survey,* vol. XV (December 1975), p. 1031.

43. *Far Eastern Economic Review,* vol. 81, no. 32 (August 13, 1973), p. 5.

44. *Dong-A Ilbo,* August 29, 31, and September 11, 1974.

45. Kim Sam-o, "Brezhnev Plays a 'Middleman' Role," *Far Eastern Economic Review,* vol. 82, no. 51 (December 24, 1973), p. 18.

46. *Dong-A Ilbo,* July 26, 1974.

47. Ibid., October 19, 1974.

48. Ibid., March 27, 1974. According to a Soviet source, China had agreed to sell about 1,000 tons of red peppers to the South Koreans. See *The Washington Post,* November 12, 1974, p. 14.

49. *Dong-A Ilbo,* September 9, 1975.

50. *Pravda,* November 24, 1974, trans. in *CDSP,* vol. XXVI, no. 47 (December 31, 1974), p. 18. Peking also claimed that the Soviet Union had low-level contacts with the South Korean government and individual South Koreans. See *The Washington Post,* November 12, 1974, p. 14.

51. Robert A. Scalapino, *Asia and the Road Ahead* (Berkeley: University of California Press, 1975), p. 176.

52. All five Soviet Siberian projects would probably require more than $7 billion in Japanese credits and equipments. *The New York Times,* April 23, 1974, pp. 1 and 61; *Pravda,* April 22, 1974, trans. in *CDSP.* vol. XXVI, no. 16 (May 15, 1974), p. 23; E. Karashchuk, "Japan's Policy in Asia," *International Affairs* (Moscow), October 1974, p. 85.

53. For an excellent analysis of the subject, see Scalapino, *Asia and the Road Ahead,* pp. 172–78.

54. *The Washington Post,* December 21, 1975, p. 2.

55. Ibid., September 11, 1975, p. 14; *Dong-A Ilbo,* September 12, 1975.

56. *The New York Times,* February 23, 1974, p. 3.

57. *The Military Balance 1975–1976* (London: The International Institute for Strategic Studies, 1975), p. 56; *Dong-A Ilbo,* June 8, 1974; *The New York Times,* February 23, 1974, p. 3.

58. *Ashai Sinbun,* March 27 and 29, 1974; *Dong-A Ilbo,* March 27, 28, and 29, 1974.

59. *Dong-A Ilbo,* March 29, 1974; *The New York Times,* February 26, 1976, pp. 43 and 47. Despite obvious evidence to the contrary, North Korea claimed that the Six-Year Plan was completed ahead of schedule. For the full text of the North Korean report on the Economic Plan, see *The People's Korea,* October 1, 1975.

60. *The Korea Herald*, February 28, 1976; *The New York Times*, February 26, 1976, pp. 43 and 47; Susumu Awanohara, "North Korea: Deeper in debt," *Far Eastern Economic Review*, vol. 88, no. 23 (June 6, 1975), p. 52. One Japanese source estimated P'yŏngyang's outstanding debt at $1.3 billion, with $550 million due to non-Communist nations and the rest owed to Communist countries.

61. Awanohara, "North Korea: Deeper in debt," p. 52.

62. *The Washington Post*, December 21, 1975, p. 2. For North Korean trade with Japan, see Table 4, at p. 96.

63. Ibid.

64. *Barron's*, May 19, 1975, p. 27; *Dong-A Ilbo*, March 10, April 23, June 24, and June 27, 1975. Yet, according to the Pentagon estimate, P'yŏngyang granted $44 million in military aid in 1975 to several African nations. Furthermore, North Korea used $75 million worth of mining and other equipments to dig the tunnels under the DMZ for clearly aggressive purposes against South Korea, at a time when P'yŏngyang was talking of coexistence with Seoul. See *Barron's*, vol. LV, no. 15 (April 12, 1976), p. 4; Rees, "North Korea: Undermining the Truce," p. 9; *The Washington Post*, February 23, 1976, p. C18.

65. Joseph Sang-hoon Chung, *The North Korean Economy: Structure and Development* (Stanford: Hoover Institution Press, 1974), pp. 112–13.

66. Tikhomirov, "People's Korea: 30 Years," pp. 52–53; *International Affairs* (Moscow), December 1972, p. 117.

67. M. Trigubenko, "The Steady Advance of People's Korea," *International Affairs* (Moscow), September 1974, p. 136.

68. Professor Donald Hellmann relates the security of the ROK to that of Japan in the following words: " . . . a military conflict [in Korea] would compel China, the Soviet Union, and the United States to lay their strategic cards on the table in ways that directly touch Japan. Whatever the specific scenario might be, Korea, more than any single issue, has the potential to provoke a major change in the direction of Japanese defense policy—to be the proximate cause for a full Japanese plunge into international politics." Donald C. Hellmann, *Japan and East Asia: The New International Order* (New York: Praeger, 1972), p. 179.

69. Robert A. Scalapino, "China and the Balance of Power," *Foreign Affairs*, vol. 52, no. 2 (January 1974), p. 357.

70. See Jack Anderson and Les Whitten, "Chinese Urge U.S. to Stay in Korea," *The Washington Post*, February 28, 1976, p. B6; Young C. Kim, "North Korea in 1974," *Asian Survey*, vol. XV (January 1975), pp. 43–44.

71. *Dong-A Ilbo*, November 21, 1973; Harold C. Hinton, "East Asia,"

in Kurt L. London, ed., *The Soviet Impact on World Politics* (New York: Hawthorn, 1974), p. 136.

72. For examples, see Chiao Kuan-hua's speeches at the U.N. General Assembly on October 2, 1974 and September 26, 1975. *The New York Times*, October 3, 1974, p. 5; *The Washington Post*, September 27, 1975, p. 16.

73. *Dong-A Ilbo*, August 31 and September 17, 1974; Pyong-choon Hahm, "Korea and the Emerging Asian Power Balance," *Foreign Affairs*, vol. 50, no. 2 (January 1972), p. 348.

BIBLIOGRAPHY

I. OFFICIAL AND SEMI-OFFICIAL PUBLICATIONS

A. Communist China

People's Republic of China. *People's Communes in China.* Peking: Foreign Languages Press, 1958.
———. *The Sino-Indian Boundary Question.* Peking: Foreign Languages Press, 1962.
———. *The Polemics of the General Line of the International Communist Movement.* Peking: Foreign Languages Press, 1965.

B. North Korea

Chosŏn Chungang T'ongsinsa ([North] Korean Central News Agency). *Chosŏn chungang nyŏngam* ([North] Korean Yearbook), 1956–1965.
Chosŏn Nodong-dang Chungang Wiwon-hoe, Dang Yŏksa Yŏnguso. *Chosŏn Nodong-dang yŏksa kyojae* (Textbook of the History of the Korean Workers' Party). P'yŏngyang: Chosŏn Nodong-dang Ch'ulp'ansa, 1964.
Democratic People's Republic of Korea. *Postwar Rehabilitation and Development of the National Economy in the Democratic People's Republic of Korea.* P'yŏngyang: Foreign Languages Publishing House, 1957.
———. *For the Peaceful Unification of the Country: Documents on the Sixth Session of the Second Supreme People's Assembly of the Democratic People's Republic of Korea.* P'yŏngyang: Foreign Languages Publishing House, 1959.
———. *History of the Just Fatherland War.* P'yŏngyang: Foreign Languages Publishing House, 1961.
———. Center for Historical Studies. *Chosŏn t'ongsa* (Outline History of Korea). P'yŏngyang: Nodong Shinmunsa, 1958. Reprinted by Hak-u Sŏbang in Tokyo, 1959.
Documents and Materials of the Third Congress of the Workers' Party of Korea: April 23–29, 1956. P'yŏngyang: Foreign Languages Publishing House, 1957.
Documents of the Fourth Congress of the Workers' Party of Korea. P'yŏngyang: Foreign Languages Publishing House, 1961.
Facts About Korea. P'yŏngyang: Foreign Languages Publishing House, 1961.

Kim Il-sŏng. *All for the Postwar Rehabilitation and Development of the National Economy.* P'yŏngyang: New Korea Press, 1954.

_____. *On Eliminating Dogmatism and Formalism and Establishing Jooche in Ideological Work.* P'yŏngyang: Foreign Languages Publishing House, 1964.

_____. *Kim Il-sŏng sŏnjip* (Selected Works of Kim Il-sŏng). 6 vols. P'yŏngyang: Chosŏn Nodong-dang Ch'ulp'ansa, 1960–1966.

_____. *Selected Works.* 5 vols. P'yŏngyang: Foreign Languages Publishing House, 1971–1972.

Kim, Suk Hyung; Kim, Heui Il; and Son, Yung Jong. *On the Grave Errors in the Descriptions on Korea of the 'World History' Edited by the U.S.S.R. Academy of Sciences.* P'yŏngyang: Foreign Languages Publishing House, 1963.

Kukka Kyehoek Wiwon-hoe, Chungang T'onggyeguk. *Chosŏn Minju Chuui Inmin Konghwaguk inmin kyŏngje palchŏn t'onggye* (Statistical Survey of the Economic Development in the Democratic People's Republic of Korea). P'yŏngyang: Kukrip Ch'ulp'ansa, 1961.

Taijung chŏngch'i yongŏ sajŏn (General Dictionary of Political Terms). P'yŏngyang: Chosŏn Nodong-dang Ch'ulp'ansa, 1964.

C. South Korea

Kongbobu (Ministry of Public Information). *Hyŏndaesa wa kongsan chuui: Hanguk'e issūsūui kongsan chuui* (Modern History of Communism in Korea). Seoul, 1968.

Ministry of Culture and Information. *Korean Unification: A Shared Responsibility.* Seoul, 1968.

Ministry of Public Information. *Intensified Aggression in Korea: A Report on Armed Infiltrators Sent by Communists in the North.* Seoul, 1968.

Oemubu (Ministry of Foreign Affairs). *Hanguk t'ong'il munje: yŏksawa munhŏn, 1943–1960.* (Problems of Korean Unification: History and Documents, 1943–1960). Seoul, Korea.

D. The United States

Nixon, Richard. *U.S. Foreign Policy for the 1970's: A Strategy for Peace.* Washington, D.C.: U.S. Government Printing Office, 1970.

U.S. Congress. House. Committee on Foreign Affairs. *Sino-Soviet Conflict.* Hearings before the subcommittee on the Far East and the Pacific, House of Representatives on H.R. 84, 89th Cong., 1st Sess., 1965.

U.S. Department of the Army. *U.S. Army Area Handbook for Korea*. Department of the Army Pamphlet no. 550–41. Washington, D.C.: U.S. Government Printing Office, 1964.

————. *U.S. Army Area Handbook for North Korea*. Washington, D.C.: U.S. Government Printing Office, 1969.

U.S. Department of Commerce, Clearinghouse for Federal Scientific and Technical Information, Joint Publications Research Service. *Economic Report on North Korea*. 1964–1966.

U.S. Department of State. *North Korea: A Case Study in the Techniques of Takeover*. Department of State Publication no. 7118, Far Eastern Series no. 103. Washington, D.C.: U.S. Government Printing Office, 1961.

————. Bureau of Intelligence and Research. *World Strength of the Communist Party Organizations*. Washington, D.C.: U.S. Government Printing Office, 1973.

E. Others

Government of India. Ministry of Information and Broadcasting. *The Chinese Threat*. New Delhi, 1963.

Second Asian Economic Seminar: P'yŏngyang. 2 vols. Colombo: The Asian Economic Bureau, 1964.

The Road to Communism: Documents of the 22nd Congress of the Communist Party of the Soviet Union, October 17–31, 1961. Moscow: Foreign Languages Publishing House, 1961.

United Nations. *Yearbook of International Trade Statistics, 1966–1974*.

II. BOOKS

Berger, Carl. *The Korean Knot: A Military-Political History*. rev. ed. Philadelphia: University of Pennsylvania Press, 1964.

Boorman, Howard, et al. *Moscow-Peking Axis*. New York: Harper and Brothers, 1957.

Boyd, R. G. *Communist China's Foreign Policy*. New York: Frederick A. Praeger, 1962.

Brzezinski, Zbigniew. *The Soviet Bloc: Unity and Conflict*. rev. and enl. ed. Cambridge: Harvard University Press, 1967.

Burchett, Wilfred G. *Again Korea*. New York: International Publishers, 1968.

Ch'eng, Chu-yuan. *Communist China's Economy, 1949–1962: Structural Changes and Crisis*. South Orange, N.J.: Seton-Hall, 1963.

_____. *Economic Relations Between Peking and Moscow, 1949–1963.* New York: Frederick A. Praeger, 1964.

Cho, Soon Sung. *Korea in World Politics, 1940–1950.* Berkeley: University of California Press, 1967.

Chung, Joseph Sang-hoon. *The North Korean Economy: Structure and Development.* Stanford: Hoover Institution Press, 1974.

_____, ed. *Patterns of Economic Development: Korea.* Kalamazoo, Michigan: Korean Research and Publication, Inc., 1966.

Clough, Ralph N. *East Asia and U.S. Security.* Washington: The Brookings Institution, 1975.

Crankshaw, Edward. *The New Cold War: Moscow and Pekin[g].* Harmondsworth, England: Penguin Books, 1963.

Dallin, Alexander, et al., eds. *Diversity in International Communism: A Documentary Record, 1961–1963.* New York: Columbia University Press, 1963.

Dallin, David J. *Soviet Russia and the Far East.* New Haven: Yale University Press, 1948.

Documents on Sino-Soviet Ideological Disputes. Seoul: Internal and External Research Institute, 1963.

Doolin, Dennis J. *Territorial Claims in the Sino-Soviet Conflict: Documents and Analysis.* Stanford: The Hoover Institute on War, Revolution and Peace, Stanford University Press, 1965.

Eckstein, Alexander. *Communist China's Economic Growth and Foreign Trade: Implications for U.S. Policy.* New York: McGraw-Hill, 1966.

Floyd, David. *Mao Against Khrushchev: A Short History of the Sino-Soviet Conflict.* New York: Frederick A. Praeger, 1964.

Garthoff, Raymond L., ed. *Sino-Soviet Military Relation.* New York: Frederick A. Praeger, 1966.

George, Alexander L. *The Chinese Communist Army in Action: The Korean War and Its Aftermath.* New York: Columbia University Press, 1967.

Griffith, William E. *Albania and the Sino-Soviet Rift.* Cambridge: The M.I.T. Press, 1963.

_____. *The Sino-Soviet Rift: Analyzed and Documented.* Cambridge: The M.I.T. Press, 1964.

_____. *World Communism Divided.* New York: Foreign Policy Associations, 1964.

_____. "Revisionism in East Europe," in Alvin Z. Rubinstein, ed. *Communist Political System.* Englewood Cliffs, N.J.: Prentice-Hall, 1966.

_____. *Sino-Soviet Relations, 1964–1965.* Cambridge: The M.I.T. Press, 1967.

Grzybowski, Kazimierz. *The Socialist Commonwealth of Nations: Organizations and Institutions.* New Haven: Yale University Press, 1964.

Han, Tae-su. *Hankuk jŏngdangsa* (The History of Korean Political Parties). Seoul: Shint'aeyangsa, 1961.

Hellmann, Donald C. *Japan and East Asia: The New International Order.* New York: Frederick A. Praeger, 1972.

Hinton, Harold C. *Communist China in World Politics.* Boston: Houghton Mifflin Co., 1966.

Honey, P. J. *Communism in North Vietnam: Its Role in the Sino-Soviet Dispute.* Cambridge: The M.I.T. Press, 1963.

Hudson, G. F., et al. *The Sino-Soviet Dispute.* New York: Frederick A. Praeger, 1961.

Ionescu, Ghita. *The Break-Up of the Soviet Empire in Eastern Europe.* Baltimore: Penguin Books, 1965.

Johnston, Douglas M., and Chiu, Hungdah, eds. *Agreements of the People's Republic of China, 1949-1967: A Calendar.* Cambridge: Harvard University Press, 1968.

Kautsky, John H. *Political Change in Underdeveloped Countries: Nationalism and Communism.* New York: John Wiley and Sons, 1962.

Khrushchev, Nikita S. *For Victory in Peaceful Competition with Capitalism.* New York: E.P. Dutton and Co., 1960.

Kim, Ch'ang-sun. *Pukhan siponyŏn sa* (Fifteen-Year History of North Korea). Seoul: Chimungak, 1961.

Kim, Chun-yŏp, and Kim, Ch'ang-sun. *Hanguk kongsan chuui undongsa* (History of Korean Communist Movement). Seoul: Center for Asian Studies, Korea University Press, 1967.

Kim, Ilpyong J. *Communist Politics in North Korea.* New York: Frederick A. Praeger, 1975.

Kim, Kwan Bong. *The Korea-Japan Treaty Crisis and the Instability of the Korean Political System.* New York: Frederic A. Praeger, 1971.

Kim, Se-Jin, and Cho, Chang-Hyun, eds. *Government and Politics of Korea.* Silver Spring, Md.: The Research Institute on Korean Affairs, 1972.

————, eds. *Korea: A Divided Nation.* Silver Spring, Md.: The Research Institute on Korean Affairs, 1976.

Kim, Young C., ed. *Major Powers and Korea.* Silver Spring, Md.: The Research Institute on Korean Affairs, 1973.

————, ed. *Foreign Policies of Korea.* Washington: Institute for Asian Studies, 1973.

Koh, Byung Chul. *The Foreign Policy of North Korea.* New York: Frederick A. Praeger, 1969.

Kux, Ernst. "East Europe's Relations with Asian Communist Countries," in Kurt London, ed. *Eastern Europe in Transition.* Baltimore: Johns Hopkins University Press, 1966.

Labedz, Leopold, ed. *International Communism After Khrushchev.* Cambridge: The M.I.T. Press, 1965.

Langer, Paul F. "Outer Mongolia, North Korea, North Vietnam," in Adam Broke, ed. *The Communist States at the Crossroads: Between Moscow and Peking.* New York: Frederick A. Praeger, 1965.

Laqueur, Walter, and Labedz, Leopold, eds. *Polycentrism: The New Factor in International Communism.* New York: Frederick A. Praeger, 1962.

Larson, David L. *The Cuban Crisis of 1962.* Boston: Houghton Mifflin, 1963.

Lee, Chong-Sik. *The Politics of Korean Nationalism.* Berkeley: University of California Press, 1963.

————. "Stalinism in the East," in Robert A. Scalapino, ed. *The Communist Revolution in Asia: Tactics, Goals, and Achievements.* Englewood Cliffs, N.J.: Prentice-Hall, 1965.

————. "The Impact of the Sino-American Détente on Korea," in Gene T. Hsiao, ed. *Sino-American Détente and Its Policy Implications.* New York: Frederick A. Praeger, 1974.

Lee, Tong-jun. *Hwansang kwa hyŏnsil* (Illusions and Reality). Seoul: Tongbang T'ongshinsa, 1961.

Lee, Luke T. *China and International Agreements: A Study of Compliance.* Durham, N.C.: Rule of Law Press, 1969.

London, Kurt, ed. *Unity and Contradiction: Major Aspects of Sino-Soviet Relations.* New York: Frederick A. Praeger, 1962.

————. *The Soviet Impact on World Politics.* New York: Hawthorn, 1974.

Lowenthal, Richard. *World Communism: The Disintegration of a Secular Faith.* New York: Oxford University Press, 1964.

Maki, John M. *Conflict and Tension in the Far East: Key Documents, 1884–1960.* Seattle: University of Washington Press, 1961.

Mayor, Peter. *Sino-Soviet Relations since the Death of Stalin.* Hong Kong: Union Research Institute, 1962.

McCune, George M., and Grey, Arthur L., Jr. *Korea Today.* Cambridge: Harvard University Press, 1950.

McCune, Shannon. *Korea's Heritage: A Regional and Social Geography.* Rutland, Vermont: Charles E. Tuttle Co., 1956.

————. *Korea: Land of Broken Calm.* Princeton: D. Van Nostrand Co., 1966.

McNeal, Robert H. *International Relations Among Communists.* Englewood Cliffs, N.J.: Prentice-Hall, 1967.

Mehnert, Klaus. *Peking and Moscow.* Translated by Leila Vennewitz. New York: G.P. Putnam's Sons, 1962.

The Military Balance 1975–1976. London: The International Institute for Strategic Studies, 1975.

Morley, James W. *Japan and Korea: America's Allies in the Pacific.* New York: Walker and Company, 1965.

Nam, Koon Woo. *The North Korean Communist Leadership, 1954–1965: A Study of Factionalism and Political Consolidation.* University, Ala.: The University of Alabama Press, 1974.

North, Robert C. *Moscow and Chinese Communists.* 2nd ed. Stanford: Stanford University Press, 1963.

———. "Polycentrism and the Sino-Soviet Controversy," in Edward M. Bennet, ed. *Polycentrism: Growing Dissidence in the Communist Bloc?* Pullman, Washington: Washington State University Press, 1967.

Oliver, Robert Tarbell. *Why War Came in Korea.* New York: Fordham University Press, 1950.

Pachter, Henry M. *Collision Course: The Cuban Missile Crisis and Coexistence,* New York: Frederick A. Praeger, 1963.

Paige, Glenn D. "North Korea and the Emulation of Russian and Chinese Behavior," in A. Doak Barnett, ed. *Communist Strategies in Asia.* New York: Frederick A. Praeger, 1963.

———. "Korea," in Cyril E. Black and Thomas P. Thornton, eds. *Communism and Revolution: The Strategic Uses of Political Violence.* Princeton: Princeton University Press, 1964.

———. *The Korean People's Democratic Republic.* Stanford: The Hoover Institution, Stanford University Press, 1966.

Pak, Tong-un. *Pukhan t'ongch'i kiguron* (On the Government Structure in North Korea). Seoul: Center for Asian Studies, Korea University Press, 1964.

Patterson, George. *Peking Versus Delhi.* London: Oxford University Press, 1964.

Ronchey, Alberto. *The Two Red Giants: An Analysis of Sino-Soviet Relations.* Translated by Raymond Rasenthal. New York: Norton, 1965.

Rudolph, Philip. *North Korea's Political and Economic Structure.* New York: International Secretariat, Institute of Pacific Relations, 1959.

Ryu, Hun. *Study of North Korea.* Seoul: Research Institute of Internal and External Affairs, 1966.

Salisbury, Harrison E. *To Peking—And Beyond: A Report on the New Asia.* New York: Capricorn Books, 1973.

Scalapino, Robert A., ed. *North Korea Today.* New York: Frederick A. Praeger, 1963.

———. *Asia and the Road Ahead.* Berkeley: University of California Press, 1975.

———, ed. *The Communist Revolution in Asia: Tactics, Goals, and Achievements.* Englewood Cliffs, N.J.: Prentice-Hall, 1965.

_____, and Lee, Chong-Sik. *Communism in Korea* (Part I and II). Berkeley: University of California Press, 1972.

Schram, Stuart R. *The Political Thought of Mao Tse-tung*. New York: Frederick A. Praeger, 1963.

Schurmann, Franz, and Schell, Orville, eds. *Communist China: Revolutionary Reconstruction and International Confrontation, 1949 to the Present*. New York: Random House, 1967.

Schwartz, Benjamin. *Chinese Communism and the Rise of Mao*. Cambridge: Harvard University Press, 1951.

Shen, Yu Dai. *Peking, Moscow and the Communist Parties of Colonial Asia*. Cambridge: Center for International Studies, The M.I.T. Press, 1954.

Snow, Edgar. *The Other Side of the River: Red China Today*. New York: Random House, 1962.

Suh, Dae-Sook. *The Korean Communist Movement, 1918-1948*. Princeton: Princeton University Press, 1967.

Suh, Nam-won. *Pukhan ui kyŏngje chŏngch'aek kwa saengsan kwalli* (Economic Policy and Production Control in North Korea). Seoul: Center for Asian Studies, Korea University Press, 1966.

Swearingen, Rodger, ed. *Soviet and Chinese Communist Power in the World Today*. New York: Basic Books, 1966.

Whiting, Allen S. *China Crosses the Yalu: The Decision to Enter the Korean War*. New York: The Macmillan Co., 1960.

Wolfe, Bertrand D. *Khrushchev and Stalin's Ghost*. New York: Frederick A. Praeger, 1957.

Wolfe, Thomas W. *The Soviet Union and the Sino-Soviet Dispute*. Santa Monica, California: The RAND Corporation, 1965.

Yang, Ho-min. *Pukhan ui ideorogi wa chŏngch'i* (Ideology and Politics in North Korea). Seoul: Center for Asian Studies, Korea University Press, 1967.

Zablocki, Clement J., ed. *The Sino-Soviet Rivalry*. New York: Frederick A. Praeger, 1966.

Zagoria, Donald S. *The Sino-Soviet Conflict, 1956-1961*. New York: Atheneum, 1966.

_____. *Vietnam Triangle: Moscow, Peking, Hanoi*. New York: Pegasus, 1967.

III. ARTICLES

An, Tai Sung. "The Sino-Soviet Dispute and Vietnam," *Orbis*, IX, no. 2 (Summer 1965), 426-36.

An, Thomas. "New Winds in P'yŏngyang?" *Problems of Communism*, XV, no. 4 (July–August 1966), 68–71.

Belyaev, I.U. "Building Socialist Industry in the Korean People's Democratic Republic." *Problems of Economics* (Moscow), I (January 1959), 33–38.

Bloomfield, Lincoln P., and Leiss, Amelia C. "Arms Control and the Developing Countries." *World Politics*, XVIII, no. 1 (October 1965), 1–19.

Bradbury, John. "Sino-Soviet Competition in North Korea." *The China Quarterly*, VI (April–June 1961), 15–28.

Brzezinski, Zbigniew. "Pattern and Limits of the Sino-Soviet Dispute." *Problems of Communism*, IX, no. 5 (September–October 1960), 1–9.

Cho, Soon Sung. "Politics of North Korea's Unification Policies, 1950–1965." *World Politics*, XIX, no. 2 (January 1967), 218–41.

————. "Japan's Two Koreas Policy and the Problems of Korean Unification." *Asian Survey*, VII (October 1967), 703–25.

————. "Korea: Election Year." *Asian Survey*, VIII (January 1968), 29–42.

————. "North and South Korea: Stepped-Up Aggression and the Search for New Security." *Asian Survey*, IX (January 1969), 29–39.

Chung, Joseph S. "The North Korean Industrial Enterprise: Control, Concentration, and Managerial Functions," in Robert K. Sakai, ed. *Studies on Asia*. Lincoln: University of Nebraska Press, 1966, 165–85.

Chung, Kiwon. "The North Korean People's Army and the Party." *The China Quarterly*, no. 14 (April–June 1963), 105–24.

————. "Japanese-North Korean Relations Today." *Asian Survey*, IV (April 1964), 788–803.

Clemens, Walter C., Jr. "The Nuclear Test Ban and Sino-Soviet Relations." *Orbis*, X, no. 1 (Spring 1966), 152–83.

————. "Khrushchev and China." *The Atlantic*, CCVII (May 1961), 43–47.

Cromley, Ray. "North Korea Sovietized." *The Wall Street Journal*, May 5, 1947.

Davidson, B. "Afro-Asian Solidarity and China." *Review of International Affairs*, XIV (November 5, 1963), 9–10.

Dernberger, Robert F. "Foreign Trade of Communist China: Factors Influencing China's Trade." *Communist Affairs*, V, no. 3 (May–June 1967), 4–7.

Devlin, Kevin. "Ten Years That Shook the World: A Movement Transformed, Some Consequences and Lessons." *Problems of Communism*, XV, no. 5 (September–October 1966), 48–49.

_____. "Which Side Are You On?" *Problems of Communism.* XVI, no. 1 (January–February 1967), 52–59.

Dubin, Wilbert B. "The Political Evolution of the P'yŏngyang Government." *Pacific Affairs,* XXIII (December 1950), 381–92.

Eckstein, Alexander. "Foreign Trade of China: A Summary Appraisal." *Communist Affairs,* V, no. 3 (May–June 1967), 9–12.

Freeberne, Michael. "Racial Issues and the Sino-Soviet Dispute," *Asian Survey,* V (August 1965), 408–16.

Fyodoror, P. "Korea: An Humane Act." *International Affairs* (Moscow), October 1958, 89–90.

George, A. L. "American Policy-Making and the North Korean Aggression." *World Politics,* VII (January 1955), 209–32.

Gittings, John. "The Great Power Triangle and Chinese Foreign Policy." *The China Quarterly,* no. 39 (July–September 1969), 41–54.

Grajdanzev, Andrew J. "Korea Divided." *Far Eastern Survey,* XIV, no. 20 (October 1954), 281–83.

Griffith, William E. "Albania: An Outcast's Defiance." *Problems of Communism,* XI, no. 3 (May–June 1962), 1–6.

_____. "The November 1960 Moscow Meeting: Preliminary Reconstruction." *The China Quarterly,* no. 11 (July–September 1962), 38–57.

Guelzo, Carl M. "Korea: the Divided People." *Yale Review,* LI (Spring 1962), 428–37.

Haggard, M. T. "North Korea's International Position." *Asian Survey,* V (August 1965), 375–88.

Halpern, A. M. "Communist China and Peaceful Coexistence." *The China Quarterly,* no. 3 (July–September 1960), 16–31.

_____. "The Emergence of an Asian Communist Coalition." *The Annals of American Academy of Political and Social Sciences,* CCIL (September 1963), 117–29.

Ham, Il-kun. "The North Korean Regime in the Sino-Soviet Dispute." *Korean Affairs,* II, no. 2 (1963), 140–49.

Hahm, Pyong-choon. "Korea and the Emerging Asian Power Balance." *Foreign Affairs,* L, no. 2 (January 1972). 339–50.

Han, Jae Duk. "Unmasking Russian Proposal for the Withdrawal of Foreign Forces in Korea." *Korean Affairs,* I, no. 1 (1962), 368–76.

_____. "Communist Life in North Korea." *Korean Journal* (Seoul), III (November 1963), 12–14.

Holubnychy, Vsevolod. "Soviet Economic Aid to North Korea." *Bulletin* (Institute for the Study of the U.S.S.R., Munich), IV (January 1957), 15–23.

Honey, P. J. "North Vietnam's Party Congress." *The China Quarterly,* no. 4 (October–December 1960), 65–75.

Kang, Young Hoon. "North Korea's Mysterious Kim Il Sung." *Communist Affairs,* II, no. 2 (March–April 1964), 21–26.

Kazuo, Takita. "North Korea: Increasing Trade With Japan." *Far Eastern Economic Review,* XXXVI, no. 2 (April 12, 1962), 51–52.

Khrushchev, Nikita S. "On Peaceful Coexistence." *Foreign Affairs,* XXXVIII, no. 1 (October 1959), 1–18.

Kim, Ch'ang-sun. "The North Korean Communist Party—Historical Analysis." *Korean Affairs,* II, no. 2 (1963), 130–39.

Kim, C. I. Eugene. "Korea in the Year of ULSA." *Asian Survey,* VI (January 1966), 34–42.

Kim, Deok. "Communist China's Intervention in the Korean War." *Korean Affairs,* II, no. 2 (1963), 212–21.

Kim, Ho Sen. "Fourth Congress of the Korean Party of Labour." *World Marxist Review,* V (January 1962), 61–63.

Kim, Ilpyong. "North Korea's Fourth Congress." *Pacific Affairs,* XXXV, no. 1 (Spring 1972), 37–50.

Kim, Il-sŏng. "The Friendship and Solidarity of the Socialist Countries." *International Affairs* (Moscow), November 1957, 65–72.

Kim, Joungwon Alexander. "The Peak of Socialism in North Korea: The Five and Seven Year Plans." *Asian Survey,* V (May 1965), 255–69.

————. "Divided Korea 1969: Consolidating for Transition." *Asian Survey,* X (January 1970), 30–42.

————. "North Korea's New Offensive." *Foreign Affairs,* XLVIII (October 1969), 166–79.

————. "Soviet Policy in North Korea." *World Politics,* XXII (January 1970), 237–54.

Kim, Roy U. T. "Sino-North Korean Relations." *Asian Survey,* VIII (August 1968), 708–22.

Kim, Young C. "North Korea in 1974." *Asian Survey,* XV (January 1975), 43–52.

————. "The Democratic People's Republic of Korea in 1975." *Asian Survey,* XVI (January 1976), 82–94.

Kimm, Ki Soo. "Impact of France's Recognition of Communist China." *Koreana Quarterly* (The International Research Council, Seoul), VI, no. 1 (Spring 1964), 24–30.

Koh, Byung Chul. "North Korea and Its Quest for Autonomy." *Pacific Affairs,* XXXVIII, nos. 3 and 4 (Fall and Winter 1965–1966), 294–306.

————. "North Korea and the Sino-Soviet Schism." *Western Political Quarterly,* XXII (December 1969), 940–62.

_____. "Dilemmas of Korean Unification." *Asian Survey,* XI (May 1971), 475-95.

_____. "North Korea: A Breakthrough in the Quest for Unity." *Asian Survey,* XIII (January 1973), 83-93.

_____. "North Korea: Profile of a Garrison State." *Problems of Communism,* XVIII (January–February 1969). 18-27.

_____. "North Korea: Old Goals and New Realities," *Asian Survey,* XIV (January 1974), 36–42.

Kulakov, I. "A Boundary Which Must Disappear." *International Affairs* (Moscow), December 1959, 86-88.

Kun, Joseph C. "North Korea's Neutral Course." *Radio Free Europe* (Munich), August 25, 1965.

_____. "North Korea: Between Moscow and Peking." *The China Quarterly,* no. 21 (July–September 1967), 48-58.

Lee, Chong-Sik. "Korean Communists and Yenan." *The China Quarterly,* no. 9 (January–March 1962), 182-92.

_____. "The Socialist Revolution in the North Korean Countryside." *Asian Survey,* II (October 1962), 9-22.

_____. "North Korea Between Dogmatism and Revisionism." *Journal of Korean Affairs,* I (April 1971), 14-24.

_____. "Korea: In Search of Stability." *Asian Survey,* IV (January 1964), 656-65.

_____. "Korea: Troubles in a Divided State." *Asian Survey,* V (January 1965), 25-32.

_____. "Kim Il-sung of North Korea." *Asian Survey,* VII (June 1967), 374-82.

_____, and Oh, Ki-Wan. "The Russian Faction in North Korea." *Asian Survey,* VIII (April 1968), 270-88.

Lee, J. K., and Wellington, Donald. "North Korea's Trade with the West: 1956-68." *Journal of Korean Affairs,* I (April 1971), 25-33.

Lee, Luke T. "Treaty Relations of the People's Republic of China: A Study of Compliance." *University of Pennsylvania Law Review,* CXVI, no. 2 (December 1967), 244-314.

Lee, Tong Won. "Sino-Soviet Dispute and the Course of North Korea." *Koreana Quarterly,* V. no. 2 (Summer 1963), 35-55.

Lewis, John W. "Communist China's Invasion of the Indian Frontier: The Framework of Motivations." *Current Scene,* II, no. 7 (January 2, 1963).

Lovell, John P., and Kim, C. I. Eugene. "The Military and Political Change in Asia." *Pacific Affairs,* XL, nos. 1 and 2 (Spring and Summer 1967), 113-24.

Lowenthal, Richard. "The Rise and Decline of International Communism." *Problems of Communism,* XII, no. 2 (March–April 1963), 28–31.

McCune, George M. "Korea: The First Year of Liberation." *Pacific Affairs,* XX, no. 1 (March 1947), 3–17.

Mosely, Philip E. "The Meaning of Coexistence." *Foreign Affairs,* XLI, no. 1 (October 1962), 36–46.

Myers, James T. "De-Stalinization and the Hero Cult of Mao Tse-tung." *Orbis,* IX, no. 2 (Summer 1965), 472–93.

Nam, Il. "The Foreign Policy of Korean People's Democratic Republic." *International Affairs* (Moscow), September 1958, 24–29.

North, Robert C. "Peking's Drive for Empire: The New Expansionism." *Problems of Communism,* IX, no. 1 (January–February 1960), 23–30.

Paige, Glenn D. "A Survey of Soviet Publications on Korea, 1950–1956." *The Journal of Asian Studies,* XVII, no. 4 (August 1958), 579–94.

———. "Korea and the Comintern, 1919–1935." *Bulletin of the Korean Research Center,* no. 13 (December 1960), 1–25.

———. "1966: Korea Creates the Future." *Asian Survey,* VII (January 1967), 21–30.

Pak, Sen Cher. "The Korean People's Struggle for the Country's Peaceful Unification and Socialism." *International Affairs* (Moscow), August 1960, 38–42.

Pak, Tong-un. "Communist China's Impact on North Korea." *The Journal of Asian Studies* (Seoul), IX, no. 3 (September 1966), 52–98.

Porter, Catherine, and Holland, William L. "North Korea's Economic Development." *Far Eastern Survey,* XXIV (November 1955), 171–73.

Pritt, D. "North Korea: Dead Myths Revived." *Labour Monthly,* IVL (July 1964), 302–10.

Rees, David. "North Korea: Undermining the Truce." *Conflict Studies,* no. 69 (March 1976), 1–14.

Robinson, Joan. "Korean Miracle." *Monthly Review,* January 1965, 541–49.

Robinson, Thomas W. "Soviet Policy in East Asia." *Problems of Communism,* XXII (November–December 1973), 32–50.

Rudolph, Philip. "North Korea and the Path to Socialism." *Pacific Affairs,* XXXII, no. 2 (June 1959), 131–43.

Rupen, Robert A. "Mongolia in the Sino-Soviet Dispute." *The China Quarterly,* no. 16 (November–December 1963), 75–85.

Scalapino, Robert A. "Which Route for Korea?" *Asian Survey,* II (September 1962), 1–13.

———. "Moscow, Peking, and the Communist Parties of Asia." *Foreign Affairs,* XLI, no. 2 (January 1963) 323–43.

———. "Korea: The Politics of Change." *Asian Survey,* III (January 1963), 31–40.

———. "Nationalism in Asia: Reality and Myth." *Orbis,* X, no. 4 (Winter 1967), 1,176–184.

———, and Lee, Chong-Sik. "The Origins of Korean Communist Movement I." *The Journal of Asian Studies,* XX, no. 1 (November 1961), 149–68.

———. "The Origins of the Korean Communist Movement II." *The Journal of Asian Studies,* XX, no. 2 (February 1962), 149–68.

Schram, Stuart R. "Mao Tse-tung as a Charismatic Leader." *Asian Survey,* VII (June 1967), 383–88.

Schram, Wilbur, and Riley, John W., Jr. "Communication in the Sovietized State, as Demonstrated in Korea." *American Sociological Review,* XVI, no. 6 (December 1951), 757–66.

Shabad, Theodore. "North Korea's Postwar Recovery." *Far Eastern Survey,* XXV (June 1956), 81–91.

Shinn, Rinn-sup. "Changing Perspectives in North Korea: Foreign and Unification Policies." *Problems of Communism,* XXII (January–February 1973), 55–77.

Simmons, Robert R. "China's Cautious Relations with North Korea and Indochina." *Asian Survey,* XI (July 1971), 629–44.

———. "North Korea: Silver Anniversary." *Asian Survey,* XI (January 1971), 104–110.

———. "North Korea: Year of the Thaw." *Asian Survey,* XII (January 1972), 16–24.

Simon, Sheldon W. "Some Aspects of China's Asian Policy in the Cultural Revolution and its Aftermath." *Pacific Affairs,* VIL (Spring 1971), 18–38.

"Strengthen the Unity of the International Communist Movement and Intensify the Revolutionary Struggle Against Imperialism." *Global Digest,* II, no. 5 (February 1, 1965), 68–71.

Suhrke, Astri. "Gratuity of Tyranny: The Korean Alliances." *World Politics,* XXV (July 1973), 508–32.

Swearingen, Rodger. "A Decade of Soviet Policy in Asia." *Current History,* XXXII, no. 186 (February 1957), 89–96.

Tang, Peter S. H. "The Soviet and Chinese Communists in Korea." *Free World Forum,* I, no. 5 (September–October 1959), 70–74.

Thomas, S. B. "Chinese Communists' Economic and Cultural Agreement with North Korea." *Pacific Affairs,* XXVII, no. 1 (March 1954), 61–65.

Thornton, Thomas P. "Foreign Relations of the Asian Communist

Satellites." *Pacific Affairs,* XXXV, no. 4 (Winter 1962–1963), 341–52.

Tikhomirov, V. "People's Korea: 30 Years." *Internatioal Affairs* (Moscow), September 1975, 51–53.

Trager, Frank N. with Robert F. Bordonaro. "The Ninth CCP Congress and the World Communist Conference and their meaning for Asia." *Orbis,* VIII (Fall 1969), 736–62.

Tretitak, Daniel. "Founding of the Sino-Albanian Entente." *The China Quarterly,* no. 10 (April–June 1962), 123–43.

Usatov, D. "In the Interest of Peace and Socialism." *International Affairs* (Moscow), August 1966, 76–77.

Walker, Richard. "Chairman Mao and the Cult of Personality." *Encounter* (June 1960), 32–38.

Washburn, John N. "Russia Looks at North Korea." *Pacific Affairs,* XX, no. 2 (June 1947), 152–60.

Wint, Guy. "China and Asia." *The China Quarterly,* no. 1 (January–March 1960), 61–71.

Wolpert, V. "Soviet Russia and the Korean Communist Party." *Pacific Affairs,* XXVIII, no. 1 (March 1950), 59–64.

———. "Turns in North Korea Trade." *Far Eastern Economic Review* (Hong Kong), no. 143 (February 13, 1964), 385–87.

Yu, Wan-shik. "Industry and Armament in North Korea." *Korean Journal,* V (October 1965), 8–21.

Zagoria, Donald S. "Sino-Soviet Friction in Underdeveloped Areas." *Problems of Communism,* X, no. 2 (March–April 1961), 1–12.

———. "Khrushchev's Attack on Albania and Sino-Soviet Relations." *The China Quarterly,* no. 8 (October–December 1961), 1–14.

———, ed. "Communist China and the Soviet Bloc." *The Annals of American Academy of Political and Social Sciences,* CCCIL (September 1963). This volume included 13 articles.

———, and Kim, Young Kun. "North Korea and the Major Powers." *Asian Survey,* XV (December 1975), 1,017–035.

Zolotaryov, V. "Economic Development in the People's Democracies." *International Affairs* (Moscow), August 1958, 72–80.

IV. PERIODICALS, NEWSPAPERS, AND OTHERS

Barron's. 1970–1975.

Christian Science Monitor. 1967–1975.

Current Background. U.S. Consulate General, Hong Kong.

Current Digest of the Soviet Press. Weekly, published by the Joint Committee on Slavic Studies. 1956–1975.

Communist China's Yearbook. Published in Hong Kong. 1961–1965.
Dong-A Ilbo. (East Asian Daily). Published in Seoul, Korea. 1957–1975.
Economist. London. 1956–1975.
Far Eastern Economic Review. Published in Hong Kong. 1962–1975.
Hung Ch'i (Red Flag). Theoretical organ of the Central Committee of the Chinese Communist Party.
Jen-min Jih-pao (People's Daily), Official newspaper of the CCP Central Committee. 1958–1975.
Korea Herald. Published in Seoul, Korea.
Korea News. Published in P'yŏngyang.
Korea Today. Monthly magazine, published by the Foreign Languages Publishing House, P'yŏngyang. 1961–1968.
Korean Central News Agency. Official North Korean News Agency, P'yŏngyang. 1956–1975.
Kŭlloja (Workers). Theoretical organ of the Central Committee of the KWP, published in P'yŏngyang. 1958–1968.
London Times. 1969–1975.
Minju Chosŏn (Democratic Korea). The organ of the DPRK, published in P'yŏngyang.
New Korea. Monthly magazine, published in P'yŏngyang. 1957–1961.
New York Times. 1958–1975.
Nodong Shinmun (Workers' Daily). The organ of the KWP Central Committee, published in P'yŏngyang. 1956–1974.
New China News Agency. Official Chinese News Agency, Peking. 1957–1974.
Peking Review. A weekly English magazine of Chinese news and views. 1958–1975.
People's Korea. Pro-North Korean weekly published in English in Japan. 1967–1975.
Pravda. 1956–1975.
Pyongyang Times. 1969–1975.
Radio Free Europe Research. 1965–1975.
Survey of China Mainland Press. U. S. Consulate General, Hong Kong. 1958–1968.
Washington Post. 1969–1975.

V. Unpublished Materials

Cho, Soon Sung. "North Korea and the Sino-Soviet Rift." Paper presented at the 20th Meeting of the Association for Asian Studies, Philadelphia, Pennsylvania, 1968.

Kim, Uoong Tack, "Sino-Soviet Dispute and North Korea." Unpublished Ph.D. Dissertation, University of Pennsylvania, 1967.

Kuark, Yoon T. "A Comparative Study of Economic Development Between North and South Korea During the Post-War Period." Unpublished M.A. Thesis, University of Minnesota, 1961.

Yim, Kwan Ha. "Korea in Japanese Foreign Policy." Paper presented at the 1973 Annual Meeting of the American Political Science Association at New Orleans.

INDEX

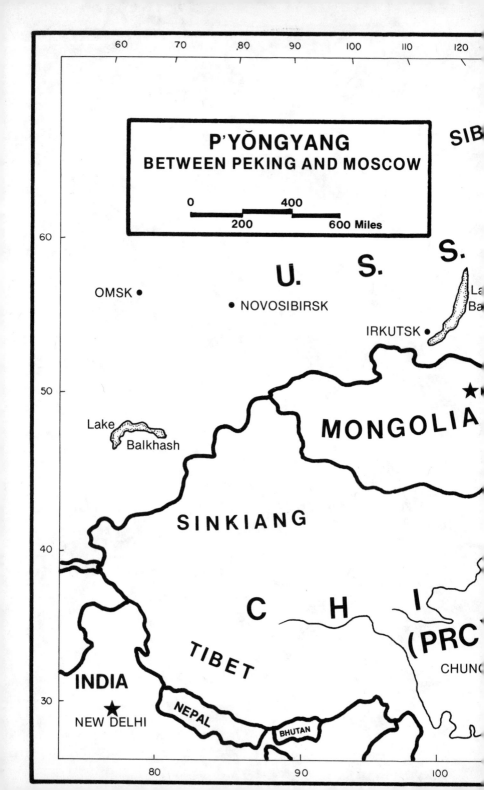